LET'S GET YOUR PARTY STARTED!

Growing up, aging, and dying — a Martian's perspective

Terryl Mackey, MD, YT*, RT*, CW*, WW*, PA*, ED*

* a highly credentialed expert on having fun with aging and dying; YT: Yoga Teacher, RT: Reiki Teacher, CW: Chicken Whisperer, WW: Worm Wrangler, PA: Party Animal, ED: Expert Dier

With ideas from many of our fellow life travelers

Let's Get Your Party Started

http://www.letsgetyourpartystartedbook.com/

Barn Swallow Publishing Company
PO Box 432
Davidsville, PA 15928
http://barnswallowpublishing.com/

Cover design by Mayapriya Long, Bookwrights

Interior design by Ken Benson

Names:	Mackey, Terryl, author.
Title:	Let's Get Your Party Started! Growing up, aging, and dying—a Martian's perspective / Terryl Mackey, MD.
Description:	First edition. | Davidsville, PA: Barn Swallow Publishing Company, [2017] | Includes bibliographical references.
Identifiers:	ISBN: 978-0-9986329-2-6 (print) | 978-0-9986329-3-3 (eBook) | LCCN: 2017943860
Subjects:	LCSH: Aging--Psychological aspects. | Death--Psychological aspects. | Fear of death. | Adulthood. | Maturation (Psychology) | Life cycle, Human--Psychological aspects. | Self-realization. | Self-actualization (Psychology) | Conduct of life. | Life skills—Handbooks, manuals, etc. | Self-help techniques. | BISAC: BODY, MIND & SPIRIT / Inspiration & Personal Growth. | FAMILY & RELATIONSHIPS / Life Stages / Later Years. | SELF-HELP / Aging. | SELF-HELP / Personal Growth / General.
Classification:	LCC: BF724.55.A35 M33 2017 | DDC: 155.67--dc23

Printed in the United States of America

2 4 6 8 9 7 5 3 1

First edition

Contents

Resources

Chapter 1

Why Party?

Birthing, aging, and dying have been around
for all of human existence

around 200,000 years.

In 1804[*] there were a lot of humans on the planet—

around 1,000,000,000.

Of those humans here in 1804, the
number who are still here:

0.

[*] The estimated date on which the first billion of us
were standing on the planet at the same time.

To date, after billions of births and deaths, no humans have escaped aging, since this process starts even before we're born. Neither have there been any humans—except those of us alive right now—who have not eventually died.

A passing Martian, on a fly-by to assess how we are doing, might wonder the following:

- Why do many young humans have a sense of urgency to live their lives fully in the first half of a lifetime that has a total expectancy of eighty to ninety years?
- Why do human young seem to consider their species to be "old" between thirty and forty years of age?
- Why do some humans in their middle years feel they are "over the hill?"
- Earthling births are celebrated. Why, then, are earthlings shocked, fearful, resigned, or angry when they consider their own aging and dying? Are these events not just as obviously a part of their life cycles?

Using a Martian-English translator, these intergalactic travelers (who are much more reflective than scary Martian movies typically depict), might be heard to wonder, "What the heck is that about?"

If you have to date not felt like celebrating the human precedent of *being born* > *growing up* > *aging* > *dying* maybe there's a different way of looking at this progression.

Martians, who are known to be intergalactic party animals might suggest: Why not party?

What's in it for you?

No matter what life stage you're currently traveling through, you will gain perspective on why humans seem to have a particularly negative attitude toward aging and dying. Then, rather than studiously avoiding the subject of aging and dying as too painful, you'll ponder some far-reaching questions . . . and be amazed by the answers you discover. You will no longer fear Martians and will come to appreciate their philosophic clarity of purpose and sunny, bon vivant dispositions. When you conclude we humans have been mistaken to attempt to frontload our lives or dread the second half of our lives, you'll get back anywhere from one day to seventy-plus years of life, which you can use for such things as fun, bold endeavors, contemplation, spiritual growth, or reckless abandon.

Who is throwing the party?

You.

You're going to get so fired up that you'll devise your own one-of-a-kind, out-of-my-way, it's-just-about-me celebration.

Whom shall you invite?

Your party, your decision. It could be just you or you could invite anyone who wishes to get more enjoyment from life.

How do you get started?

Let's play a game of Question the Assumed.

To challenge your negative assumptions on aging and dying, I'm introducing what I believe to be a great party game called Question the Assumed in which the object is twofold:

1. To question what we don't usually question; and
2. To answer the question in an innovative, thought-provoking way.

Hmm . . . to question what we don't usually question. You might ask: "How do I do that?" In playing Question the Assumed, I found it entertaining to question and re-examine what I had previously considered an obvious conclusion from the circumstance, or to do the same mental exercise by challenging any one of my absolute truths. In so doing, I could at times come up with potential answers that were challenging, thought provoking, and unexpectedly crazy-fun. Being an itinerant party animal, the crazy-fun thing appealed to me, so I began to play in earnest. Okay, ready to give the game a try? Here's a quick example game: While you're driving along, someone cuts you off in traffic, and you assume he's a jerk. Hmm. But what if he's not a jerk?

Then, oh reader and soon-to-be party animal, you must be brave, you must attempt to argue in support of the view opposite to your natural inclination. Wow! Think of a reason that he might not actually be a jerk. This is not easy to do, you say. Ah, got it! Maybe he's driving fast to the hospital for the birth of his first child. Or maybe he's rushing home to feed his gerbil. WARNING: The game can get very difficult to play if you really do agree wholeheartedly with the original assumption. Driving along, someone cuts you off in traffic; you think *He really is a jerk. I'll bet he doesn't even own a gerbil.* To practice, I challenge you to play the actual game of Question the Assumed, the contest that got the party started and then led to this book.

It's admittedly tough to come up with arguments sufficient to convince ourselves and others that aging and dying are worth celebrating. Begin by asking yourself about any assumption you've never questioned, in this case the following:

When reflecting on the three main life processes (birth, aging, and dying), why do we celebrate only one of the three?

Have we humans amputated half of our lives by relegating any age that's "not young" to the scrapheap of life?

Have we thereby done a disservice to the following groups:

The young (the invincible), who feel pressure to live complete lives by age twenty-nine, dread aging, and say that they studiously avoid even the contemplation of aging because "I don't feel that I will live that long"?

The middle-aged (the sucker-punched), many of whom say, "I never thought I would live this long," who are shocked and dismayed that they're no longer young, and express the feeling that they're "over the hill"—and sliding down a precipitous slope?

The aged (the kicked-to-the-curb), who echo the middle-aged in saying, "I never thought I would live this long," who find that society neither respects nor appreciates them, and worse, who find that they don't respect or appreciate themselves?

The lights fade . . . the music starts . . .

(your party planner is seen dancing with reckless abandon)

the DJ overrides the music to shout,

"Let's get this party started!"

the music stops abruptly; the lights snap back on . . . . .

Oh? So, you see no reason to party, since so far all you have are questions (provocative, to be sure)—but no answers have been forthcoming to persuade you that aging and dying are worth celebrating?

And you didn't know that you had a party planner?

No, you are not being rude, and yes, thanks, I do consider myself a pretty good dancer.

Even starting to question what we haven't before questioned opens unprecedented avenues of thought. As we begin to explore the basis of our personal and societal gloom-and-doom attitudes toward the stages that we all go through, we make room for a life-changing awareness of the beauty of our entire lives, from birth through and including death. What if there's not only no reason to fear or merely tolerate the natural progression of our lives as sadly inevitable but also reasons to celebrate the entire continuum of our lives from birth through death?

Let's address your second point first. You didn't know you had a party planner? Obviously since this is your party, you get to decide whether to hire me. You can plan the party on your own, but you don't seem convinced that there's even a reason to party in the first place. Since it's a new concept for you to celebrate aging and dying,

I thought I might lend my services. As an applicant for the job of party planner, I'll give you a quick review of my credentials in, and expertise on, having fun with life reflection, aging, and dying. Given that you are a non-partier, you might be unfamiliar with my credentials which will be discussed in more detail later: YT—Yoga Teacher, RT—Reiki Teacher, CW—Chicken Whisperer, WW—Worm Wrangler, PA—Party Animal, and ED—Expert Dier.

The main credential that allows me to speak knowledgeably of dying is that last one, my status as ED (Expert Dier). I have almost died several times, and a few other incidents were close. With my OJT, that is, On the Job Training, I initially reassured myself that my ED status was a slam-dunk for getting a toehold on credibility in the soon-to-be-lucrative-and-highly-sought-after field of "Fun with Aging and Dying." On reflection, however, I became concerned that some might challenge my "dier" expertise, since I am "not quite dead yet," as Monty Python would say. Always one to seek the wise counsel of others, I polled a group of folks, none of whom had come even remotely close to dying, for their opinions of my aforementioned expertise. Their conclusion was that, albeit rudimentary, my knowledge and experience of nearly dying qualify me as a de facto expert.

So, since I am a self-described and peer-reviewed expert on aging and dying, it's my hope that you'll remain engaged long enough to find out why it's time to get your party started. As a backdrop, you might question the process by which I concluded that aging and dying are worthy of much celebration. Nearly dying creates an existential opportunity to reflect on the entire living/aging/dying process through which we humans pass. Since my next go at dying might be completely successful, I thought of things I'd like to do or accomplish before I become completely dead—the proverbial bucket list. Among the tasks that I set for myself was my burning desire to have something unprecedented—an Original Thought.

I wondered whether I could have an original thought—not just an original thought to me but a purely original thought, one that no one has ever thought before. Obviously, some people have had original/unprecedented/unique thoughts in the past (e.g., Copernicus, Galileo, da Vinci, and Einstein) and thus have moved the world forward with their philosophies, experiments, and scientific theories. Humbly, I am not trying to be remembered in perpetuity as a brilliant philosopher . . . but twenty minutes of fame might be nice. However, the task of having an original thought today seems even more daunting than it may have been for these historical pioneers whose pool of competitors was about 6 or 7 billion fewer people back then. Even if I have an original thought, there's a good chance that others on the planet are having exactly the same original thought at the same moment as I am. Hmm.

I waited awhile and didn't notice any thought that seemed the least bit original. Never particularly patient, I devised the Question the Assumed game as a shortcut to a unique thought. I chose to challenge my most cherished opinions, and even what I know as Truths, with questions like: "What if?" "Where did?" "How come?" "Why?" "Could it be?" Any of my random, tightly held opinions, when noted, could be cause for pause. I'd ask myself, "What if I'm wrong?" I would then attempt to argue the view opposite to that which I held.

Playing Question the Assumed after one of my dying episodes, I began to wonder why most people fear dying, which led me to: "Why do most people fear aging in general?" It was then that I came up with what was, at least for me, a novel thought: "What if there is reason not only to not fear but to actually celebrate aging and dying?" I had successfully achieved the first object of the game: To question what I don't usually question. The pressure was on. Could I achieve the second object—to respond with an original, thought-provoking answer? Could I refute the entrenched idea that aging and dying pretty much suck? It was certainly ingrained in me (and my gestalt was that most people agreed with me) as a no-brainer that to be young is the best we can be, that aging is to be avoided, and death is the ignominious end to a lifespan that should have ended at thirty. In fact, have you noticed that in our culture there is little conceptualization of life as a continuum? It's almost like there are two species of humans, the young and the old, with the nebulous middle-aged frantically trying to be included with the young. They bemoan that youth has somehow tragically slipped away from them and try to gain traction as they teeter toward the abyss of old age.

The preceding paragraph might look pretty outrageous in black and white, as we give voice to the not-actively-acknowledged but nevertheless observed actions of those in youth, middle-age, and old-age. If, however, you

- Reflect on it yourself,
- Assess the semantics of advertisements across all media,
- Observe TV depictions that celebrate youth, denigrate aging, and infantilize elders, or
- Poll other people across the lifecycle,

you'll find that the above conclusions are not far off the mark.

The downside is that it's no anomaly that any random Martian on his fly-by journey would wonder why we aren't getting this party of our full life started. The upside is that the Martian pilot has probably convinced his fellow Martians that they should not even consider an invasion of Earth, because we must be crazy. But, even at the risk of a Martian invasion, why don't we rethink this whole birth/aging/dying thing?

I came up with a new way to perceive our life cycle so we could indeed celebrate the entirety of our lives. Also, I pondered how the problem of misperceiving our life span has come about and some means by which we can address the many negative issues that have resulted, in all phases of the cycle, from our negative attitude toward aging and dying.

Author's Note

1. It is not my intention to advocate, negate, or debate metaphysical, philosophical, or religious beliefs; neither is it my purpose to support or challenge the thoughts of agnostics or atheists.
2. The following ideas are merely food for thought for those of us who like to dream of a world of possibilities without necessarily reaching an opinion or conclusion.
3. I'm not claiming to be an expert on anything beyond my own personal expertise with nearly dying. As to any references in this book, please read the specific author's comments directly and bear in mind that I don't necessarily subscribe to his or her opinion.
4. If this book makes you angry, please stop reading, give away or burn the book, and find something more enjoyable to do.
5. If this book makes you think, especially new thoughts, keep reading. You will learn much about yourself. As you do, you'll likely discard negative perceptions of our life cycle, and thus will begin to celebrate every phase of your life.
6. As you begin to reflect, you might start to look forward to aging and dying—not to hasten them, but to peacefully and joyfully look forward to them as meaningful and vital life stages.

We earthlings have a big problem: Lots of folks are unhappy overall, but especially about aging in general and dying as a specific point of disgruntlement. My precedent is never to present a problem without at the same time offering a potential solution. Because I thought other people might agree that aging and dying are thorny issues worth addressing, it seemed appropriate to take a poll of other people's opinions for validation. I started interviewing people from their teens to their nineties and found that they too felt personal and perceived societal angst regarding our life cycle.

One of the interviewees, Charlie, a sixteen-year-old girl whom you'll "meet" more formally in chapter 9, had a mellow, matter-of-fact tone to her voice as she answered the survey questions. Because she had a test the next day, Charlie agreed to twenty minutes for the interview; she ended up speaking to me for two and a half hours. For her, like the many other interviewees, it seemed that the interviews were a welcome opportunity to talk aloud about subjects rarely thought of and never addressed in detailed conversation. Many interviewees admitted that until I asked the survey questions, they had actively avoided thinking about what, to them, had been the taboo subjects of their own aging and dying. The open-ended interview questions allowed each an opportunity to explore his or her aversion to considering these vital human topics. I was humbled to witness their transitions from sadness and/or fear to humor, acceptance, and even a modicum of excitement about what they discovered about themselves in the course of the discussions (appendix 5 includes more information about the interviews).

The shortest interview was forty-five minutes, the average was two hours, and the longest was four and a half hours. I have included the interview questions in the resources section. One interviewee, Laura, a sixty-eight-year-old Reiki teacher, decided to use these questions during the holidays to spark a more in-depth communication with family members who were planning to visit her. Based on my own experiences and life reflection, this book offers ideas for averting our current trajectory of pessimism. As well, you'll have access to the philosophies and wisdom of those people I interviewed. Where should we start?

Party Planning

1. Questions posed in this book might be ones you have never pondered.
2. You'll get the most benefit from jotting down your answers as you consider new perspectives.
3. At the back of the book is a resources section. Footnotes and asterisks can be distracting, so, while some references are cited, others are simply included in the references section. If you want to look at the definition of a word, you'll likely find it in the definitions section. The resources section is expansive, but not exhaustive, so you might need to do a little research now and again. Each division is alphabetized for easy reference.
4. The resources section includes commentary in the following subsections:
    a. Definitions: Some uppity writers use uppity terms that they do not define. This author is not uppity but loves vocabulary and sometimes uses potentially uppity words, so pertinent definitions can be found in this subsection. Also, I have a pet peeve when folks use terms without defining them, particularly if the words are integral to their message. Because language is ancient, even "easy" words like *fear* or *habit* are subject to interpretation. Words in common use can mean different things to different people.

b. Quotations: Favorite quotations that seem applicable to the content of this book from a diverse group of authors venerated for their creative thinking.

c. Topics of Interest: Supplemental information regarding topics mentioned in the book.

d. Scientific, Philosophical, or Psychological Concepts: Expansion on concepts only briefly mentioned in the body of the text.

e. Supporting Data: Miscellaneous references to relevant data.

f. References: Information on books referenced in the text, as well as information on books not referenced in the text, which you might enjoy as cool, funny, interesting, or thought-provoking. This section also includes funny or philosophical movies and Web references.

So, let's get started.

Is it a valid observation that we treat the age groups like two species of humans, the young and the old, with the young oblivious to the fact that they are on the same continuum of aging that converts all of us from young to old? Can you suspend your personal and cultural programming regarding these life stages? Can you let me not necessarily persuade you of the answers but share the questions that launched me into being an Aging and Dying Party Animal? Can you then use your imagination to answer the questions and discover your reasons to celebrate?

Do We Need New Nomenclature?

All the terms—*youth, middle-aged,* and *old,* or *elderly*—have some pejorative connotations.

1. Youth, to some older-aged interviewees, signifies a group of people who are inexperienced, uninformed, entitled, or selfish. According to seventy-eight-year-old L.N., "Most of the younger people do not appreciate their youth and are clueless that they too will one day be old."
2. Some youthful interviewees characterize middle age with terms such as middle-age spread, a condition in which those of middle age tend to let themselves go physically. Birthdays typically demonstrate a theme with over-the-hill connotations, with gifts like adult diapers and other items portending the birthday celebrant's descent into the realm of the old.
3. Old age is the most denigrated of all categories, with descriptions from some of the youth surveyed characterizing the old as being, dull, sad, not relevant, a drain on the rest of us, uninformed, entitled, or selfish. [*Hmm. Note the interesting overlap in both generations' negative views of each other.*]

Could it be that the cross-generational disparagement is fueled by terminology that is habituated and unexamined? What if we could come up with new terminology? If we can't find globally recognized terms of endearment, respect, and veneration for each category of our life cycle, perhaps we could coin brand-new terms with positive definitions for each.

First, we would need a consensus as to the range of each age category before we could come up with new nomenclature. This categorization wouldn't be an issue if we cherished each age and viewed the ages of our life as a continuum. Since we do not, however, what if we clearly identify the age divisions to instead reframe the demarcations as positive place markers? If we recognized and looked forward to each marker age, could the celebration change our perceptions and thereby allow us to see a seamless positive progression of aging? It's interesting that Google delineates middle age as ages forty-five to sixty-five, identifying this range as "the period between early adulthood and old age." There doesn't seem to be consensus on demarcations of youth other than that it occurs prior to middle age. The same is true of old age: It's characterized as the age group that follows middle age. [*Hmm, that seems odd, no clear numerical delineation. Let's examine that.*]

The average life expectancy is approximately 81 years for females and 76 for males. The midpoints of those life expectancies, and, one would think, the mathematically accurate midpoint of middle age would therefore be 40 years for females and 38 for males. Interestingly, middle age is commonly felt to extend from 45 years to 65 years old. The midpoint of the twenty-year total range would be 55 years of age. However, using the actual life expectancies, ten years on either side of the true midpoint of life expectancies would make middle age encompass the range of 30–50 years of age for women and 28–48 for men.

[*Wow! No one would want to be considered middle-aged when only twenty-eight or thirty, but maybe this is part of the angst young folks feel as they approach age thirty. Even though it's not defined as such, the young are in fact entering chronological middle age when they reach thirty.*]

What about redefining each of the age demarcations for youth, middle age, and older age? If we could come to a consensus, what advantages might there be? Could it be that if we had clear age divisions and if folks were excited about reaching each landmark age, the dates could be positively anticipated? Making plans for each age transition can give rise to a celebratory event—a "rite of passage"—that will be discussed below. The age group demarcations that follow are based on empirical reasoning, in that I could find no clear or adequate references. The categories I propose are:

1. **Very Young**—up to age 13 [*1st formal rite of passage at 13*]
2. **Young with Minimal Experience**—ages 13 to 29 [*2nd formal rite of passage at 30*]
3. **Young with Experience**—ages 30 to 44 [*3rd formal rite of passage at 45*]
4. **Middle age**—45 to 65 years (Google definition) [*4th formal rite of passage at 65*]
5. **Old age**
   a. 66 to 81 years for females (average age of female life expectancy 81.21) [*5th formal rite of passage at 81*]
   b. 66 to 76 years for males (average age of male life expectancy 76.37) [*5th formal rite of passage at 76*]
6. **Old-Advanced**—older than 76 for males, older than 81 for females [*6th formal rite of passage at death*]

What if we replaced the tired English terms in the above chart regarding the life cycle? The English terms *youth, aging, middle age, old age, aging, dotage, elderly, old, and others* have been bandied about for centuries and are therefore no longer pertinent or consistently definable due to the lack of clarity as to when each age begins and ends. These and other such words that denote age classifications invite the baggage of hundreds of years of interpretation and oft-times carry pejorative connotations. For example, "aging" is a term accurate even for the very young because every day children are aging and every day they learn from their life adventures and their milestones: To walk, to talk, to read, to skip, and so on; however, young people are rarely said to be aging. To date, the term "aging" has been used only in reference to those of more advanced age. This perpetuates the dichotomy between young and old rather than identifying aging as a continuous process.

It's easier to stereotype if we use language-weary terms that are unexamined and which perpetuate a label (Hmm, maybe even a libel). As examples, in recent years several cultures have advocated the use of more accurate terminology to describe themselves, such as Native American instead of Indian or Asian rather than Oriental. We could decide to use unique, complimentary, and accurate terminology to describe aging if we adopt kinder, inventive, and more accurate language.

Recently I heard the terms "Sage-ing" rather than "Age-ing" from a book by Zalman Schachter-Shalomi and Ronald Miller entitled *From AGE-ing to SAGE-ing, A Revolutionary approach to Growing Older.* Please see the book particulars in the resources. My definition of "sage" means wise, with wisdom acquired through reflection on life's experiences. What a lovely and accurate term for all of us humans, young or old, as we become wiser with each adventure. Therefore, the young and the old can both be accurately said to be aging, but by far the more accurate and positive term is "sage-ing."

Identifying what "sage" you are rather that what age you are would, with advancing age, connote improvement rather than decay. "I am not aging; I am sage-ing" allows for the upward positive movement of passing years to offset any of the previously considered ill effects of the physical aspect of aging. So, thanks to authors Schachter-Shalomi and Miller, we have one good term to replace "age" and "aging." All right, my new nomenclature buddies, help me out here. We need to replace all the previously noted terms. I think the French might be able to help.

In a moment of self-imposed hilarity, I decided that everything sounds better to me when said by the French, so what if we came up with terms from the French language? As one of those rejected-as-crass Americans lacking fluency in the French language, I couldn't come up with appropriate French terms with the satisfyingly melodic syllables I crave. What to do? . . . What to do? I began to apply random French words, whose sounds I found particularly appealing, to replace the English terms. Take, for instance, the cool-sounding French term *accoutrement,* pronounced "ack-coo-treh-mah," to replace the English terms *old, elderly,* and *aged.*

"Accoutrement" is an example of the delightfully entertaining French precedent of biting off a word's last syllable and adding a sound inconsistent with the spelling. Such is the case for the "mah" sound, which must be said with sexy gusto. So even though the definition of accoutrement has nothing to do with aging, dying, or death, what if we unrefined, unknowing Americans adopted this French term to replace the English terms? I would therefore not be approaching the chronological category of that ugly English term, *old age.* I would instead be classified as entering the lovely sounding category of *accoutrement.* In like manner, we could rename each of the above-defined age groups with terms purloined from French or some other global language that has terms of endearment, respect, and veneration for each category of our life cycle. On second thought, to keep the French happy and not confuse everyone who's multilingual, we might be wiser to follow author Kurt Vonnegut's precedent of making up new terms, coined to replace the inexact and judgmental English terms currently used for life-cycle taxonomy. The category "youth," for example, seems way too broad to help us identify, understand, and embrace this part of our life cycle.

I suggest three totally different terms to identify the three divisions of youth. How about "larva" for the very young (to sage thirteen), "pupa" for the young with minimal experience (sages thirteen to twenty-nine), and "butterfly" for young with experience (sages thirty to forty-four)? No? Okay how about "seed, sprout, and plant"? We face a similar task in assigning appropriate nomenclature to the two categories of old-sage. How about "maximus" and "maximus prime"?

Can we at least get rid of the term "elderly" right now, please? I have worked hard to hopefully earn the title of Elder, which sounds so very much better, don't you think? I hope I've gotten the idea of improving terminology across because that just blew out my brain coming up with the analogy. Since I'm very protective of my neurons, I would ask you to come up with some better terminology. Then the potential terms could be submitted to an ad hoc terminology improvement committee committed to the quest of ferreting out the perfectly purloined or cunningly coined phrases for the age categories.

If we could come to a consensus on our life-cycle landmark ages and had friendlier terminology for each stage, what advantages might there be?

If we were looking forward to each stage as we advanced through the paths of our lives, could we wildly and joyously anticipate all of them? Would we look forward to the increasing sage number each year? What if we were to meaningfully mark the milestones with private, thoughtful rites of passage? I attach the caveat "private" because this could get really competitive and lose all meaning if we try to outperform each other with our more expensive and/or showy celebrations of frivolous and superficial pomp and circumstance.

Greetings, earthlings, I am MN26X. The very confused and sometimes amusing earthling has occasionally referenced me in a "what if?" manner, clearly not really believing that I exist at all. Thinking it amusing, in order to avoid the tired 21st-century cliche of "let's go global," she went beyond an orbiting satellite's perspective, even farther into space, to capriciously channel what a Martian might say on observing some of humanity's idiosyncrasies and downright cosmically weird attitudes toward their lives and life spans. Her approach preempted an even more tired cliche of "not seeing the forest for the trees." I must admit that on my occasional flights over your lovely planet I have been quite confused; but I have figured it out.

You folks have lost your manual, right? Martians have an operational manual when we arrive, much like you receive with an earthling washing machine, so that you know what is expected of you, the owner-operator, as you go through the cycles using all the dials and controls effectively. Hmm . . . no manual. No wonder you humans keep getting into the same problems over and over again while thinking that the situations are unique. Well, my advice is that since each of you is an exceptionally unprecedented individual, both genetically and experientially, you might be well served to fashion your own manual. Within that, however, remember that a few billion other humans have walked or are walking in shoes similar to yours and that their life paths can be reviewed to help you with making your own life manual. Looking to their "good" and "bad" ideas and actions in forming their life paths could net some excellent material as you begin to construct your own manual for a life well lived.

Maybe the Party Animal has some thoughts on this. What if you started by looking at everything from a different perspective? Oh, no! What if . . .? That raucous human party animal is beginning to rewire my Martian logic circuits. I am out of here; I will check you out on my next fly-by.

(Excerpts from the Martian Manual are included as appendix 1.)

Chapter 2

Let's Get into the Party Mood

You have tentatively given me the job of party planner. I suspect that you have afforded me that status for two reasons:

1. Because of my lofty credentials mentioned in chapter 1; and
2. My party animal persona, which is at once a heady mix of the whimsical, existentially thoughtful, and (only a wee bit—but tolerably and ingratiatingly so) irritatingly optimistic about aging and dying.

Of course, my tenure as party planner hinges on whether you decide to party, so I guess my first job is to get you into the party mood by playing a round of Question the Assumed. Being the author of the game provides no traction for winning, as I found when I drew the card bearing the assumption "Being young is better than being old." I had difficulty disagreeing with the statement. I was convinced that we humans are pleased about being young but generally afraid of aging, being old, and dying. I could think of obvious reasons to agree with the negatively biased assumptions regarding issues such as failing eyesight, body parts becoming gravitationally contested, pain, graying hair, or becoming human wallpaper—overlooked and disregarded. So, when I chose to play in earnest, I had to be able to reject my dismay at growing older by finding answers that could persuade me that being young is not better than being old. It took me a lot longer than the game's three-minute time allotment to come up with some convincing arguments to substantiate the corollary to the card's assumption.

I started by examining why I came to agree with those who said being young is superior to being old. Hmm. I wondered why my attitude toward aging, old age, and dying, and what I perceived as the general public's attitude toward them, are so pervasively negative. Until recent history it didn't seem that this negative attitude was the case, and even today in other cultures the process of aging is not seen with the jaundiced eye with which we see the later portions of our life continuum.

One interviewee, Chima, a twenty-eight-year-old from Nigeria, explained his respect for his parents, whom he considers to be his wise and caring mentors. Chima was puzzled about the lack of respect he detects in the U.S. for our elders. He said that when he has traveled back to Nigeria for visits, he has noted that people of that country have respect for the aged even if the elder persons are homeless, for the very fact that they have survived to reach their current age.

- Reader, please grab your pen to answer the following questions: Why are gray hair, aging bodies, and previously rounded derrieres now taking on a square geometry, and wrinkles usually considered terrible, since these are all integral aspects of human lives?

- Could and should we begin to venerate these heretofore physical pejoratives as actually being positive markers of the journey to advanced age?
- Are there no potential gains of becoming aged, or are the gains ordinarily overlooked?
- Could we begin to venerate aging and the aged appropriately to the point that young people would have plastic surgery to look like the older, wiser, and more respected members of society? Wow, now that's an unprecedented thought!

After answering all those questions, I took a nap and then wrote a poem.

Being young is not an accomplishment.
Being old is not a failure.
Existence is a continuum.
Life fully lived a goal.

But wait . . . this line of reasoning led to an even more profound question: Could we take it a step further and propose that maybe all our life processes not only could be but should be celebrated? I expanded this original thought through the following questions, which I submit for your consideration:

Since there are actually five, not just three phases of life—gestation (the pregnancy), birth, aging, dying, and death—why is it that we consistently celebrate only birth (and birthdays until about age twenty-nine)?

Why do we not celebrate gestation, aging, dying, and death?

What if there's reason to celebrate all of it?

During pregnancy, the baby is getting older (a.k.a. aging) with each day of life, until the time of birth. After we are born, we are getting older (a.k.a. aging) with each day of life, until the time of death. But after a certain point, although we are still getting older (a.k.a. aging) with each day of life, the terms "older" and "aging" take on undesirable connotations. With each day of gestation until the time of birth the baby is developing something new. Wow, way cool; babies don't know that they're developing something new each day. With each day of life until the time of death the adult is developing something new. Wow, not cool; adults are also unaware that they're developing something new each day. Granted, the baby might be developing a finger or a toenail, and adults might just be developing bad attitudes, but the similarity is there. What information do we lack that would make the perception of the entirety of our lives not only more palatable but also deserving of joyful anticipation rather than dread? Here's an intriguing line of thought: one could wonder if there is something parallel about how we develop before birth and how we develop after birth.

We celebrate birth and some birthdays, but we don't celebrate the baby during pregnancy (a.k.a. gestation). We can't perceive what it must be like to be cooped up in a really tight space growing body parts about which we have no knowledge or apparent need. So, let's examine gestation, the first life phase, from the baby's anatomic and philosophic perspectives. Mind you, this is part of the crazy-fun, speculating about what you might have been observing or thinking while in the womb.

Gestation

Floating along, you saw no particular reason to celebrate.

Your mother might or might not have been celebrating the pregnancy, depending on whether she was throwing up constantly or feeling like a beached whale, but the pregnancy was pretty much all about her from the rest of the world's perspective. There were obvious physical changes happening to your mother, and we observers could communicate face to face with her as she went through the joys and travails of pregnancy. Other people anticipated your advent, but while you were still in the womb they were unable to see or communicate directly with you. You have no memory of the time you spent in your mother's womb, so you have no concept of what it was like to be a baby before birth. In fact, none of us has any memory of our own gestation or of our first year or two of life, so it's understandable that we adults don't consider the gestation from the baby's perspective. It's a time totally removed from our awareness and as such is not a time that we've even thought to celebrate.

But what's going on in there? You can track the days of development on software applications, but these provide only objective, scientifically established dates of developmental achievement. Although helpful in following the progress of the fetus, the resources are, of course, unable to provide the subjective elements of the baby's journey. If we were aware of our own time in the womb, what would we have observed?

At first, the new attributes you developed were obvious, physical things like an eye or a toe, but later, when the superstructure of your body was complete, what you developed each day as you floated along in the amniotic sac was much more subtle. In medical terminology, during gestation, which is the time during which the mother is pregnant, the baby (or fetus) is considered to be *in utero.* The term "in utero" is given to the time during which the baby is floating in an amniotic sac and is fed and oxygenated by the placenta and umbilical cord within the mother's uterus (or womb). If you could remember your gestational observations, you were forming a body, which was getting progressively larger. As well, numerous other developmental events that were absolutely necessary for life were coming on line, about which you could not possibly have been aware. The exhaustive list of developmental milestones is beyond the scope of this book, but some of the biggies are noted below.

The Five Senses

Taste: Taste buds are forming, but there is nothing to taste, so this one is definitely not even on the radar of possible cool abilities to have.

Smell: Since you are completely enveloped in a liquid environment, there's no pre-birth opportunity to detect aroma or know that you even have a nose that you will one day breathe through, sneeze, or blow.

Sight: There is generally nothing but darkness upon which to gaze even if the non-noticed eyes were to open. And because you therefore could not see in utero as you can after birth, the above discussed theoretical awareness of your body parts forming and getting larger would not have been possible either.

Touch: You might have felt the warm fluid in which you floated, but without ever having had any other contrasting sensations, like cold or pain, it's unlikely that you'd have an awareness of warmth or touch.

Hearing: Of the five senses this is the only one "on line" enough in which you, the baby, had you had language, could have said, "Hmm. I think I heard something!" You would have been very aware of your mother's heartbeat and the swishing of her blood through her blood vessels. You might also have been aware of a similar sound, only louder, as the blood from your mother rushed via the placenta and umbilical cord to feed and oxygenate you and thereby sustain your life. It's likely as well that you could have detected random loud noises such as the blowing of a car horn, but that sound would probably have been reduced to the level of a vibration as it was transmitted through all the layers of your mom's skin, muscle, and the fluid that separated you from the outer world. There might have been distant, muffled sounds of people's voices, which would not have been identifiable to you as voices, since you were unaware that anyone or anything existed outside the confines of the uterus.

The Body

The details of forming a body could fill a book, but let's consider a few examples. Unbeknownst to you, vocal cords were forming, but no sounds could be made within the liquid environment, so even if you'd had the capacity of language, you couldn't say, "Hmm." You would have had the ability to move your head, neck, torso, arms, legs, fingers, and toes, but these were only slightly moveable because you were tightly constrained by the small space in the uterus. You developed lungs, but you couldn't breathe, as you were essentially "underwater" in the amniotic fluid.

The Mind

Mental abilities were latent, but without language, thought as we know it wasn't possible. Try to think something right now without putting words to the thought. It's like taking a picture, but not one that you can put into memory, because our memories are processed via language. You, as an adult, can and do have sensory-triggered memories, but they are tied to language-accessed thought and, of course, are not available to the baby in utero whose sensory input is not yet accessible.

As the forty-week mark of gestation approaches, development is complete. The placenta, amniotic sac, and umbilical cord have aged and are about to be jettisoned as the birth process ends. You didn't know why the heck you were doing it, but you wiggled into a dive stance. You turned your head down toward the lowest portion of the uterus as you and your mom's body prepared for the process of birth. The brain (with its surrounding skull bones) is the largest part of a baby's body. Your head became the battering ram against the interior physical confines of your mom's thick muscular uterine wall, in order to open the "door" (also known as the *os*, Latin for "opening") of the uterine cervix. The uterine cervix is somewhat akin to a thick rubber band of muscle, which has kept the "door" tightly closed during gestation so your amniotic fluid (a.k.a. water) couldn't leak out.

Over time, once the process began, the muscular wall of the uterus and the cervix thinned out with the stretching caused by your big head, which was sort of stuck in the constriction of your mom's pelvic bones and the os. After hours of pounding on it by your head, the cervical os, which had been tightly closed, began to open. As the uterine contractions continued and your head created more downward pressure, the os opened more and more until it was large enough that your head could descend into the vagina. This is, generally, when the amniotic sac breaks due to the lack of support—now that the os is open. It's sort of like holding an inflated balloon halfway while squeezing toward the end; a process that ultimately creates so much internal pressure that the balloon wall ruptures due to the pressure. When your amniotic sac ruptured, the fluid in which you were floating rushed out. This is referred to as when the "water breaks."

The bones of your skull slid over each other as your skull and brain were compressed to fit through the relatively tiny birth canal. The baby, you, who had previously been floating, not knowing the sensation of pain or the emotion of fear, likely experienced both now. If nothing else, the fear and stress felt by your mother were likely communicated to you as well. We can all recognize that it is painful for the mother to deliver a fully-grown baby through a very small aperture. You entered this world through a 10-cm opening—at 2.54 cm per inch—the diameter of that opening was approximately 3.93701 inches! Surely it must stretch a little more than that as your head moved all the way into the opening, but this is where the measurement starts. By the way, it might be nice to take a moment to mentally thank your mother for her efforts.

Those contractions of the uterus that pushed you out the door were obviously painful for your mother. But what about you? Don't you think that the experience might have been painful to you as well? Think about the pressure of a sinus headache, then consider the vise in which your head was clamped, as well as your whole body, for the timespan during which your mom and you labored, typically 12–36 hours. What's worse is that intermittently the pressure became excruciatingly higher as the uterine contractions, which wax and wane, clamped down even more. Your head and body, over that really, really long time, were systematically lengthened and squeezed down in order for you to be pushed through the cervical os and then through the birth canal, known as the vagina.

So even though the pregnancy, for you, was pretty great, you were unaware of what was going on developmentally (ergo no obvious reason to party or room for a party hat anyway), and you didn't know what was about to happen as you went from oblivious floating to being rudely pushed out of your toasty little home (from your perspective an ignominious rejection).

This birth talk gets pretty heavy, so how about engaging CW (Chicken Whisperer) mode? You can start by viewing funny chicken videos on YouTube. The antics of these prehistoric animals, which are descended from the dinosaurs, will make you laugh. Laughter will give your poor brain a respite from the heavy lifting of thought regarding gestation. You could write a poem. Here is mine:

Advised to make the journey the destination
I sit contentedly rocking.
In my lap sits my cuddled chicken,
A Barred Plymouth Rock of characteristic
black-and-white-striped plumage.
She tips her head toward me.
Tiny dinosaur eyes
black, inquisitive,
blink slowly bottom to top
questioning my motives.

For those who've never viewed a chicken up close, because of their wide-set eyes they must turn one eye toward you, making it appear that they are not sure of your legitimacy. Only by being close can you notice that instead of the human precedent of closing our eyes from top to bottom, theirs close from the base toward the top. I have speculated that the reason is to watch for hawks or other predators.

At this point, a nap might be in order, you have some hard work of thinking ahead.

Birth

Initially, from your perspective, there was NO obvious reason to cheer.

Finally, you popped out into the world. It's hard to imagine how strange and unsettling that experience must have been. For the first time, you felt air as it wafted over your moist skin, exposing you to your first encounter with the sensation of cold. Opening your eyes must have hurt no matter how dim the light of the birthing room, much like an adult's eyes exposed to bright sunlight after being in a dark cave. Even quiet noise may have seemed extremely loud to your new ears, but at the same time, the loss of hearing your mother's heartbeat must have seemed unnervingly quiet. After the months of weightless compression and hours of getting squeezed in a vise, it must have been terrifying to feel gravity. Your extremities, so long appliquéd to your body, splayed out as gravity was fully felt, giving you the sensation of falling. It's no wonder that babies like to be tightly wrapped up to feel the comfortable compression of the swaddling blanket, which envelopes us like the snug and cozy uterus.

So, a baby's time, your time, in utero, comes to an end with a "bang" literally and figuratively. Unbeknownst to you, there have been months of physical preparation as you developed lots of potentially cool capabilities, but it was not until you went through the angst and pain of leaving the uterus that you had any possibility of awareness of your innumerable abilities. In protest to the indignities, pain, and surreal environment you entered, you likely wailed loudly. You expanded your lungs for the first time with life-giving oxygen, a process that was probably painful as the air sacs of the lungs were forced open. As you cried out for the first time, you used vocal cords you didn't know you possessed. This probably startled you further at the sound of your first self-generated noise and with the intensity of your emotions.

After Birth

Finally, you began to see reasons to start celebrating.

Taste: Taste was brought to awareness as you nursed for the first time.

Smell: You could smell your mother's skin and likely were acutely aware of other aromas that an adult's overburdened sense of smell would presumably no longer detect.

Sight: Your pupils, now accommodated to the brightness of the lights, did not hurt as your eyes opened to see light, color, movement, objects, and people. Can you even imagine how that dazzling display of movement and color must have felt to you as a brand-new little human?

Touch: As a baby, you were quickly cuddled into heated blankets and laid against your mother's warm skin.

Hearing: It would have been soothing to hear the comforting sound of your mother's heartbeat again. Quiet cooing sounds, which your mom made to soothe you (and possibly also the sound of soft music in the background), introduced you to hearing.

The excitement after birth was about you, the cute little baby. While you were trying to take in the new environment, the placenta, umbilical cord, and amniotic sac in which you incubated and which, until the moment of your birth were vital to your survival, were quickly discarded. It's so odd that the minute you were born, these structures, from one minute to the next, were no longer necessary for the continuation of your life. In fact, stranger still is that these previously life-giving structures would have impeded your survival. If they were to somehow have remained attached, they would have become encumbrances that would not have allowed you to embark on your new life as a breathing, moving, feeling, conscious person.

For the majority of babies, birth is an event celebrated by family and friends. Perhaps for you, balloons of pink or blue flew over your new home, and cardboard storks announced your arrival. In our culture, each subsequent birth anniversary is celebrated with birthday parties, which are considered fun until about our twenty-ninth birthday, but even those are generally superficial affairs. The anniversary date of your birth is commemorated with cake, party games, party hats, and a gathering of friends and family. There is frivolity and some cavorting, but rarely is there an in-depth, self-generated, retrospective evaluation of our lives and accomplishments to that date. It's unlikely that birthday festivities are a time of meaningful pause to celebrate one's life journey. Rarely do we reflect on what we have liked about the path of our lives thus far; neither is there an examination of what we have learned from our adversities. On our birthday, it's rare that we take even a brief time to consider the course we might desire for our lives over the next year or the next decade. It's akin to getting onto an airplane with no destination in mind; you might end up in a place you never intended, or you just might crash and burn on your way to nowhere.

As birthday number thirty approaches—party over.

Many of us dread aging to thirty, becoming middle-aged at some ill-defined point, or crossing into old age. I wonder if it dawns on the twenty-nine-year-old who looks to his thirtieth birthday with trepidation that he probably has another sixty birthdays ahead of him to dread? Maybe he could consider O.G.'s perspective.

Interviewee O.G., age sixty-three, stated, "Old age is mathematical; it is N + 20. When I was forty-three, I considered old age to be sixty-three. Now that I am the N of sixty-three (obviously, my assessment at forty-three was wrong—I am at most just entering middle age); eighty-three is when I will hit old age. Of course, when I hit N=83, I suspect that my assessment will be that old age will begin at 103!" Despite his creative mathematics, O.G. wished to be known to you by his nickname of the last twenty years: Old Guy. In other words, like the rest of us, "Old Guy" never wants to become old, and neither, by his calculations, shall he do so.

As a party planner, it seemed my duty to examine ways to relook at aging in such a persuasive manner that we would go from celebrating every birthday until age twenty-nine to "major party mode" for every year thereafter. Because of my now second-nature examination of the why of things, it seemed best to contest the "young versus old" pattern of birthday celebration. We can thereby recognize the reality of our life cycle as a continuum. I wondered, since babies in utero are developing capabilities to be used after they pop into the world, about which they are unaware, could we as adults be going through a similar developmental process?

You lived your full *in utero* life in about nine months. The in utero time is, by convention, divided into what are called trimesters, a period of three months each, as divisions of pregnancy. Your first three months as a young fetus, i.e., the first trimester, were marked by the very active, physically obvious building of the superstructure and the non-visualized infrastructure of your body. You started as a few cells, which basically weighed nothing. A mere twelve weeks later you had developed a brain, a heart, lungs, abdominal organs, nerves, and muscles. At the end of the first trimester, you were about 3½ inches from the crown of your head to your rump, and you weighed in at about 1½ ounces.

As you matured, you entered the second trimester and thereby became a "middle-aged" fetus. In these middle three months of in utero growth you were working on further developing your infrastructure. By that time, you had grown from about 3½ inches to a whopping 9 inches from your crown to rump, and your weight had increased from around one ounce to two pounds.

You then entered your third trimester, the final months of gestation, in which you as an older fetus continued to grow. Among many other events, your lungs continued to develop, your brain and body increased in size and volume, your nervous system matured, and your cartilaginous arms and legs converted to bone. You started your last trimester at less than 10 inches long and about two pounds—not much bigger than a large hotdog. By the end of your time in utero, around nine-ish months of gestational age, you were a fully formed baby, 18–20 inches long and weighing around 6½ to 8 lbs. At that point you had "aged out" of your time in the uterus and were ready to be born.

You might wish to take a walk, contemplate your navel, or rest awhile as you view another funny chicken video; a clear head and an open mind are requisites for the next chapter.

Chapter 3
Reasons for the Party

If you want to peek at how old you will likely live to be, check in the resources section for a copy of the Social Security website actuarial table, which lists life expectancy for each chronological year of life. The average human life expectancy in the U.S. (76 for males and 82 for females) is skewed, because to arrive at the average all deaths must be counted, including premature deaths, i.e., those from childhood or young adult diseases or accidents or pandemonium at any age. When those premature deaths are removed, the resulting average life expectancy goes up.

As an example, the table shows that at age sixteen a man's life expectancy is 16 + 61, a total of 77 years. However, once men get beyond the age of fast cars and "I am invincible" choices such as lighting their flatus with matches, overall life expectancy goes up and approaches that of women. Good news, guys, it's not that your bodies are inferior to and don't last as long as women's, it's just that you don't initially make the best decisions for longevity. For men who live to be 88, the life expectancy is about 4½ years, or 92½. For women at age sixteen, life expectancy is 16 + 66 for a total of 82 years, but once you are past the childbearing years, you too have a better chance of living longer. If you live to be 88, your life expectancy is another 5½ years, or 93½. Therefore, excluding the premature deaths, overall life expectancy for both sexes is a bit closer to 90 years.

Here's an amazing supposition to ponder: There is no doubt that all the nine-ish months of gestation, all three trimesters are important to the launching of a healthy infant. Could it be that all the nine-ish decades of adult life, all three "trimesters," i.e., youth, middle age, and elder years, are important to the launching of a healthy adult? Granted, after death we're not too healthy in this world's terms since we are dead, but just work with me for a minute. What if this corporeal life that we live as adults, right now, is parallel to the process of development of the in utero fetus who launches into this world at birth? What happens when we die? Some people take umbrage at even speculating that there's something more in store for us after we die. Other people come down on the side of our continuing on as a soul or a spirit. Some facetiously theorize that we might become a quark or photon.

A Note to Agnostics and Atheists

Hang with me for the next few sentences, and then you can tear this book asunder if you choose. It is the religions of the world that variously posit that we are reincarnated or go to heaven or hell or nirvana. In a recent Scientific American article entitled "Afterlife for Atheists," the author explores the hypothesis that a brain's connectome might be preserved beyond death. A connectome is a comprehensive map of neural connections in the brain, and may be thought of as its "wiring diagram."

So maybe those who doubt the existence of a "supreme being" might want to get with the program to celebrate and treasure this life as if it is going to translate to the next realm. Connectome preservation has not been perfected yet, but what if the technology becomes available shortly before you exit the world? Just in case it does, you might want to maximize learning and adventures in this life. Wouldn't that be a kick in the pants if the only ones who actually have an afterlife are atheists who choose to preserve their brains, and everyone else just becomes compost?

On a more serious note, religions uniformly emphasize the importance of what we do in this world and how it impacts our fate in the afterlife. So, whether our perspectives include religious concepts, philosophical conjecture, or atheism, no human knows for sure what lies beyond death. When we die, we might just stop as a life force, or we might endure in some capacity. No one and no religion can prove that our life continues, and if so, in what form we might exist. Equally, no one, no agnostic, no atheist, can prove that we do not continue to exist in some form.

Here's an interesting thought for you. If we do continue beyond death, could we adults be developing, during our adult lifetimes, capabilities we are unaware of? We did not know it, but when we were in utero we were getting prepared for launch. Immediately after birth, as we exited our in utero world, the placenta, amniotic sac, and umbilical cord that brought us here were unceremoniously discarded. These components were not only no longer necessary but also we couldn't survive had we remained contained with them. Similarly, our bodies are jettisoned as we leave this world. As we exited the uterus, we took a lot of what proved to be good stuff with us. As we exit this world could we again be taking some good stuff with us, and if so, what? If we can wrap our heads around the idea of developing attributes as adults that might be necessary or at least helpful for our next journey, we need a term to identify this time of ongoing adult metamorphosis.

[*What to call it? Hmm. I have it! Let's call it—ta-dah!*]

In Utero II

The complex intrauterine system of your placenta, amniotic sac, and umbilical cord was the only means by which to complete your preparation for birth (your in utero development). Similarly, your physical body provides the only means by which you can complete your life journey as an adult. Therefore, in a nod to symmetry, let's designate your developmental time in the womb as In Utero I and, as a metaphor, recognize the similarities of your adult lifetime as your In Utero II journey.

Time Out

Let's stop using our brains for a while. You have an option. We can talk about my WW degree in worm wrangling or we can go to YT (Yoga Teacher) mode and do a little meditation. By the way, there's a wonderfully funny book by Dan Harris entitled 10% Happier, in which the author details his hilarious, self-deprecating foray into meditation. If you've considered meditating but have found the prospect scary, frustrating, or impossible, and you want to laugh and learn something at the same time, start with Harris's book. On second thought, although meditation, a yoga practice dating back thousands of years and known to be restful for the brain, would be perfect right now, teaching yoga is a little beyond the scope of a paragraph.

So, let me give you a lesson to ponder leisurely, one that I learned from worms. In a new garden spot, I was chagrined that the previous owner's pesticide and herbicide usage had decimated the worm population. I ordered thousands of red wrigglers to repopulate the area. If you're unaware of the importance of earthworms, or would like to visit a lovely site to reaffirm your status as a worm lover, please see "Why are earthworms important?" by the Earthworm Society of Britain (Resources - Topics of Interest - Earthworm Society of Britain). Several months later the worms were doing well, until we had a week of torrential rainfall. (Worms need moist soil, but water-saturated ground can kill them.) The first clear morning, I took a much-needed walk in the sunshine. I was upset to find that a large percentage of my little worm buddies had gone to "high ground" on the driveway and were now stranded as the sun began to cook them.

I ran hither and yon trying to pluck them from sure death, only to find that the little critters seemed to be flattening themselves defensively. So, if the worms were trying to keep me from picking them up, they succeeded by making it very difficult to grip them. My rescue operation was much stymied, and thus a smaller percentage were rescued than would have been had they just cooperated.

On later reflection, I learned several lessons from the encounter, but the following is probably the most pertinent for purposes of this book. I'm not sure I ever want this lesson to come in handy, but if I have almost drowned, then almost cooked, and a Martian 10,000 times bigger than I am tries to pick me up, I think I will let him—I'm screwed anyway and maybe Martians are friendly.

For those who don't understand my meaning, other than the hilarity of the visual, here goes: Folks, if things are going poorly for you, climb to high ground. Do not "Stop. Hunker down. Give up." High ground can take many forms, but my inference, drawn from the behavior of the worms, was not to sit around and complain of the rain and the potential for drowning. Do something. If you think you're safe once you get there, keep looking for alternatives, because what at first looks like a safe place may in turn become a "hot seat." And finally, the safest place might look scary. Take a chance. You have nothing to lose if you keep trying and everything to lose if you don't.

When working backward, re-examining a situation, or quite honestly examining it for the first time as we just did for your time in the womb, we confirm what we know and speculate on what we don't know. While in your mother's uterus, you developed a lot of useful attributes: Your brain, limbs, sense organs, circulatory system, respiratory system, gastrointestinal system, and genitourinary system. You developed an entire human body and mind with all the amazing potential you ultimately possessed as you entered this world. Whether hale, frail, large, small, damaged, or malformed, our physical body is the only means by which our mind, intellect, and life force can exist.

After your birth, ending In Utero I, the process of physical growth and development continued as you rapidly grew, adding length to your arms, fingers, toes, legs, and spine. The volume of your brain and body expanded. Most of us develop motor skills necessary for sequential crawling, walking, and running, and eventually abilities that combine such skills, to allow participation in complex sports, dance, playing a piano, and countless other activities. But whether such skills started and remain strong or if they are now frail or damaged (or even have been since birth), your physical body is still the container in which your life essence is housed. As your brain continued to grow, you developed full consciousness with thought, language, and skills in mathematical processing, general cognition, and reasoning.

On average, it takes only a few months to begin to communicate beyond just having to cry for attention. (Check out baby sign language in chapter 4.) By age two, you may have had a vocabulary of twenty-five to 250 words. Have you ever asked your family what your first word was? And when they first heard you say it? Can you recall your first memory?

There's no question that after gestation we continue to develop physically, mentally, and emotionally as children and young adults. In fact, the frontal lobe of the brain isn't fully mature until our mid-twenties. But what if we continue to develop important abilities in the middle and older ages, and what if this development in our later years is vital to becoming a complete human?

Talk about a crazy-fun topic to speculate about.

The baby at birth takes along many developing body parts and abilities as it enters this adventure of life. What might we adults take with us as we launch? Let's go back to look at those senses you developed during In Utero I, which you've used extensively during In Utero II. Could you take these along if there is something beyond this life?

The Senses

It doesn't seem that we could take our senses with us, since the five senses are perceived through organic sense organs such as the eyes and nose. Hmm. But if these touchstones by which you perceive the world are gone, could it be that they are stored in memory? What if those senses of an adult are rudimentary, so that in a future iteration of our individual selves we'll be able to see a much broader spectrum of colors or, like whales, send and hear sounds over hundreds of miles.

The Mind

During gestation (In Utero I), you floated in the amniotic sac within the uterus, and you were incapable of free movement. Were you able to learn or think? As you entered your In Utero II phase, your brain began to recognize patterns of action and sound. Minds, at some point come on line with a cascade of thought that doesn't cease until we die. The mind floats free with curiosity and possibilities. The brain is organic and therefore will decay at death, but is consciousness brain-derived, a form of energy, or something beyond the brain's function of thought?

Some children have an "imaginary" friend with whom they converse as they would with a person standing adjacent to them. Is the "imaginary" friend real?

When does the imaginary friend go away, or does he or she go from externalized to internalized as an "inner monologue?"

At what age does a child begin to perceive the inner monologue?

Do all adults have that inner monologue, "that voice in our head?"

Is our inner monologue actually a dialogue?

Where does the imaginary friend, the inner monologue, or the inner dialogue originate?

Is the inner monologue or dialogue our awareness of "self"? Consciousness is defined as the awareness by the mind of itself and the world. Or is there someone in there with us? Hmm. Spooky thought.

What is perception, and where is it stored? During gestation, In Utero I, you perceived, at best, a two-dimensional world, which became your three-dimensional world as you entered In Utero II. Could it be that in your next destination you will perceive a fourth, fifth, or sixth dimension?

Memory

Our memory is the sum total of who we are as humans. Our memories are the essence of us. Memory stores a life of learning and sensing and striving. It also stores our relationships with other humans, especially those whom we love, nature, and animals. Our entire life is stored in memory circuits in the brain and therefore can be lost to disease, but does the brain have a backup, like a computer's hard drive, so we can retrieve it later? What if we take all the memories and all the ideas we've had, the entire content of what we read, and our abilities to create and enjoy music, art, or dance with us?

Emotion

Are emotions a function of or beyond the brain? During fetal development, In Utero I, you didn't feel the emotions of happiness, sadness, exhilaration, anger, loneliness, compassion, or empathy. During In Utero II you feel all these emotions strongly. In fact, if consciousness is our life essence, the emotions might be argued to be the reason we exist. In his book *Mindsight,* Dan Siegal recounts the story of a woman who became essentially an automaton when her frontal lobe was damaged, resulting in an inability to feel emotion. The tragic story is required reading for anyone who wants to understand the complexity of human emotion. Emotions develop in this life, but are they transferable? We consider love an emotion, but is it something beyond thought or emotion?

You, as a developing baby during In Utero I, were unaware of many latent abilities that would later become essential. What latent abilities might you be developing as an adult of which you have no awareness or only a rudimentary one? Could there be aspects of your existence whose full impact cannot be known until you begin your existence elsewhere? An example might be your sixth sense, the one termed gut feeling, gut instinct, a "knowing," or intuition, and on which you and the rest of us rely much more than most of us are aware. You receive sensory input through your nose, ears, skin, taste buds, and eyes. This sixth sense, however, is not legitimized by a concrete sense organ as our five major senses are. Could it be that we "pooh-pooh" (get it? gut feeling?) the sixth sense because we don't know where it resides and don't buy into the stomach area as being the origin? Like some of the *Star Trek* species, could it be that we'll communicate in the next phase of existence without voice as we know it now? Maybe we'll communicate through our sixth sense.

I know this is getting "out there," but what the heck, it's fun to think about "what if?" Is there a seventh, eighth, or ninth sense developing during In Utero II, like telepathy or synchronicity or déjà vu, of which you're unaware, just as you were unaware of your five developing senses during In Utero I? Most of us have had the occasion of thinking of someone we haven't seen in a long time, only to have that person appear shortly thereafter. Do you note the phenomenon in passing but not delve into the full nature of relevant possibilities? You probably experience a quickly discounted thought such as *It's cool that I was just thinking of you,* but it's doubtful that you engage in studied reflection on what this experience means or why it happens.

Could musical abilities be vital to our next realm? One musician interviewee said he feels that future corporeal humans might communicate more with music than voice. Could such attributes be translated and enhanced beyond this life? These are some of the highly speculative "What Ifs." However, what about now, in this lifetime?

Could the contemplative time of our adult "second and third trimesters" be the most important part of our In Utero II development? With aging comes a decline of youthful bravado as the gradual degeneration of the body, pain in the joints, or the pain of disease causes recognition within us of our eventual mortality. Whereas in youth most of us did not even consider aging or dying, those who age but who do not "give up or get mad" about their aging often begin to reflect more on the meaning of life and any mission they might like to accomplish before they die.

Most of us can be physically active, and those of us whose bodies don't cooperate struggle to attain physical movement. After being cooped up during In Utero I, a part of the enthusiasm of youth may be the sheer joy of unrestrained movement, engendering an accompanying feeling of invincibility for youth driven by strong, healthy bodies and hormonal-induced emotional lability. We sometimes lack judgment because we cannot conceptualize the processes of aging or death. As youngsters, we're filled with the joy of life, an emotion that can result in bold adventures and occasional disasters. Youth is often a time characterized by minimal reflection on the continuum of life and the inevitability of death. Maybe youth, which is a pretty cool time with all the freedom of body and mind, identifies a stage of life both to be enjoyed and to be overcome. In the middle and older ages, without these youth-associated "encumbrances," we can begin to reflect on our life process in the broader scope, and endeavor toward further character development and experiential wisdom. Our thoughts start to move toward an introspective discourse as we begin to realize that we are, in fact, mortal.

Just as it was painful for a time during In Utero I when our bodies were squeezed down into a squished and pummeled tubular form to get through the birth canal, we suffer pain as our bodies are dying to this world. Just as the pain of the contractions of birth once came to an end, so too does the pain of the transition of the body into death. Pain can be described as physical or mental suffering caused by illness, injury, or emotional distress. I'm pretty sure that no humans, neither any of the billions before us nor the billions who share the world now, have avoided the experience of pain. Sure we need pain meds, but are they overused? Is our body trying to tell us something? Is pain the only way our body can get our mind's attention? Could much of our pain be alleviated by not resisting pain as vehemently as we do?

Hmm. Here we go again; no human escapes having pain. So, if we all suffer pain, could there be a reason? As interviewee T.N. stated, "Since pain is universal, could there be something that we gain from it, like grit or resilience?" What if we didn't resist but yielded to and reflected on the pain to learn from it? Radical thought: Why do we call it suffering? What if one of our best teachers is pain? What if we welcomed it, studied it within ourselves, then embraced and/or conquered it?

One philosopher, Shinzen Young, directs the individual to look mentally at an area of pain and to observe it without resistance. Interestingly enough, for many who do focus directly on the pain without resisting it, the pain is perceived as decreasing in intensity. Does pain in fact diminish with our intervention, or do we just perceive it as such? Could it be through soldiering on and not giving in to physical or emotional pain that we can become more compassionate regarding the pain of others? Could it be that by surmounting pain we become more courageous and more resilient to life's later untoward events? Again, to quote T.N., "No one ever said it (life) was going to be easy. Maybe the struggle is the point."

Could it be that compassion, courage, and resilience travel on with us? If you consider the last two trimesters of In Utero II, your middle and older years, to be equally if not more important than your first trimester (youth), how differently would you approach your most meaningful life phases? What if we adopted a perspective that we have a job to do? Maybe we are to experience all that life has to offer, good and bad, to become as developed as we can be in this existence. What if we took the attitude of runners who run through the finish line? If runners were planning to stop directly on the finish line, they would have to slow their pace in anticipation of it, and to do so would make them lose the race. Maybe the challenge for us is to consider our lives as akin to a race in which we run toward the finish line, not as a downhill course into death but as a run-through, developing a really cool skill set of life accomplishments that just might come in handy if we do travel on.

What if we don't travel on? If we don't have awareness on the other side of death, we won't know it and therefore we won't be disappointed. But maintaining the attitude that we might be in for a pleasant time could help us all live life to the fullest while we are on earth.

My Truly Original Thought

My Truly Original Thought is that we could be developing capabilities during this lifetime that parallel those of the growing fetus. This speculation is why I became a Party Animal when it comes to aging and dying. Since I have hopefully done a terrific job of persuading you that there should be a party, I consider myself your bona fide party planner. In a similar vein, if you think there's reason to party or if you think there's not, you're right. I hope you can see that there is reason to party as you live your life expecting each day to be full of experiences—the good and the bad—from which you glean wisdom, angst, joy, and sorrow to keep you moving forward. Sometimes people learn the most from the adverse events of their lives. Sometimes these events, viewed in retrospect, are seen as pivotal to a subsequent positive circumstance, such as a divorce that you didn't want allowing you the freedom to find your soul mate. Or an untoward event might afford you an easy lesson that steers you away from a future, similar but far worse consequence. These events help you accrue the tools in your toolbox for an awfully good life in the here and now and these tools might be super-helpful if we pop out into a next domain. We can't know if we will live one more minute or another hundred years. Humanity would be well served to come to grips with the fact that much of our existence is unknowable.

What if you re-looked at any obstacles that have been placed in your path, or that you have placed in your path, that have, to date, kept you from leading your happiest, most fulfilled life? What if you determined to rid yourself of these hindrances to forge a new path? If you can see more reasons to look at your life as a continuum, with each portion incredibly important to a life well lived, how would you maximize every moment? Would you travel more? Would you travel less? Would you exercise more (which can be a bit painful in the here and now—just look at the faces and bodies, particularly the feet of those who have just finished a marathon—ouch)? Would you exercise less (hurt less now but hurt more later when you're older, in pain, and can't move as you once could)?

Can you envision your life as an In Utero II journey? If, at your current age, you knew that the remaining years of your life were the most important, how would you change in attitude or trajectory? Would lifelong learning, reading to reflect, and seeking experiences of all kinds become paramount concerns to maximize this life as well as whatever adventure might follow?

Chapter 4

Watch Out for the Party Crashers

No matter your current age, if you can't think of aging and dying in a positive light, there may be some party crashers destroying your party mood. Consider this statement:

We humans tend to do what we have always done.

Our cave ancestors figured out a strategy when they were in need of a snack: "Hungry—really hungry. Super-tired of pterodactyl salad every night. Hmm. Mastodon burger sounds delectable. What to do? Let's run a herd of mastodons off the cliff. Fire up the barbie!" Once our cave brethren learned to stampede mastodons off cliffs, even to question why they were going to the metaphorical grocery store in such a manner would have required some novel thought processes. It seems that the initial outlay of brain energy to learn something new requires increased fuel for thinking, i.e., glucose derived from what we eat. But once the brain is trained to the new skill, the energy required to repeat the learned skill goes down substantially. Back to our cave folks: "Hungry. Need mastodon. Run fifteen or so off cliff. Fire up the barbie" may have become one of the first prehistoric habits formed.

By definition, doing something the same way over and over as a regular practice, especially one that's hard to give up, is known as a habit. Sadly, due to this unexamined "off-cliff" habit of our ancestors, we no longer have cute little hairy mastodons running around. We modern humans haven't learned any generalized lessons from the mastodon debacle and to this day tend to "do what we have always done." In his intriguing bestseller *The Power of Habit,* Charles Duhigg delves into the reasons, consequences, and power behind the habits we form (Resources – References – Books – Duhigg). He contends that much of what we do every day is a repeat of what we did the day before. It's a bit scary to think that half of the thousands of actions we take each day and the thousands of thoughts we think each day (such as how we tie our shoes, the path we drive to work, or what we say in conversation) is a duplicate of yesterday's actions and thoughts. But not only yesterday; we may have repeated them every day for years. Worse yet, we're often unaware that what we're doing is just a habit. We think we're having new thoughts, making novel decisions, and carrying out unprecedented actions, when in fact we're oftentimes actually recycling the old.

Party Crasher #1: Habit

On the other hand, we humans also tend to habitually suppress thinking about anything that upsets us. You, like many of those interviewed, might actively avoid contemplating aging and dying if you view them negatively. This life-reflection avoidance is a habit—a covert, subliminal, sneaky party crashing habit that has prevented you from even considering that your whole life cycle could be audacious. If you recognized that this aversion is a habit, might you attempt to re-examine your life and its trajectory in a more positive manner?

Could it be that it's a habit to view various aspects of the latter parts of the life cycle negatively?

Could it be that since there are many who suffer age-related memory loss that we've formed a habit of treating all the aged as if they do not have their faculties?

Could it be that we, having seen older people who've gotten into the habit of not exercising, presume, as we get closer to our elder years, that that's the way of being old? Must we assume the habit of not exercising as well which has been modeled for us? Since we've seen elders who move slowly and carefully because they might break something, do we presume that we are doomed to the same fate? Must we groan when we move from one position to the next?

M.T., sixty-two, said she recently noted that each time she arose from the floor to pursue her eighteen-month-old stepgranddaughter, she did so slowly and with an accompanying little groan. M.T. asked herself why, and decided that she'd gotten into this as a habit. The next time she arose, she chose not to moan and to get up with a spring in her step. She was surprised that not only was it easier to get up but she also saw no reason why she'd been groaning before. M.T. said that in so doing she had fun challenging her assumptions (yes, she had played the assumption game) and declared, "As a child I wanted to be a grownup, not a groan up!"

The more fragile we perceive ourselves to be, the more fragile we act. We then by default become more fragile—physically, emotionally, and mentally—because we quit exercising our bodies and minds. Instead of looking to the stereotyped elderly, what if we start seeking more positive elder models. Many elders continue to perform amazing physical feats that few sedentary, deconditioned teens can accomplish. One woman chose at age sixty-seven to become a bodybuilder, a habit she has continued. At eighty-plus years old she is amazingly strong and has a figure that many twenty-year-olds would aspire to. A few years ago, a ninety-two-year-old woman completed a marathon. One ninety-six-year-old man still climbs mountains. For fun, go on the Internet to see these and others in their older years who are proving what can and should be done at their age. Shouldn't these highly motivated seniors be the rule rather than the exception? (See Resources – Topics of Interest – Elder Athletes.)

Could it be that we have a habit of thinking elder bodies and faces unattractive? Ancient pottery is considered beautiful even if the vessels have a crazed surface or portions thereof are broken. These bits of human-made works, which have survived a hazardous journey through time, are considered precious works of art. Why? You could just as easily consider them trash. Are they revered because someone told us they should be? Is it because others made a habit of thinking of these containers as special and we have continued that habit? Could we elder people treat ourselves as treasures, be treated as treasures by those who will one day be old as well, and thereby form a habit for humanity of honoring the aged if for no other reason than that they've survived a hazardous journey through time?

If habits can be party crashers, what other examples might we identify?

Quite a few of the interviewees for this book used the term "dread" when asked about their own attitude and their perception of society's attitude toward aging and dying. The words *dread, anxiety, nervousness, tension, worry,* and *stress* are euphemisms for fear. If we say we dread something, it's milder and less embarrassing than saying we're afraid. Remember in childhood we never wanted to be called a "scaredy cat." In our society, few people want to show weakness by admitting that they're afraid.

Could fear have been the reason we formed the habit of avoiding life reflection?

Could being fearful, when there's no need, be a habit?

Party Crasher #2: Fear

During In Utero I and after birth, babies appear to lack the capacity to fear, and toddlers are noted to be pretty fearless. If fear is not necessarily a natural emotion, could it be a learned behavior? Hmm. If fear is a learned behavior, at what age did we learn it? As a baby and then as an early toddler, you didn't have the language necessary to form thoughts as you now know them. No doubt you had some sort of thought process going on; otherwise you could not eventually have put all the pieces of the communication puzzle together. Brilliant researchers have theorized that babies process language internally before they develop the brain circuits and/or anatomic voice maturity to speak the language of adults. Based on that theory, now known to be fact, babies as young as six to seven months whose vocal repertoire is limited to laughably disjointed syllables, squeaks, and guttural screeching have been successfully trained in sign language to communicate their concrete needs, for example, that they are thirsty, hungry, or tired.

It's unlikely that you were learning to fear until you were at least old enough for autonomous movement. Independent exploration through crawling, reaching, pulling up, and walking exposes babies to more and more hazardous items and situations. This exposure, of course, freaks out parents, but babies are quite blasé with respect to dangers posed by such things as dogs, fire, swimming pools, and numerous other potential threats. As babies, you and I were just too busy having fun and trying to make sense of gigabytes of information to fear dog bites or drowning.

Stop for a second to think (better if you write) of a list of all the things you fear. Is your list short or long? Hmm. How do you define fear? Decide for yourself, then you can check out the 93 million search results available on Google that define and discuss this emotion. As I use *fear* in this book, it is a normal protective human emotion, which we learn over time. The unpleasant emotional and physical feelings associated with the emotion of fear stem from the core belief that you are in a dangerous situation that can cause physical or emotional pain. Fear is really, really good if we apply it sparingly to events that we can impact.

As cavemen and cavewomen, if we didn't have a healthy dose of fear (fear of hunger, wild animals, and the like) we wouldn't have survived as a species. One hundred percent of "cave-folks" lived with a high-percentage chance of morbidity and/or mortality every day. Statistically, we modern "man-cave-folks" have less to fear.

[*Oh, you don't believe me? Remember, it took over 100,000 years to reach our first billion people on the planet. Now we are adding another billion people about every twelve years. Obviously, we're not dying at the rate that we used to. But we sure are a fearful lot, aren't we?*]

We aren't born with innate fears, so why are we adults so fearful? Somewhere on the continuum of baby to adult we learned to fear. The worst that you've been taught and have assimilated from the mass hysteria of your similarly taught brethren and from media in all forms is:

Free-form, pervasive, relentless fear.

The "lessons" for appropriate fears have been lost among the background clutter of potential fears. [*Chicken Whisperer wisdom: You might want to take a re-look at the fable of Chicken Little. Is the sky really falling?*]

Thanks to the Digital Revolution's media coverage, we are alerted moment to moment of travails from every corner of an entire planet; however, such sources of information provide no measure of relative risk. Much of our modern fear is well founded, but the percentage chance of any particular event directly affecting us is often extremely small. Out of 7 billion people, if even 1,000 have significant issues that are reported on a given day, the actual number of persons involved is .00001428% or 1.4×10^{-5} percent. Yet, on hearing the media coverage of the event, we go into high-alert status as we hit the ungoverned "fear button." It's like having only an on/off fear switch with no modulating rheostat. As a result, our bodies begin to pump out stress hormones, engage the fight-or-flight responses of our sympathetic nervous system (Resources – Definitions), and occupy our already overtaxed brains with gloomy ruminations. How much should we worry?

Through media exposure it appears that our chances of directly suffering the in-reality-unlikely event are quite high. What if TV commentators (who once upon a time were called reporters) were required to assign a number to the risk of your encountering a similar event? For example, tsunami risk: Is it 100%? Or perhaps .00001%? What if the "commentator" was required to "comment" on a specific action plan for you to take on behalf of yourself, your family, the injured person in a report, or how to avoid the adverse event completely? This requirement would avoid the feeling of helplessness and hopelessness that often follows bad news that we cannot positively impact.

If fear is a learned behavior—who teaches it?

Let's examine learned fear across the spectrum of baby to adult. Even if you don't have children or don't like children, you used to be one. Therefore, to read about the thought processes of babies and children is pertinent to your understanding about how we humans "think what we think" about fear.

Babies and Toddlers

Babies' brains are truly blank canvases on which we adults begin to paint our worldviews. Especially in the last few decades we've begun to understand neurological development and recognize the critical window of opportunity we have to shape healthy, happy baby brains. Very few parents plan to get it wrong when it comes to giving their children the best-case nurturing to launch their offspring toward a successful adult life. Most parents set about to teach and nurture their beloved children to the best of their abilities, but sometimes our unexamined actions have negative consequences. Sadly, we take this tabula rasa, this beautiful blank slate, and begin to sully it with our own subliminally communicated and overtly stated fears. Are parental fears and habits affecting babies, children, and teens? Do parents "check out" to the detriment of our children by using drugs or alcohol or through unexamined mindless hours spent on television, sports events, gaming, and other media programming because we don't want to focus on the many fears of living in our fast-paced, ever-changing world?

In the *Journal of Translational Psychiatry,* an article speaks to a growing concern that young children may be experiencing speech delay because of the amount of distracted parenting due to cell phone usage (See Resources – References – Parenting and Cell Phones). Hmm. We're so busy texting, reading emails, and the like that we're not interacting socially with our children. Do we need to focus on long-term parenting effects rather than short-term outcomes? A baby or toddler is rarely allowed to freely embrace all aspects of his or her environment. Just imagine the joy of learning and perseverance demonstrated when a child discovers that turning a faucet "on" results in water gushing forth and that turning it "off" stops the water. A baby can repeat the on/off experiment for an amazingly prolonged time as he or she learns the wonders of water and the lessons of cause and effect. Sadly, the baby usually continues until the parent says stop because the parent is impatient to check email, do the dishes, or engage in some other worthy adult venture. Parents sometimes forget that experiences we consider routine or mundane are novel and wonderful for a baby. What do babies or toddlers learn about impatience and the "power-over" wielded by the parent who interrupts their innocent and exciting experiments? And what do they not learn about the science of cause and effect, autonomy, leadership, and personal boundaries?

We parents leave seductive trinkets in front of our offspring and are dismayed when the baby reaches for them; then we start with the inevitable "No." Toddlers often begin to fear that command because of the emotionally charged manner in which the lone syllable is delivered by the parent (whom, of course, the child wishes to please). The generalized message of repeatedly saying no is "watch out; not safe; don't follow your heart, mind, or imagination; be cautious; or "experimenting is not encouraged in this house." Soon, before the toddler reaches for something novel, interesting, or beautiful, he or she begins to look to the parent for approval or disapproval. Toddlers rapidly develop a fear of the negative consequences of exploring their environment and of upsetting the beloved parent. Could this reaction stymie the baby's critical thinking skills, which are borne of self-taught assessments of cause and effect? Overly involved parenting styles can usurp a child's decision-making autonomy. Because children are not allowed to get into benign predicaments from which they can free themselves, they don't learn to avoid the situation in the first place; neither do they gain the feeling of personal power when they rescue themselves.

Children

The original 1980s work of Cline and Fey in *Parenting with Love and Logic* recommended ways to nurture autonomy in young children. Their contention was that parents do a disservice to their children up to age eighteen if they don't allow them to experience the consequences of their decisions. By experiencing minor negative consequences of personal choice at a young age, children develop the necessary skills to assess risk as they enter late childhood or adolescence. The long-term effect of rescuing children from the consequences of their own decisions is to render them less able to weigh risks and benefits of personal decisions that they must make as adults.

What if you help your child to be aware of a hazard and how to avoid it, but are careful not to foster fear? [*The following observations and suggestions about parenting without fear are strictly my opinion and therefore for you to entertain, adopt, or adapt to your own needs, or discard after studied thought.*]

The mnemonic "Stop, Drop, and Roll" is taught to children so they can act reflexively if their clothes catch fire. This learned response instilled into their computer-bank brains teaches an appropriate action plan that children can apply to keep them safer. Could it be, on the other hand, that "Stranger Danger," a phrase evidently coined in the 1960s, is a well-intentioned travesty? With their natural curiosity, babies and toddlers frequently demonstrate wide-eyed engagement as they spy new things and new people in their environment. When children meet an adult (later to be identified by the disparaging term "Stranger"), they look directly into the unknown person's eyes, to the benefit and amazement of both. Typically, for the first two years of life the child and we doting onlookers get to gaze at each other in mutual adoration. Around age three, however, many children are taught the singsong, highly memorable "Stranger Danger" phrase.

Subsequently, when a young child meets an unknown adult's eyes, both the adult and child initially smile, and then the child gets a look of confusion in his or her eyes. It's sad to watch as the internal thought loop, "Stranger Danger," starts to play through the child's mind. At some level the child perceives this previously instilled message of fear to conflict with the real-time, real-life fun he is having, but the child dutifully ducks his or her head, no longer making eye contact, and complies with the brainwashing admonition to not gaze upon someone who represents danger. Poor babies: They were having a grand old time and now they're on high alert. They experience fear. The child studiously avoids looking back toward the unknown-but-almost-got-suckered-into-liking person who is actually a Stranger! This internalized message regarding strangers begets a globalized message: "Stay vigilant—I am not safe—Don't trust anyone."

A lot of well-meaning adults are now shying away from even looking at children. The reason is twofold:

To avoid frightening the child; and

In self-defense, so as not to be made to feel like a child molester as the child suddenly looks away in terror.

This is especially an issue for elders who as children were cosseted and adored by grandparents, aunts, uncles, and random older strangers. The instinct of the elder is to adore random children just as they themselves were adored.

The mnemonic "Stop, Drop, and Roll" is a memory aid of actions to be taken in the unlikely event of catching fire. The mnemonic does not teach "Fear Fire." Instead it identifies a hazard and an appropriate action plan. However, the use of the phrase "Stranger Danger" is a tragic irony in that most child molesters are not Strangers but known family or friends. The phrase does not identify a specific hazard or an action plan, but it fosters a nonspecific fear of every unfamiliar person on the planet, essentially all 7 billion of the child's contemporaries. The phrase becomes ingrained, and the globalized message undermines the child's sense of safety in his or her world. How does this message, which is so entrenched in childhood, affect teens and adults?

Well-motivated adults should be curious about where the heck the Law of You Must Teach "Helpful" Mnemonics arises? Was the phrase "Stranger Danger" vetted with controlled scientific studies, or did someone or some group assume it to be a great idea? And even if the phrase was found efficacious in preventing child endangerment, was there a scientifically appropriate companion study of the endangerment posed by making children fear humanity? [*Hmm. Is Stranger Danger a statistically and logically faulty concept? Can it produce great harm to a child's sense of safety? Why do good parents and teachers feel compelled to teach the phrase in order to "protect" the child?*]

Are parents who wish to teach tolerance to their children instead teaching them just the opposite? Can you be tolerant of people when you fear them? Children may have a sixth sense that an adult whom they are gazing upon cares about them and wishes them well, but when their instincts conflict with their memorized automatic script of fear toward strangers, do they also learn not to trust themselves?

As children become older they learn to fear not only the people and situations in their local environment, such as strangers, other students, teachers, failure in general, bullies, not making the team, or not being liked but also learn to fear global problems and complex social issues. Just because children appear to be absorbed in various activities doesn't mean they're not listening to everything they hear. Mom, Dad, and the news programs the parents watch (and that the child inevitably overhears) expose children to topics too complicated for them to understand. Children's perceptions are much more concrete than those of adults because of their immature neurologic developmental level (chapter 9 provides more in-depth discussion). These adult concepts are to a child both abstract and nebulous; however, even though they don't understand the issues, children typically incorporate parental anxiety.

Do children have the intellectual capacity to weigh the personal risk of global events when they overhear news programming the parent is listening to? For example, why should a child in Montana fear a tsunami? Do children thus fail to develop their own internal barometers of safe/unsafe, right/wrong, or fear/no fear when warranted? As children grow could they thereby be unable to internalize their own boundaries? If children were allowed to observe cause and effect, allowed to fail, and allowed to develop critical thinking skills to extricate themselves from difficult situations, might these lessons be applied to future challenges? Could unsuccessful attempts be viewed not as failures but as opportunities for learning? Could learning from such experiences increase competency for the future and avoid developing fear of failure?

Teens and Adults

Teens, by definition, are individuals between thirteen and nineteen years of age. The interesting thing is that "teens" as a recognized separate age group did not exist until the 1930s when high school was mandated. Prior to that time a person of those ages could choose to stay in school or enter the workforce. Before this interesting social development, children transitioned into adulthood when they were ready or when it was necessary. The actual term "teen" as we know it was not in common use until the 1940s. This process partitioned what was previously experienced as a gradual continuum of growth.

It's sad to see teens who aren't following their own paths and passions but are instead governed by the expectations of their peer group. The consensus of the peer group is that they will never get old. Are teens emotionally locked into their age group? Some young interviewees disparage elders as if they have "failed" to stay young. A few seem arrogant and condescending as if they are the planet's first bad-asses. If they were to reflect on the long lineage of human bad-asses, teens might discover that some of the "old geezers" they reject as wimps were in fact their own generation's bad-ass equivalents. Other teens feel that they are "evolved" with a social conscience and acceptance of others. However, they limit their human-to-human contact via preferential use of "social" media (which could in fact be termed "antisocial" media), video games, and TV programming. More and more due to technology we experience less and less actual human interaction.

It seems that we are in some ways more connected in that we can converse with anyone on the planet within seconds; however, that very "connection" is driving more social isolation. Due in part to texting we are reduced to "text bites" (akin to sound bites), little snippets of written communication that are becoming the preference to voicemail or direct real-time voice communication. Observe people at restaurants: They're often head-down looking at electronic devices, making no or little eye contact with the person seated with them. Without eye contact and verbal dialogue there is no observation of the nuances of language, which are transmitted via voice inflection, facial expression, and body language, all integral to human communication. In an intriguing book entitled *Blink,* Malcolm Gladwell discusses the observation and science of human communication that occur in the blink of an eye when looking directly at someone.

How many times do you check your cell phone each day? Would you estimate twenty times? Fifty? New research conducted by British psychologist Dr. Sally Andrews found that young adults use their smartphones roughly twice as often as they guessed. The participants in her study checked their cell phones an average of eighty-five times a day.

Dr. Andrews suggested that cell phone usage is driven by habit and is so automatic that users don't realize how much they use their phones. Another British psychologist, Dr. Richard House, found that people spend up to a third of their waking hours using their cell phones. Dr. House is concerned about the impact of such excessive use.

Research on the effects of technology has identified impairments in areas such as memory, creativity, and thought processing. Dr. Andrews suggests that reasoning and analytic thinking are impacted by having such ready access to online search engines. (For sources of the above comments see Resources – References – Web – Andrews, "Beyond Self-Report: Tools to Compare.")

Are young people failing to learn social cues that are integral to a sense of trust in the stability of the world and for successful human communication? Could it be that fear for the planet, global warming, the economy, politics, school performance, and peer acceptance, among many other fears, is fueling the high incidence of teen suicide? The statistics on adolescent suicide are terrifying, or should be. The following is excerpted from the CDC website, which explores suicide in all age groups.

Among students in grades 9–12 in the U.S. during 2013–2014

- 17.0% of students seriously considered attempting suicide in the previous 12 months (22.4% of females and 11.6% of males).
- 13.6% of students planned their potential suicide in the previous 12 months (16.9% of females and 10.3% of males).
- 8.0% of students attempted suicide one or more times in the previous 12 months (10.6% of females and 5.4% of males).
- 2.7% of students made a suicide attempt that resulted in an injury, poisoning, or an overdose that required medical attention (3.6% of females and 1.8% of males).

(Resources – Supporting Data – CDC Suicide Data Sheet)

Something is desperately wrong when teenagers are in such emotional pain that they prefer death to living.

You were taught to fear as a child by well-meaning parents and teachers, and you learned the lesson well, so well that you don't even recognize fear, partly because of the euphemisms we discussed, which include worry, stress, and anxiety under which it is disguised. Worry can evolve into a lifelong daily habit and for some a paralyzing moment-to-moment burden impacting work, self-worth, and relationships. It's no wonder that anxiety (fear) is the largest of the mental illness categories. In addition to traditional therapy and/or medications, there are multiple complementary ways to approach recovery from anxiety. In that anxiety is a huge issue for a large segment of the population, we will delve into it in more detail in chapters 5 and 6. Fortunately, a non-pharmaceutical, immediately available, free treatment for anxiety is pranayama. As one of the limbs of yoga, pranayama has been around for upward of 5,000 years and has recently attained scientific legitimacy. Pranayama addresses awareness and exercise of the breath (Resources – Scientific, Philosophical or Psychological Concepts – Yoga).

As a yoga teacher, I am a proponent of the fascinating maneuvers to alter and strengthen our breathing in pranayama. Of the many breath exercises and resultant outcomes, some specific breathing techniques are used to decrease anxiety. The following exercise engages the parasympathetic nervous system, which is the more vegetative nerve system (sort of the anti-stress mode). With this system, the heart slows and breathing becomes deeper as blood is shunted to core functions such as digestion. On the other hand, the sympathetic nervous system kicks in with increased heart rate and breathing rate (the fight-or-flight mode) when, for example, you see a snake or a jerk cuts you off in traffic.

4-7-9 Breathing Exercise

Take a deep breath during a count of 4. Hold for a count of 7. Then slowly exhale for a count of 9. This can be repeated three more times during any one session, because to do more can make those of us who breathe shallowly have symptoms of hyperventilation. But the good news is that you can do the three-step exercise at different times throughout the day. No one will know that you are increasing the oxygen content of your brain, thereby calming yourself and possibly gaining a few IQ points.

Since habit and fear are impediments to a life well lived, how can we recognize these challenges within our children, ourselves, and our society?

What can we do about negative habits, nonproductive fears, and the habit of being fearful?

Chapter 5

Where's the Bouncer?

In the last chapter, we found that fear and habit are party crashers that undermine the intent to celebrate our lives beyond age thirty. So, where's the bouncer? We need a "big beefy guy" attitude to toss out these insidious obstacles. It's sadly comical how much we worry about worrying. Paraphrasing, there is a saying: "Worry (a.k.a. fear) is creativity all dressed up with no place to go." Fear with no action (i.e., no place to go) leads people to feel helpless—then hopeless.

In chapter 4 we discussed the party crashers, the worst of which was learned fear. To analyze and resolve fear, critical thinking skills are needed. There are many definitions of "critical thinking." In fact, a recent Google search of the phrase returned 71,300,000 hits, including sites on how to teach critical thinking skills. The word "critical" can be characterized as the objective analysis and evaluation of an issue in order to form a judgment. Some definitions of critical thinking are just long, conceptually generic laundry lists of attributes. The way critical thinking is used in this book is as follows:

- To think critically is a learned process that results in mental flexibility and confidence to act.

- Critical thinking is the mental process we use to interpret novel observations or actions and thereby make sense of our daily experiences.
- Critical thinkers can reference historical information and experiences, ones that they can apply to current observations, to anticipate future events.
- Using numerous apparently disjointed bits of information that might or might not be related, critical thinkers can arrive at new ideas.
- When thinking in an analytical manner, the critical thinker can organize and construct action plans, make decisions, and evaluate ideas.
- Critical thinkers have the ability to think beyond currently accepted lines of thought.

The following is a generic plan for using critical thinking skills, which can be adapted to a variety of situations.

Action Plan Using Critical Thinking Skills

1. Identify the issue to be considered.
2. Assess the risk, including whether the risk is related to doing something or doing nothing at all.
    a. Is there a problem?
    b. What is the percentage chance of harm?
3. Arrive at an action plan. Consider alternative actions; make up your own or gather ideas to assist in making your own.

4. Carry out the action plan.
5. Adjust the plan as needed, based on changing circumstances.

In the following sections, this action plan will be adapted to situations appropriate for various age groups, including babies and toddlers, children, early teens, as well as older teens and adults. Remember, this is a template that can be adapted to a broad spectrum of situations.

Babies and toddlers

1. Identify the issue: How can we avoid the pitfalls of inadvertently teaching fear to our children? Babies and toddlers love to meticulously explore (especially with their mouths) anything new to them.
2. Assess the risk:
    a. Is the problem real or perceived? The risk to babies and toddlers is quite real if they're left to their own devices in that they have no understanding or fear of very real hazards.
    b. What is the likelihood of harm? There's a significant likelihood of injury if babies and toddlers are not observed closely. However, there is a second problem, which often goes unrecognized: a significant risk of timidity and loss of autonomy if they're not allowed to "explore their world freely."
3. Arrive at an action plan:

    Suggestion: Clear the path in advance, before babies and toddlers enter a new space. Remove items that are potentially harmful or that seduce attention such as shiny, breakable items. Then let your child explore. Your job as parent is not only to watch but also to anticipate a child's potential trajectory around a room. As an example, you see your child headed in the direction of an electrical outlet. You've placed covers on the outlets, but even these can be enticing for little explorers. Before your tyke gets to the potentially dangerous situation or object, subtly move a piece of furniture, such as an ottoman, to block the path to the outlet. That way your toddler will never get to the outlet that would otherwise have been discovered and that he or she might have drooled upon. If you are observant and do not communicate your own fears or reactively admonish the child, he or she will feel safe and will be safe. If you are watching, children will feel safe—they'll never even know that they could be hurt by the electricity, and they'll remain safe because you're doing your job in anticipating and removing harmful, yet attractive, enticements from their path.

4. Carry out the action plan. This is where you as the parent decide whether the action plan is appropriate or whether to modify it.

5. Adjust the plan as needed. If you are at someone else's home, one that has not been childproofed, your level of vigilance will need to increase proportionally.

It's your job to protect your children not only from danger but also from fear.

Infants and toddlers are too young to understand electricity. Why not wait until language is sufficiently developed to explain it to them? Granted, these fearless explorers will ultimately need to learn that electric outlets are to be avoided, but give them a year or two of unbridled freedom until they're able to understand appropriate verbal communication. Who knows? Maybe we wouldn't have the "terrible twos" if these short-adult children weren't so frustrated with us tall-children parents who stymie their joy and learning with a barrage of "No, no, no." When language and their processing capacity for abstract thought are such that they can understand, children will be able to put "No" in perspective. Then the admonitions of danger will be episodic, have to do with specific risks, and, one hopes, be accompanied by your instruction on developing future action plans. "No" applied too early and too liberally can undermine the child's self-confidence as well as his or her freedom to explore, experiment, and learn critical thinking skills.

Another example of creatively protecting and allowing your little ones to flourish:

1. Identification of the problem: Babies and toddlers, who are used to relatively small play areas, seem to go joyfully crazy in the wide-open spaces of an airport. Appropriately, parents try to corral or capture their beloved offspring to keep them out of harm's way. Then they try to redirect the children (they chase or grab them, which is the physical equivalent of the verbal "No"), which never seems to work with these determined short-adult children. Typically, children see this as a game and continue play by immediately escaping again. If toddlers can't escape, they scream in protest at the inhibition of their freedom.

2. Assess the risk:

    a. Is the problem real or perceived? Yes, the threat is real.

    b. What is the likelihood of harm? High. There could be a catastrophic collision with a busy traveler trying to catch a flight. There's also a less obvious risk to the child, i.e., the risk of squelching his or her perceived freedom and joyful exploration.

3. Arrive at an action plan: In an actual airport situation a child can be better protected from injury by use of what is pejoratively called a "leash." Actually, the tether allows the child relative freedom, yet it maintains necessary parental control. However, to foster a child's joyful exploration and maintain autonomy, ingenious parents might recreate the airport atmosphere in a protected manner. Get the toddler into large, open, safe places, like fenced yards (which have been pre-inspected for hazards) or large parks. Then, parents (even better if other family or friends can be conscripted) form a "perimeter of safety" at intervals around the child. Such intervention lets the child feel totally free since he or she doesn't know that caregivers are watching like hawks for any possible threat. Instead of correcting the child, whom the parent perceives is heading for a hazard, one parent provides distraction by acting foolishly and wonderfully childlike (a very healthy action for the psyche of us tall-children adults). The other parent then surreptitiously removes or covers up the hazard that was so enticingly perceived (or about to be) by the child.

4. Carry out the action plan. This is where you, the parent, decide whether the action plan is appropriate or whether to modify it.

5. Adjust the plan as needed.

We read the directions on how to bake a cake (which in the long run matters not a whit) before we bake it. Why do we not apply the same principle to raising our beloved children? Where is the required-reading manual for parenting? Parents, who rarely have formal training in childrearing, tend not to "read the directions" on how best to raise a happy, healthy, intrepid explorer child who will grow into a happy, healthy adult critical thinker. Albert Einstein, one of the finest minds in both science and philosophy, observed that independent critical thinking is vital for the development of a young human.

Providing theories about childhood and adolescent brain development is important. However, some expert, supposedly factual how-to primers on childrearing are more in the realm of opinion. Unfortunately, there is also a downside to seeking out the numerous books and Internet articles for "expert" opinions. Sometimes the experts' ideas are wrong in general or specifically wrong for your child; however, even bad recipes can provide food for thought. Parents can choose whether to accept or reject the expert opinion, because parents are the final experts on raising their own child. Still, to never study parenting skills leads to lost opportunities. Let us apply the action-planning process described previously.

1. Identify the problem: It's amazing and sadly pervasive that parents who wish to do the right thing by their child may fail to adequately explore the many resources on "how to parent." Parents can miss opportunities by not studying a child's brain development and may inadvertently teach their child to fear.

2. Assess the risk:

    a. Is the problem real or perceived? When you consider the issues facing children, teens, and young adults, it's evident that many of these individuals are not prepared for those life phases.

    b. What is the likelihood of harm? In chapter 4, an excerpt from the CDC provides alarming statistics on teenage suicide.

3. Arrive at an action plan: Try to read prospectively, in advance of childhood stages, starting when the child is still in the

In Utero I phase, as to the most proactive ways to nurture healthy babies. While your baby is still a baby, begin to read parenting strategies for toddlers. Continue to anticipate and plan for the milestones they need to achieve as they progress through their transition to adulthood.

4. Carry out the action plan. Take the opportunity to study those resources you find appropriate for your child.

5. Adjust the plan as needed.

Babies have more brain cells than they need for many reasons, one of which is to have backup cells if there's an injury early on. As an example, a baby with intractable seizures underwent a massive surgical reduction of tissue on one side of the brain, resulting in a resolution of the seizures. With the infant brain's ability to grow new pathways, development was relatively normal. The capability of the brain to adapt to injury is due to brain plasticity which denotes the ability of the brain to adapt to changes, even significant injuries, by reforming itself.

In babies, brain plasticity is made possible by the multitude of redundant neural synapses. As the infant matures, these synapses (or nerve-cell-to-nerve-cell connections) go through a process called apoptosis. Apoptosis is not a decay of the extra brain synapses; it's very akin to pruning an apple tree. Much like the tree, unused or duplicated pathways (branches) are removed so the child's brain (young tree) becomes more streamlined. As a result, the baby's brain moves along a developmental pathway that, subsequent to the apoptosis, allows the necessary scaffolding for higher-order thought. This pruning sets the stage for the next important phase, "the terrible twos." This rather infamous age is actually not terrible at all except in the parents' perception. Parents are chagrined because they lose the malleable, silly-putty infant to gain an obstinate, demanding, fearless explorer of his or her childhood universe. A second major phase of apoptosis that occurs in adolescence will be discussed later.

In the previous chapter, we talked about the risks of inadvertently teaching fear to children, specifically the fear of unknown adults.

What if children were taught that the hazard of encountering a person of malintent is relatively small, but real, and were encouraged to use their gut-level intuition about such encounters?

Suggestions

In a manner appropriate for their age level, give children an action plan to recognize truly dangerous situations such as inappropriate touching. Inform them that you are able to assess situations and that while they're with you they can feel free to look at or talk to folks. In fact, even encourage it! Oh, the joy, the human connection, and the life lessons they will learn from random strangers of good intent.

Explain to young children that when they're alone or with a caregiver other than you, there are sadly a few people who are not of good intent, and that, since they are too young to know the difference, it's better not to engage unknown persons by eye contact or by talking to them. Even then, however, begin to encourage trusting their instincts if they get a feeling of not being safe.

Speak to your child as if he or she were a short adult. If you think about it, that's more true than not. Encourage children to let you know if they don't understand. Also, they have fantastic memories—think back to what you remember from your childhood. By your instilling safety-action plans, not generic fears, you ready their computer-bank-brains should the need arise.

The toddler experienced the first major period of apoptosis. Early teens go through a second period of apoptosis as they enter the very important phase of adolescence, a stage characterized by separation from their parents' influence, resulting in individuation (being distinguished from everyone else). As teens begin to separate their identities from those of their parents, they develop their adult personalities, think deeply on their life philosophies, and begin to assume their adult life roles.

As much as we parents want to keep our children close to us, we do them a disservice if we don't help them to separate from us. Successful separation, particularly in the phases of early childhood and adolescence, require continued development of critical thinking skills to transition to adulthood. Most parents want their children to develop leadership skills, but some sabotage their own efforts by fostering an environment of fear that insidiously erodes the natural self-confidence necessary to think independently. When children who lack a sense of autonomy get beyond their parents' radar, they are not leaders. Children who aren't encouraged or allowed to think freely, make their own choices, take responsibility, and experience consequences do not learn to choose their own path or to trust their own instincts and assessments. When the parent is absent, children, preteens, teenagers, or young adults who are taught-to-be-followers transfer their dependency for motivation and validation to their respective peer groups. This is likely one of the reasons that some first-year college students flunk out of school. These young students, who have escaped Mom and Dad, want to fit in with peers. The student may feel uncomfortable forging his or her own path or standing up to peer pressure. These taught-to-be-followers look to the "leader," who may disparage studying or encourage risky behavior. [Hmm. Could the double whammies of not having an internalized nidus of judgment (lack of critical thinking skills) and the conviction that the world is unsafe (fear of their fellow humans) have some impact on teenage drug and alcohol use and suicidal behavior?]

Of the many challenges facing teens and adults, one area that gets disproportionate media coverage, is that of disasters. There are innumerable opportunities for catastrophic events such as tsunamis, comets, tornados, random assaults, and pandemics. You notice I did not say disaster. These events have been happening since the world began and will continue for as long as the earth survives; that's why they call them natural. Depending upon where you chose to live, your chances of a particular event occurring increase or decrease. If you're living in "tornado alley," by a volcano, on a fault line, or at or under sea level, and are fearful that these events might occur, you might want to rethink your life strategy for housing.

Some of our modern fear is based in reality, but the percentage chance of any particular event directly impacting us is often extremely small, yet through media exposure it appears that our chances of directly suffering the in-reality-unlikely event are quite high.

Using critical thinking skills, the following provides an example of risk assessment and action planning:

1. If you fear a tsunami: do you live in a tsunami area?
    a. No? Good. There's a zero percent chance of harm to you and your family—quit worrying.
    b. Yes? Bad news. You might want to move.
        i. What if you can't move? Take out "insurance" by deciding in advance that you will run away from, rather than toward, the coast as the water is swept out (which occurs shortly before the huge coastward surge.)
        ii. For even better insurance, keep a boat, ropes, and/or a tsunami capsule handy.

2. Do you fear a comet? Just get over it, because we cannot directly "impact" this one.
    a. If a comet hits, there's a 100% chance that we will not make it—so hello dinosaurs, goodbye world.
    b. But there is almost a 0% chance that you'll die from a comet striking in the next seventy years. [*Whew, I feel better. You can take this fear off your plate.*]

We have other valid fears, and we can take action steps to alleviate much of the threat, or at least ameliorate its impact, by purchasing property, car, and life insurance or flood and earthquake insurance. Then, for the most part, we quit worrying, drive down the road, sing along with the radio, and think about our destination or the day's tasks, not considering that at any moment we could experience a flood, have our house blown away, or be hit by another car. These risks are real but relatively unlikely. Perhaps you can decrease fear by conceptualizing a new kind of insurance:

"Don't expect someone else to take care of you" insurance.

Personally assess the level of threat that any potential event poses to you, your loved ones, your country, other countries, people of the world, or your planet. Think deeply on the measures you personally can take to affect a positive outcome. Make an action plan, and commit to populating your plan as much as possible, such as by stocking supplies and water in case of tornados, earthquakes, or other natural events.

Don't be fatalistic and surmise that you won't survive an untoward event. You probably will survive, and, by the way, it will suck if you're hungry or thirsty and no governmental aid is forthcoming for days to weeks. If you look at every major disaster of the last twenty years, no matter how much the government prepared and no matter how many supplies it has stockpiled to help, there's always a lag time between the untoward event and the actual aid getting to all the people in need.

Your "insurance" is putting the necessary steps into action. To get effective car insurance, you must pay for it. You consider the premiums to be the cost of doing business and hope you never need to get a return on your investment. Similarly, if you take responsibility to protect you and your family, you need to spend the time, effort, and money necessary to gain the security of being prepared. You'll very likely never experience the planned-for disaster, but the premium, i.e., the money you spent for the supplies, will help you attain a feeling of calm self-assurance in that you've prepared. If you have a family, being prepared and having a non-fearful demeanor are gifts for them and yourself in the event of untoward circumstances.

A brief disaster protocol, which I wrote to get you started, is provided in appendix 3. You can also delve into the excellent resources readily available to you. The Federal Emergency Management Agency, known as FEMA, has a website containing suggestions for you to be able take care of you and your family were there a natural or manmade disaster. FEMA's website also has links to other helpful preparatory agencies and computer applications, or "apps," (Resources – Topics of Interest – FEMA Disaster Resources). As well, there are many disaster preparedness books available in which the authors have done the brainwork of figuring out what would help most in any given situation (ergo less brain output on your part).

Can we quit fearing and just start noticing? There are many, many potential risks that we can fear. The human brain is wired to recognize threats, so no doubt thoughts of potential hazards will continue to pop into your mind. If we ruminate on the various potential threats, we're likely to feel helpless, hopeless, and trapped by our fears, a process that can lead to chronic anxiety and depression. When the fear of tsunamis, terrorism, or tornados comes into your mind, try the following:

Repeat the feared event out loud, then add the word "and."

For example, I fear tornados . . . and . . .

After the *and,* add: the likelihood of tornados in New York is very low.

or

Say aloud the action you've already put into place to effect a more positive outcome. For example, I fear tornados . . . and since I live in Oklahoma, I've reinforced my closet so my family can seek refuge there during a storm.

or

If you haven't yet carried out the positive action, identify the next steps you plan to do, and name a date by which you plan to accomplish them. For example, I fear tornados . . . *and* I will buy a tornado storm shelter by May 1.

The *and* statement gives you the action step (worry dressed up with a place to go), which is so important in converting anxiety to appropriate action. When the fear of all these serious but unlikely potential events is dealt with, what about lesser but more likely fears? These would include fear of the loss of a job, fear of retiring, fear of not retiring, fear of failure, fear of not making the team, fear of not being liked, and so on. Did you notice that some of these fears are similar to those of our childhood? The same tool, discussed above, can be applied to these more common day-to-day fears.

Retirement

To begin: Assess the risk, use the *and* tool, and engage your "Don't expect someone else to take care of you" insurance. Then arrive at your action plan.

1. Identify the issue: Retirement
2. Risk assessment:
    a. You want to retire but can't afford to.
    b. You don't want to retire.
3. Arrive at an action plan:
    a. If you want to retire, aggressively save money for retirement. Sacrifice now, big-time, for that dream retirement, including possibly working overtime or taking a second job. You might want to read about financial planning or seek the counsel of financial planners.
    b. If you don't want to retire and don't need to physically, don't. Or, you could choose to have your "backup" job plans already in place. That way, if you can no longer perform a physically demanding job such as construction, you could transition to something less strenuous such as buying rental properties.
4. Carry out the action plan.
5. Adjust the plan as needed.

Aging, Dying, and Death

Of all our fears, perhaps the most limiting is the fear of aging, dying, and death, in part because there's no insurance policy or action plan to prevent their inevitability. Hmm. Like the result of a potential comet impact, since there's an absolute certainty that we aren't going to make it out alive, we should probably quit worrying about it. If fear is a learned behavior—let's unlearn it. We can use fear effectively for things we can impact. We can unlearn fear if we assess risk and make an action plan, whereas the abstract and smaller concrete fears might or might not happen, and percentages say most are unlikely to happen to you.

How cool would it be to have, like a dog, no idea that your life has an expiration date? Maybe that's why man's best friend is always so happy. Canines don't worry that in dog-years they're getting gray in the muzzle or approaching the end of their life expectancies. But since we're not as lucky as dogs, how great would it be to live your life every day as if you had just one more day, and at the same time live as if you were going to live to be one hundred years old? If you thought you had just one more day, what would you do? Some interviewees said they'd seek time with family and friends and mend relationships that needed repair. Others said they'd spend every last moment enjoying the beauty of the world, which they had to date overlooked. If you anticipated living to be one hundred, would you take much better care of your body and mind? Some of the more elderly interviewees with humor, but also perhaps a bit of melancholy, observed, "Had I known I would live this long, I'd have taken better care of myself." Other elders voiced that their main regrets were opportunities lost due to surmountable fears.

What would you do right now if you gave up fear? Charlie, the sixteen-year-old interviewee, gave up fear for the forty days of Lent. What if you became fearful, mentally identified that the fear was an emotion, and even for a moment gave it up? And could you then decide not to take back the fear?

> *Avoiding danger is no safer in the long run than outright exposure. The fearful are caught as often as the bold. Life is either a daring adventure, or nothing.*
>
> —Helen Keller

We can choose to recognize that the whole life cycle has a purpose. If we make our lives purposeful, we will benefit greatly by enjoying every moment rather than fearing what we cannot avert. If you adopt the attitude that we're still growing new human capacity during In Utero II, the fear of aging, dying, and death can melt away. If you're religious, you likely don't fear death in the same way that nonreligious people do; however, I've known many religious folks, and some were pretty fearful regarding their own and their loved ones' deaths. Wouldn't it be freeing to anticipate, plan for, and enjoy the living and dying processes with gusto—no fear, sadness, hopelessness, no sense of being cheated, no helplessness, no anger, and no fruitless gnashing of teeth?

One of the greatest constraints to a life well lived is fear.

Chapter 6
So Your Party Hat Keeps Falling Off?

If you've been reflecting on your answers to questions thus far raised and have resolved that you will celebrate the upcoming phases of your life, have your party hat on, and are looking around for appropriate libations to toast the festivities, let's get rolling. A list of potential festivities from which you can tailor just the right party for you is available in later chapters and in appendix 6, but if you're even a teeny bit worried that your party hat sits rakishly askew, you might want to check out this chapter before proceeding directly to the merriment.

You're beginning another chapter in a book of "Why?" and "What if?" You've had much to consider:

- What you were doing to amuse yourself during your three trimesters of In Utero I;
- What party hat you wished to choose when you considered that we adults might just be continuing to develop lots of cool "stuff" in the three trimesters of In Utero II;

- That the party crashers of fear and habit can be very sneaky; and
- That it can take the attitude of a "big beefy bouncer" critical thinker to rid yourself of party crashers.

We've explored some of the ways in which we have passively absorbed habits, fears, and attitudes from peers, society, family, and others. Are you forging a life in the here and now of your choosing? Are you the author of your life story, or do you remain captive to a story written by others? We can't free ourselves if we don't think to try. As an exercise, how about taking a minute to think of your response to the incomplete statement "I am ______."

Please jot down your answer before proceeding.

Did you just provide a response, or did you question, I am (who?) or I am (what?)?

Why can't this idiot party planner be a bit more specific? To which I say, Duh, that's the point. I'm doing the heavy lifting here. Just provide the requested information, please. So, have I stalled you long enough before you read the next paragraph that you've filled in the box with a response?

In the books of our lives, the "who" of us is sometimes obvious to us and to others. For example, you might say:

I am an accountant, mechanic, mother, doctor, farmer, or artist.

In other words, do you feel that the essence of who you are is your profession or role in life? Do you feel identified by your title, or is it just a subtitle of who you are?

Sometimes the title by which we identify ourselves might match our feeling of who we are. Is your I am ______ a title congruent with your passion? Does your passion reveal the I am ______ of you, or is it a subset of who you feel you are?

For example:

I am an artist who does accounting, a woodworker who does mechanics, or a dancer who is a mother as well.

If you really drill down, you might discover that the I am ______ of you might be unsettling:

I am an alcoholic; I am disabled; I am angry, sad, lonely, helpless, or depressed. Or, I am a failure; I am old; I am middle-aged; I am a victim of abuse; I am retired; I am too young to do that; I am the perpetrator of abuse; I am mentally ill; I am a diabetic; I am too old to do that; or I am drug addicted.

Until you ponder your I am ______ statement, you might not be aware that you were thinking of yourself in a negative manner, not by the essence of you, not by your accomplishments, not by your passion, but in fact by labels, many of which have negative connotations. Some of us might not be able to clearly state the nature of our passions. On the other hand, we might have been so downtrodden that even if we could name the passion, for example, dancer, the follow-up phrase might be "But I can never be a dancer because I can't earn a living as a dancer. Another person might comment, "I am an alcoholic"; "I am lonely"; "I am stuck in my life." Have you figured out the essence of who you are? If not, could it be that there are active, self-inflicted thought processes and emotions of anger, sadness, guilt, and victimization, resulting from our labels, which limit our full potentials?

Most of us are like Achilles in that we are reasonably strong, resilient, and yes, even courageous, but unlike Achilles, we just don't realize it. As this ancient hero had his physically vulnerable heel, we often have a "mental/emotional/spiritual" weak spot that is the hinge point of who we think we are and through which we can be saved or destroyed. Sometimes we feel guilty about the label by which we call ourselves or the events that led to us to think of ourselves in this way, so that the I am of us is guarded from other people and ourselves.

- You might secretly drink or use drugs, but you're not an alcoholic or drug abuser, right? Because you "have control of it," right?
- You might never have told anyone that you were raped, as if it were somehow your fault.
- You might think it would be your undoing to really "own it," to recognize or acknowledge any of your mind-branded but unspoken labels.
- Would you risk disapproval, loss of job, or loss of dignity if coworkers or family knew the real "you"?
- Would you be undone if people discovered that your public persona, I am Joe the accountant, hides your secret self-label, I am Joe the alcoholic?

There's no denying that you were a victim if someone else physically or emotionally abused you or that the reasons that led to your substance abuse might have been an attempt to escape from your mind's replaying of those events. People who criticize our inability to "get over it" are oblivious, unhelpful, and unkind; however, we can do even more damage to ourselves than these outside critics can by applying cruel and untrue labels to ourselves. When asked to tell the yoga class one thing about herself, Dorothy (age eighty-six) paused, said she couldn't think of anything, paused again, and then stated, "I am stupid." Often we do not notice that we're abusing ourselves. We would never say to others what we say to and about ourselves because the same statements would be hurtful to them.

We suffer in silence. Our inner monologue of personal abuse loops over and over—all day, every day—undermining our confidence, our choices, and our potential joy. Our minds can create havoc very quietly, unobserved by others, with no one to object to the inflammatory and untrue barrage against us. There's no outside judge or jury to determine guilt or innocence, because we serve as both. We can neither expect nor receive a fair trial.

O.E., a fifty-three-year-old interviewee, bemoaned: "I want to move to Illinois but I can't get a job in my area, welding. I can't get a different job because I'm too old to learn new skills. I'd like to move my girlfriend, who's in Illinois, to my home in Indiana, but I'm still married. I'd like to get a divorce, but my wife might keep all of her family property." When O.E.'s friend of many years, to whom he complained of his plight, offered suggestions such as training for another job or not having a girlfriend at the same time as having a wife, O.E. rejected each suggested potential solution with reasons why it wouldn't work. He tearfully went on to say, "I worry so much that I don't sleep well. I'm sad, depressed, and angry. I'm miserable. I just don't know what to do."

You might reject your own or other people's potential solutions because you feel that nothing will work for you. There's no way out . . . you're stuck. As interviewee Leigh stated when asked about her read on people becoming "stuck" in their lives, such as O.E., she suggested that the individual quit arguing for the problem and argue instead for the solution. She added, "When you find yourself in a hole, quit digging." The welder discussed above has effectively placed himself in a hole of his own digging by his thought process. If our Martian buddy were to ponder this thought process, would he scratch his head in confusion? Does the way we think, not just our thoughts, limit our possibilities in life?

Some people with anxiety or depression do not improve on medications or only partially get better. Don't you think that's generally because they have a reason or a bunch of reasons to be anxious or depressed, and pills don't change their reality? If you live in constant fear, you lose hope. Some people are the victims of their circumstances, can't see a way out, and give up. But is everything we think true? Dorothy was not "stupid," she was bright and engaging once the yoga teacher (your's truly) got her talking and laughing about some funny stories from her childhood. Does our thought process shape our perception? As an example, a minor auto accident might be perceived by one person as catastrophic, yet someone else experiencing a similar accident might view the accident as a relatively small problem. Cognitive behavioral therapy was developed to address the process of thought that shapes different perceptions of a similar event. In other words, if one person thinks that there's a catastrophe and the other person feels the incident is no big deal, it's not the incident but the thought process of each individual that shapes perception.

Cognitive Behavioral Therapy (CBT), suggested originally by Aaron Beck, Ph.D., was a major breakthrough in psychological therapy. Cognitive refers to intellectual activity such as thinking, reasoning, or remembering. The CBT approach to the recognition and treatment of problematic thought processing has proven so successful over time that it has been applied to many other thought-derived issues beyond anxiety and depression. CBT has become the most widely utilized and researched approach of psychotherapeutic methods. It has been found to be useful in the treatment of generalized anxiety disorder, depression, posttraumatic stress disorder, suicidal thoughts, substance abuse, and other conditions.

[Regarding Cognitive Behavioral Therapy, MN26X might observe, "Surely the study of thought must be a required foundational component of Earth's school curricula. No? Really? Wouldn't it be a brilliant strategy for every human to study his or her own pattern of thought, since all humans think?"]

Individuals who don't have experience with CBT often believe that emotions are triggered directly by an event. Research, however, found that the thoughts about a situation, not the situation itself, give rise to emotions. How we perceive an event is critical to the emotions we attach to it and ultimately the behaviors we attach to the emotion. Granted there are events like the death of a loved one that trigger thoughts of loss and sorrow; however, many lesser events can trigger negative thoughts that are disproportionate to the magnitude of the event.

Negative thoughts that occur repeatedly and automatically have been termed thinking errors or cognitive distortions, which, like a pair of tinted glasses, filter how we see a situation. With clear lenses you see white as white, but yellow lenses give you the perception that the object is yellow. Only when the yellow lenses are removed do you see the true color as white. Mental filters, these yellow-tinted lenses, "color" thoughts in a negative manner, resulting in negative emotions.

Research has identified a host of these thinking errors such as "all or none thinking." As an example, a person might have twenty-five good things happen in a day and only one bad thing but consider the day a failure because of the one bad event. Another pattern of thinking error that was identified was choosing to ignore positive events. For example, *Sure I got a raise, but it wasn't as much as I deserved.* It was found that these thoughts happened automatically (i.e., by habit) and that the person was unaware of the habituated thought pattern. The consequence was that events triggered habitual perceptions leading to negative emotions.

After an untoward event such as a fender-bender, a person might, for example, identify his or her emotion as despair, anger, or rage. When asked to notice the thought occurring just before the negative emotion (the thought related to the fender-bender, not the accident itself), the driver might drill down to the automatic perspective *I always screw up.* On further assessment, the driver might identify a core self-belief such as *I am a failure.* Asked to assign a percentage as to how much he believed the negative conclusion drawn using the lens of these mental filters, the driver might estimate his belief that he's a failure at 80 percent. Asked then to arrive at arguments to counter the perception of being a failure, the driver might say, "I haven't had an accident before. My record is clean. I was able to swerve to get mostly out of the way." After this exercise of rejecting the automatic thought, the driver, on re-looking at the same accident, might assign a percentage as to how much he believed his own negative script (I am a failure). The assessed percentage can sometimes drop by half or more in less than five minutes (40 percent in this example).

Over time, when people note feelings of sadness, anger, and hopelessness, they practice identifying whether the emotion was precipitated by a negative automatic thought. If the welder described above lost his job, he might notice that his thought was *I will never get another job.* If he realized that he was applying an automatic negative thought, e.g. catastrophizing, cognitive therapy provides the tools to substantiate the evidence to the contrary to refute his overstated conclusion. This technique of reflective self-examination has consistently been able to defeat automatic personal conclusions and negative emotions that can lead to negative behaviors such as substance abuse. Such reflection can limit the vicious or woebegone voices in the heads of people with thinking disorders. Self-defeating and self-punishing monologues, when brought into the light of awareness rather than hidden in the dark recesses of the mind, are more easily refuted. (See Resources – Scientific, Philosophical, or Psychological Concepts.)

Some of the other categories of problematic thought distortion include jumping to conclusions, "should" statements, and guess what? Labeling! We all commit these thinking errors to some extent. Cognitive behavioral strategies can help *all of us* identify the unhelpful thoughts that can distort our perception of events. Each reader is encouraged to further explore what CBT might have to offer him or her. There are many books available, including Beck's original works, David Burns's *Feeling Good: The New Mood Therapy,* Internet resources, and Cognitive Behavioral Therapy online treatment websites, that can further your use of this valuable tool.

Could techniques such as CBT free you from a self-imposed burden of fear, victimization, blame, or shame, allowing you to pursue your passions in life? Let's take on some specific issues identified in the above examples.

Has someone harmed you? Maybe the best vengeance against any perpetrator is to lay down the heavy burden of your heretofore self-imposed label, "I am a victim," by stating instead, "I was victimized and I am a strong, resilient, talented, and worthy individual. I am not a victim. I will not accept a label. I refuse to let you (the jerk that did the dirty deed—whether it be a person or life in general) write the story of my life any longer. It is my life, my story, my script. No matter what was dealt to me, I can choose not to make it the defining moment of my life." The answer for Anna, age fifty, was illuminating: "When I was forty-nine, I would have answered, 'I am depressed. I am a victim of abuse.' Now I would say, 'I am just me. I'm a life traveler with a mission to have fun, suffer some, learn much, love much, and give much.' "

When someone is victimized, he or she is often advised or self-admonished to "forgive and forget." Hmm. So, the victim who suffered an injury is now disparaged by other people or society if she doesn't forgive and forget. Really? Did it ever occur to anyone who so states that he or she has just damaged the injured individual again? Do you know where the phrase "forgive and forget" comes from? Take a guess. The admonition to "forgive and forget" is incorrectly identified by many to be a verse in the Bible. According to various websites, the phrase derives from the book *Don Quixote* by Miguel de Cervantes and the play *King Lear* by William Shakespeare. Isn't it interesting that our society holds itself to a truism found in fictional literature and is not an edict from God?

Forgiveness is generally defined as a deliberate decision to let go of resentment or as a feeling of vengeance toward those who have harmed you, regardless of whether the forgiveness is deserved. Forgiveness doesn't mean that you're obligated to forget, nor does it mean condoning or excusing offenses. Forgiveness, which can help repair a damaged relationship, doesn't oblige you to reconcile with the person who harmed you, neither does forgiveness release them from legal accountability. The act of forgiving another individual can release you from corrosive anger.

Being directed to forgive either the perpetrator, or to forgive yourself for being the perpetrator, as in the following sniper's story, is no easy task.

Shortly before he died, Don, an eighty-six-year-old WWII veteran, finally told his family just a little about his military service. Don was only an eighteen-year-old when he was drafted into the army. He had been raised on a farm and was an amazingly good shot when hunting for the family table. In the army, he was assigned to be a sniper. He had no choice in the matter. To refuse would have been punishable as treasonous. When he came home four years later, at age twenty-two, he refused to talk about the war. On his eighty-sixth birthday, Don spoke of his lifetime of sadness and guilt for his actions in the war. After sixty-five years, Don's family realized that he had been suffering from post-traumatic stress disorder (PTSD). Don was not only grieving those deaths but also tearfully wondering what would happen to him as a result of the suffering he'd caused others.

There are many sources available to explore the topic of forgiveness, and self-forgiveness. As you explore "expert opinion," you can ultimately decide to forgive or not to forgive, because you are the final expert on your life. However, studying rather than "staying in your head," with continuous negative scripts that are never resolved, can help you gain clarity and objectivity. It may be that self-forgiveness entails making amends as best you can, as in the Twelve Steps for addiction recovery (Resource – Scientific, Philosophical, or Psychological Concepts – Twelve Step Program). If you are addicted to anything—substances, anger, problematic relationships, self-abuse, among many others—"working" at recovery each day is important lest you become complacent and backslide. Can we choose whether to continue to be locked into the labels of victim or perpetrator? Habit and fear might have kept us there, but now that you recognize that you have a choice, you have the opportunity to change the script.

Could striving be another self-inflicted abuse?

The definition of *strive* is to make great efforts to achieve or to obtain something, to struggle, or fight vigorously. Synonyms include: To go all out, to force, to be intent upon, quest after, or to set your sights on. All the great accomplishments of our own lives and those of others that have resulted in our modern society have come through striving. But sometimes individuals begin to strive for something and if they don't get what they want, they become obsessed with the lack thereof. Some may strive for goals such as to retire, while others strive never to retire; some strive to get married; others strive to have a child; and still others may strive to attain and/or retain physical prowess, to get a certain job or earn an academic degree, or to be youthful in appearance or behavior. Sometimes what we strive for is attainable or potentially attainable, while at other times the goal cannot be accomplished. For some, the "failure" to attain what we seek makes us want the goal even more. A vicious cycle of striving and obsessing can follow. Repeated "failing" is accompanied by the concomitant emotions of disappointment, anger, and victimization that can destroy happiness. As we keep our focus on the goal, we might miss opportunities to attain what might actually be our true goal. We would be well served to recognize the distinction between the positive aspects of striving and the negative consequences of obsessing. If we continue to strive for a goal that's unattainable, we might exclude other, attainable and perhaps more fulfilling, goals.

We've conceptualized that all three trimesters of our In Utero II adult life are vital. Could it be that the adversity is a necessary part of our maturation through the progression of the trimesters? Could failing to get what we're striving for be considered adversity?

As a youth, Morgan Brian, who became a member of the U.S. Women's Soccer Team, was the only one of her entire club team not to advance in a competition. Her coach evidently said that she could pout or use the failure as motivation to improve. Morgan began to train in earnest, and by the next year she made her state team. Shortly thereafter she qualified for a regional team and ultimately made the US Women's National Team (see http://www.ussoccer.com/players/2014/03/15/05/05/morgan-brian#tab-1).

Morgan Brian used the adversity of being the only one on her team not to have made the roster as a springboard to action. Her mentor didn't coddle her, he challenged her commitment; she decided to work harder toward her goal and thereby achieved national ranking.

When does the upside of striving against adversity become the downside of obsessing despite reality? It's a question each of us must personally answer. Maybe happiness lies in continuing to strive but also celebrating defeats. If you strive to be an amazing soccer player and work hard to make it happen, you could also practice piano so that if your soccer career stagnated you could pursue a career in music. If you strive to have a child, instead of despairing each month that you haven't gotten pregnant, you might volunteer a day in a shelter for handicapped children. If you strive to look young, you might have surgery to alter your whole face or surgery just to look less tired. On the other hand, you could just get a little more rest. The downside to the decision to have surgery is that you might have a bad outcome or experience the cosmic joke that no one even notices that you had the surgery. Maybe we should strive to keep our minds young by maintaining a childlike curiosity and refusing to let life events steal our innocence. Maybe we can strive to keep our bodies young through exercise, healthy food, and a commitment to "live happy" so the wrinkles on our face reflect the brushstrokes of years well spent. Could Eleanor Roosevelt have been correct when she said, "Beautiful young people are accidents of nature, but beautiful old people are works of art"?

We have suffered from many emotional and physical adversities. Many of us have been unable to extricate ourselves from the resultant labels and emotional burdens and thought-fashioned constraints on our life options. If we continue to rail against our past experience (our own misdeeds, the whims of fate, or the transgressions of others), such events persist as part of our current reality and we continue to suffer.

One interviewee, B.G. (age sixty-seven) said of her life, "When I laid out the hideous and the horrible, the magical and the marvelous events of my life . . . the more intense the challenge the more profound the portal that opened behind it." She went on to say that some of the best achievements in her life stemmed from the worst, most horrible circumstances. She was surprised because at the time of the event she would never have perceived the horrible to eventually result in anything at all good. Her initial script was that of addiction. Compassionate and wise, she has spent the last thirty years teaching others the steps she learned in her own harrowing journey to sobriety.

Helen Keller, born in 1880, is one of the greatest examples of someone who not only overcame adversity but also thrived despite and possibly because of it. Helen was only nineteen months old when she contracted an illness that left her blind, deaf, and mute. She overcame her handicaps with the aid of a teacher named Anne Sullivan, who was also visually impaired. Miss Keller wrote her autobiography when she was twenty-two. In it, she spoke of the "magical" moment when she made the connection between cold liquid flowing over her one hand with the signs Miss Sullivan was drawing on her other palm (an episode reenacted in the 1962 movie *The Miracle Worker*). Miss Sullivan had thereby unlocked Ms. Keller's amazing intellect. She, who had been thought severely mentally retarded, overcame her disabilities to graduate cum laude from Radcliffe and to become one of the 20th century's most memorable and admirable constituents.

The following quotations from Ms. Keller seem particularly pertinent to the discussion of adversity:

Everything has its wonders, even darkness and silence, and I learn, whatever state I may be in, therein to be content.

We could never learn to be brave and patient, if there were only joy in the world.

The only thing worse than being blind is having sight but no vision.

Perhaps her most applicable words of wisdom are:

The marvelous richness of human experience would lose something of rewarding joy if there were no limitations to overcome. The hilltop hour would not be half so wonderful if there were no dark valleys to traverse.

Chapter 7

What if You Were a Honeybee?

You might wonder about being asked to speculate on your life as a honeybee in a book dedicated to getting the most out of being a human. It's amazing to watch the intricate and coordinated activity of more than 100,000 bees that each day work ceaselessly and collegially in a space of just a few cubic feet. Bee society and the human condition are independently complex and not comparable overall, but there's something we used to have in common with the bees: Bees clearly know their relationship to the hive and thereby what's expected of them as individuals. Throughout our history, humans have known their relationship to the rest of humanity and what was expected of them as individuals. I'm speaking specifically about the relatively clear expectations, responsibilities, and rewards inherent to humans as they progressed through their youth, middle, and elder years. Bees must have the order and stability of the hive, the foundation of their society, lest they become disoriented. If the beehive is moved even a foot away from its normal position, or the box in which the hive is housed is painted a different color, the bees can get completely lost. Therein lies one of the challenges of the current human condition as it relates to growing up, aging, and dying: The members of our human hive have had their home base shifted. Metaphorically speaking, the foundation of human society has been moved miles from where it was located, and painted with very different colors. As a result, humans are disoriented in general, but some have become completely lost.

Over most of the 200,000-ish years of our human society, we were nomadic hunters and gatherers. About 10,000 years ago societies began to shift to agriculture, transitioning to what was deemed an agrarian society, one whose economy is based on producing and maintaining crops and farmland. Such communities have been the most common form of socioeconomic organization for most of recorded human history. A slow transition began several thousand years ago, as humans started to develop cities and commerce in addition to the agrarian economy.

The average span of a generation of humans is approximately thirty years, for example: First generation, grandparents; second generation, parents; third generation, children, and fourth generation, grandchildren. If you divide thirty years per generation into the total time that humans have existed, there have been over 6,000 generations. In the last 10,000 years, as humans became organized into agrarian societies, there have been approximately 300 generations who filled the roles needed for the success of farming communities. In the last few thousand years there have been approximately fifty generations of families structured around mixed agrarian and early commercial societies. Within these societal shifts, interdependence among all age groups in families and societies has continued to be the norm.

Throughout the approximate 6,000 generations, young adults and middle-aged members carried out much of the labor necessary for the family's survival. Needed assistance was, however, provided by the youngest, and more significantly, by the eldest family members. Children were truly needed to do their part in making the family successful by performing such chores as tending gardens, feeding chickens, family pets, and some livestock, which were eventually harvested, and cooking or cleaning. Food came from harvesting the cows or chickens, and pets eventually died; as a result, children had a more elemental relationship with life and death. Often the elder members of the family were not only appreciated for their contribution to the family's livelihood but also venerated for their efforts on behalf of its welfare. Elders were the keepers of the family history, which was passed on in an oral tradition. Elders' memories were important for the transfer of much-needed knowledge of the farm or family business management. Elders had the long view of such activities as tending crops and livestock, processing and storage of food, production of clothing, and other related tasks, as well as wisdom regarding physical health, childbearing, and childrearing. But more important than written knowledge of facts, elders were treasured for their experiential wisdom, through which they could offer family guidance in a variety of circumstances.

There was a symbiotic affection and appreciation for the various ages of family members. When grandparents became infirm and died, lessons in pragmatism and the naturalistic order of aging, infirmity, and death were understood by even the youngest of the family. Whether we now applaud or denigrate agrarian familial relationships, those interactions clearly provided stability and mutual respect.

The family dynamic began to change dramatically with the advent of the Industrial Revolution. The term "revolution" has been defined in several ways; the most appropriate to this discussion is a sudden, complete and at times extreme shift in the way people live and work. The Industrial Revolution, which occurred in the late 18th century (first in England), was characterized by the introduction of machinery powered by external sources of energy such as steam. This change fundamentally altered the entire concept of how people worked. Young adults and people whose livelihood had been dependent on farming began to move to the cities for work. Over the next 200 years this migration away from the farm resulted in major shifts in family dynamics, particularly in that there was less need for elders to perform physical work and to share their knowledge of farming. Elders were, however, still the keepers of the stories, and continued to serve as repositories of the knowledge and accrued wisdom of their lives and of their ancestors'. The means of communication remained a direct oral tradition.

In 1790 farmers made up 90 percent of the labor force in the United States. By 1840 farmers were 69 percent of the labor force. Since then the U.S. has experienced a steady decline in the agrarian population, yet even in 1910 farmers still made up a third of the labor force. The number of farms has declined by 3.25 million since 1950, with the largest decrease (1.7 million) occurring between 1950 and 1960. An additional drop of 1 million occurred in the 1960s, followed by a half million more in the 1970s.

With the significant workforce changes since the 1950s, the constitution of the nuclear and extended family in the United States has been transformed. Nuclear family refers to the basic social unit composed of a couple and their dependent children. In our Western culture, the extended family generally refers to grandparents, uncles, aunts, and cousins, who don't necessarily and in fact rarely live in the same household. It is interesting, however, that the accepted definition of the extended family for most cultures refers to the same cohort of people, but all living nearby or in the same household.

Historically the natural order was for all generations to participate in the care of the whole family. According to interviewee F.M. (age fifty), whose family is of mixed Portuguese and Hispanic heritage, even now in the Hispanic population there's no question that all family members are expected to participate in the care of their entire family. F.M. stated that there's no conscious decision to venerate and care for the elder members of the family and community; that to do so is "just expected." She went on to say, "In fact, anyone who does not care for their aging family members is considered an embarrassment, and those individuals are subsequently shunned by the rest of the family and community." F.M. related multiple stories of such support to validate that caring for elder members is the rule, not the exception. She shared also that members of the community outside the family often contribute to the support of aging neighbors who have no family.

One moving account described the care of F.M.'s paternal grandmother's mother, whose six surviving children spent many years caring for her until her death at age one hundred. "Every day, for many years, every child went to visit her." But perhaps the most poignant display of love and dedication was the story F.M. related of her friend Norma's mother. Norma's eight children hired two caretakers for their mother, who suffered from Alzheimer's disease. The children not only shared the financial responsibilities for the caretakers but at least one of the children was also in the home at all times.

After a historical precedent of 6,000 generations of the interdependent agrarian lifestyle, in less than six generations all members of society have been impacted by the transition to an industrial social model. Two vital subsets of the family, children and elders, are no longer considered productive contributors. A downstream effect for the young and middle-aged breadwinners whose livelihood is dependent on jobs outside the home is that childcare and eldercare have become significant financial drains on the family. What has evolved is that the very young and elders are now cared for (or not) by non-family, institutional caretakers and are completely isolated from the symbiotic relationship that the young and the aged could experience in the agrarian model of society.

Interviewee E.N., age eighty-four, talked about her paternal grandfather who lived on the family farm with her parents and her eight siblings. E.N. spoke with reverence of her beloved grandfather, who always had time to spend with her in conversation at a time when her parents, who ran the subsistence-level farm, had very little time to spend with any one child. In fact, E.N. could remember only three times in her life when she had been alone with her father. She spoke in wonder of her blind grandfather's ability always to know which grandchild was in the room by their steps and by touching their arms. She said she had learned many life lessons from him. As an example, she recounted an incident with one of her elementary school classmates. In retrospect, she acknowledged that her grandfather helped her realize that she had been unkind. Asked whether she felt rebuked by her grandfather, E.N. looked surprised and said she had never felt that he'd ever been anything but gentle with his comments and concerned for her welfare.

K.R., age twenty-five, whose extended family lives in Mexico, has fond memories of spending time as a child each summer with his cousins and grandparents in a "round-robin" fashion. He spoke with respect of the older members of the family, whom he came to know to a depth that would never have been achieved otherwise. Currently, many nuclear and extended family members are scattered across the nation or even the globe. The cross-generational support and appreciation of past generations has been lost due to a transition away from the agrarian, interdependent family dynamic as well as a loss of proximity.

Interviewee D.B., a.k.a. "The Machinist," a sixty-two-year-old grandfather, is a primarily self-trained large-machine-repair troubleshooter. He's held in high esteem for his wisdom and practicality by a young, formally trained engineer protégé who thinks of his mentor as a "natural engineer." The engineer seeks out D.B.'s stories of growing up on a farm, an experience quite foreign to the young protégé who was raised in a city. The young man values the story telling in which D.B inserts practical wisdom, life lessons and humor. D.B. bemoaned that his daughter, with whom he shares a loving relationship, lives over a thousand miles from him. He doesn't see his grandchildren more than once or twice a year. He is sad that his grandchildren don't know him, or he them, in other than a superficial manner.

The machinist also said that his daughter doesn't seek stories of the nuclear or extended family, neither does she seek his counsel in matters of parenting. He stated that she prefers unvetted Internet sources for guidance in childrearing. Her lack of interest results in a painful loss to the grandfather, an amazing storyteller, who holds the oral history of being raised by his grandparents on the family farm. D.B. won't be able to pass on the legacy of his grandchildren's ancestors. D.B. said of his grandfather, an orphan of Cherokee descent known as J.H., "He was born during the days of horse and buggy but lived to witness a man on the moon." When D.B. passes away the stories will be lost forever.

For the past two to three generations, young people have not been raised with easy access to constant and mutually respectful older members of the extended family. Some of the young expressed in their interviews that they disparaged elder members of society as "old, sad, and not only unnecessary in society but a drain on shrinking revenues and resources." Several young interviewees who espoused a more positive perception of the elderly stated, "With age comes wisdom." Yet none of these young participants could recall a time when they had asked advice of any elders. Asked where they did seek information, they all identified routine use of the Internet, even though they didn't know the source or veracity of the advice received. It's not surprising that the elderly, especially those no longer in the workforce, feel they are no longer needed. Because the family paradigm of rural cross-generational interdependence is no longer the norm, elders who no longer feel necessary are sadly correct.

The Digital Revolution began in earnest for the majority of humanity with the advent of cell phones and personal computers. It is estimated that there were about 10 million cell phone subscribers (well less than 1% of the world's population) in the early 1990s. Within twenty years, that number had grown to over 25 percent of the world's population (a hundredfold increase). There are similar statistics regarding the dramatic increase in use of the Internet.

In less than one generation, human society may have been changed more than at any other time in history. This is particularly true regarding the volume of information available and how we access and share it. The elder responsibility and privilege of being the keepers of the stories has been irretrievably usurped by the infinite capabilities of computer memory storage. It's no wonder that many in our current world feel unsettled. Personal, familial, social, and cultural precedents of thousands of years have changed drastically over an unprecedented short time.

Wow! What the heck just happened? All of human society has been caught off guard. We didn't have even a few generations to "take a breath" to assimilate social shifting so we could begin to adapt and accept the new roles, expectations, responsibilities, and rewards of a changing technological and digitally savvy society. The term "culture shock" comes to mind. It's a term that's been bandied about for the last fifty years as the structures of families, societies, and countries have changed dramatically. Culture shock is characterized by uncertainty and anxiety due to rapid changes in society without adequate preparation.

Beginning around the turn of the last century, mavens such as Emily Post were there to give us advice on "the polite manner" of speaking on the telephone or "the rules" for setting a proper dinner table. With the welcomed breakdown of arbitrary societal rules and the advent of computers, cell phones, the Internet, and social media, humanity is being jump-started into evolutionary changes of lifestyle, family composition, and human-to-human communication. Previous rules have been nullified. We have no experience on which to base our current trends, and without some sort of compass, members of our culture are experiencing anxiety about their personal and societal trajectories.

In 2014, for the first time in more than 130 years, adults ages eighteen to thirty-four were more likely to be living in their parents' homes than be living with a spouse or partner in their own households (Resources – References – Web – Fry). Some might observe that this pattern appears similar to the structure of the agrarian family. In the agrarian model, however, the young adult had passed through developmental and increasingly responsible steps to assume an adult role. In the new societal construct, some of these young adults have abdicated the role of responsible adults and are often dependent and underachieving. Are they unwilling or unable to forge a life of their own?

While cultural change has affected all ages within society, elders have experienced the most disorienting and negative effects. In a culture increasingly enamored of youth, elders began to lose their voice in that they were no longer respected members of society. The older generation has become fearful of loss of affection, dignity, self-worth, and of being relevant in society. Adding to the apprehension of the elders who perceive that they aren't respected by the other age groups is the reality that elders don't have the level of ego integrity and thereby self-respect that they possessed in their own youth and middle years. Seniors began to give their voice away because they no longer respected themselves enough to fight for their rightful place in society.

One of the obvious examples of seniors' discomfort with their role has been in relation to the Digital Revolution. Some elders have come to embrace portions of the digital age, but the use thereof is not a natural language for them as it is for most children and teens who've grown up using computers and electronic media. The structure of the brain has been altered from the pre-technologic to post-technologic pathways. Some elder interviewees even admitted that they are "afraid" of computers. Many elders feel inadequate in the digital age; some apologetically say they're unable to use computers or cell phones or social media, and preface discussions regarding these with "I am a computer illiterate."

Many seniors also faced a fundamental loss of autonomy. Despite what appeared at the time to be good financial planning, they experienced an unanticipated adverse financial environment at the same time as profound social changes. When they were no longer able to remain in the traditional expanded family home and could not afford their own homes, society began to warehouse them in nursing homes.

As some seniors became fearful and hopeless, they also became helpless. Many complained about illnesses (which were made worse because they had lost anything else to focus upon), allowing them to be discriminated against and infantilized. A vicious cycle began. Some of the elderly became so overwhelmed that they quit trying to help themselves, a decision that shifted a heavy burden to the family members who tried to help them.

While the loss of respect because of these societal changes has been damaging, a much more devastating specter faces seniors, the fear that we may lose our minds. Dementias are becoming so prevalent that each time we lose our car keys we begin to wonder if we are on a downhill slide to ignominy through the loss of our memories.

Darn it, the old saying "Life sucks and then you die" really is true! Sorry, folks. I may have just lost my party planner license, without which I can no longer provide my mildly amusing pithy commentary on life. Before I leave in disgrace, however, let's divide up. The first one third of you are in charge of worry. You there—the next one third of you—take it up a notch. Your role is to freeze in place but also manage to tremble in fear. The rest of us, how about we just whine with the injustice of it all? Oops, I didn't see you last few over there—how about you folks come up with a suitable dirge? Yes, that's right. You're in charge of making up a mournful song fitting the occasion. Hurry up, please. It doesn't have to be perfect. I must get home to flail about, moan, and gnash my teeth. A slow, sad song that starts softly is heard: "Whoa-ee-o, Our respect is gone. Whoa-ee-o, Our dignity and derrieres have slipped. Whoa-ee-o, We are doomed, for sure. Whoa-ee-o, (building to a crescendo) There is no hope. We might as well eat a worm."

Stop the music!

Oh, gee, that was close. I almost went down the rabbit hole of despair! Thank goodness I take exception to anyone's even considering eating a worm! That reminds me of my worms who flattened out and not only gave up but also resisted any attempts at outside help from this large benign human. We just need to get creative to solve this dilemma.

Before we go all gloom and doom, consider the fact that with knowledge comes power. If we all become aware of the above-noted reasons for elder fears, we can begin to address the problems that have resulted. Those of us who are sixty-five or older may have lost our voices and been marginalized in society because of social change and technological advances. However, we elders need to remember that we not only still hold a valuable place in our families and in society but also possess wisdom, affection, and the long view of the last century, which are vital to the mental health and happiness of the generations who'll follow in our footsteps. We are the keepers of the stories, the richness of which cannot be found on the Internet. We became lost as the life path we were accustomed to and for which we required no road map took an unexpected, uncharted, disorienting, and thus frightening new direction. We momentarily gave away our voices when we lost confidence in our own value. Notice the qualifier "momentarily" because we just have to remember how important we are. As soon as we find our sea legs, so to speak, we can get on with the business of being Wise Ones again. So, where do we start?

Sea legs refers to the ability developed by those at sea to adjust to the motion of a ship, allowing them to walk and to avoid seasickness. Recent social changes could be compared to the unpredictable pitch and yaw of a boat in relation to the movement of the sea. For someone to stand successfully on a moving deck requires time to adjust to the movement. Balance and flexibility (not locking one's knees) are key to compensating successfully for the rocking deck.

Elder Boat Wisdom

1. Recognize that you are on a boat that has encountered some rough seas, and

2. Carry on by flexibly seeking balance as you allow yourself to adjust smoothly to the rocking of the waves.

The next few chapters will give you some ideas about the keeping calm part, and the last chapters will give you some ideas for carrying on. Socially we will not en masse be going back to an agricultural-modeled lifestyle. If, however, we recognize familial affiliation as foundational throughout human history, we might make more of an effort to tighten our splayed family bonds.

What if?

What if we begin to recognize the importance of honoring and rekindling the bonds inherent to our family of origin, that is, your Large "F" Family (the family structure in which you grew up)? Whether genetically related or socially blended families that have been mixed, merged, or mingled, the family of origin is a valuable anchor for our lives. Your unique family circumstances will shape your decisions, but here are some ideas.

Rank living close to family as a priority. People don't generally choose to make a bad decision. Instead, they usually take the information available and weigh the importance of each fact or opinion to make the best, most informed decision at the time. How each part of the information is ranked is the key to being satisfied with the decision you ultimately make. Let's take the case of deciding whether to move across the country—away from family—to seek a new job opportunity. Granted, you might choose a higher-paying job, but consider also that the cost of childcare, which might be supplied by a family member for free, might offset the higher salary. A more subliminal "cost" of the move could be the loss of the family support system, e.g., family members who are willing to pitch in during a crisis. Prior to your reflecting on the importance of family, the parameter of proximity to family might have been of secondary importance to that of the salary. When all parts of the decision are weighed, you might still decide to move for the higher-paid job, but you'll at least be aware of the impact on the family.

The maximum distance most people will travel routinely to visit their family is about a one-hour drive; however, in many cases family members, nuclear or extended, now live hundreds, if not thousands, of miles from each other. Additionally, sometimes the family of origin is not available due to death or problematic relationships. Even the most functional families can have some dysfunctional aspects, which can be benefited by family therapy. Please see the resources section for a detailed discussion of psychologist Virginia Satir's approach to problematic aspects within families. If, however, your "F" family of origin is toxic, it might be better to distance yourself from those relationships. Yet, the need for a family-like structure is possibly even more important for those who have not experienced a healthy "F" family dynamic. If psychologists like Abraham Maslow are correct that the need for familial connection is foundational for human development, and you cannot live in close proximity to your family, is there a potential solution? [*Note:* *Familial connection is included in the first level of Maslow's proposed seven-level hierarchy of human needs. See below as well as resources for further discussion.*]

What if?

What if you don't have an established large "F" family available to you? Would it be worth making the effort to establish a small "f" family? I define an "f" family as a group of cross-generational friends. When you move to a new area, you generally make friends within an age group similar to yours. Have we been accidentally trained to stay in our single generation silos?

Originally, rural schools were of the one-room schoolhouse model, wherein one teacher taught grades one through twelve. The older students taught and interacted with the younger children in the class. Several generations ago, stratification of age groups began as schoolchildren were divided into single-age grades, a pattern that persists through college. Not until people enter the workforce do they begin to interact with young and middle-aged fellow workers. Even then, younger entry-level employees are largely segregated from the middle-aged, C-suite, management.

These friends are often merely casual acquaintances. What if you were to seek out friendships in the age groups of family members who are physically or emotionally distant from you? As an example: A young couple in their early thirties might seek out friends who are in the age group of their own parents, aunts, uncles, and even their grandparents. Friends of their own age group could, of course, fill in for missing siblings. Could the supportive alliances of cross-generational friends, our intentionally created small "f" family, give us the joy of sharing our lives in the easier times and help us with stability as we seek to balance on our sea legs in the more turbulent times?

What if?

Elders have historically served as mentors to the young, but what if we instead seek out youth mentors for us elders? "Mentoring" is a teaching process, but the definition is subject to debate. Mentorship pairs a more experienced or knowledgeable person with a person of less experience or knowledge.

We generally think of mentors as older, more seasoned individuals who impart knowledge and wisdom to younger individuals, but the mentor can be a person of any age who is willing to share his or her knowledge with another.

Youth can help elders by sharing youthful remembrance and engagement in lighthearted fun as well as sharing their computer skills. When reflecting on an elder's difficulty with technology, possibly a better message would be "Using computers is not my native language as it is for you. I'm sure I could learn it over time. Perhaps you could teach me those skills and I could in turn teach you some of the skills that have been lost to younger generations." Elders can mentor parenting skills, gardening, canning, provide insight regarding career paths, and share experiences or philosophic conclusions of a long-lived life.

How about we elders become wise enough to recognize what we don't know, introspective enough to figure out how we got to such a sorry spot, and humble enough to consider the perspectives of those younger than ourselves? We don't want to fall on the altar of worshiping youth, but rather take their wise counsel mixed with our own wisdom to forge a new path that will be better for us and for them. As the saying goes, "If you think you have won or you think you have lost, you are right." I particularly think of this with respect to Olympic silver medalists, wondering as I gaze on these people who've worked so hard and achieved so much whether they celebrate the silver or mourn the gold. Do you celebrate or mourn your life to date? And, if so far you or the world has screwed it up for you, could it be that it's the last portion of your life, and what you do with it that is the most important portion as you journey on? Let's teach by example and be the mentors and grandparents who live such full, brave, and meaningful lives that those in the young and middle years will no longer dread but anticipate the full spectrum of their lives.

Interviewees of all ages were asked if they would be willing to serve as mentors to those older than they are. Margie, age ninety-two, said that she would serve as a youth mentor to anyone older than she, but added that she didn't anticipate a large pool of applicants. Margie refuses to give up or give in to cancer, a bad hip, the excruciating pain of trigeminal neuralgia, and a life-threatening heart condition, among many other maladies, any of which would put a person much younger than she under the covers. In a world where there are too many woebegone naysayers and too few heroes to emulate, Margie's infectious chortling laugh and joie de vivre can give people of every age a target to shoot for if they wish to live a full, exciting, and meaningful life. [*Okay, that's it! Look at the pronunciation of "joie de vivre"—ZHwä də 'vēvrə. That's just too cool! I'm officially putting "learn French" on my bucket list.*]

When Margie was asked what she might share with her older mentees, she said that she highly recommends practicing dying and went on to demonstrate lying on the couch with her eyes closed in blissful moribund repose. Her less humorous but more profound response was that, as elders, we have many job responsibilities, but maybe two of the most important are: to model how to die with grace and dignity and how to be completely and enthusiastically alive when we die.

Chapter 8

The Biggest "What Ifs" of All

You've been flexing and strengthening your mental muscles in preparation for this chapter, which is designed to engage your critical thinking skills, challenge your assumptions, and have a bit of fun with some pretty big "what ifs." As you are guided by your curiosity and imagination, you'll create a thread of thoughtful content and a line of inquiry that's never been and never will be mapped again in human history. This sounds overstated, but think about it: When you were born, to whom you were born, the content of your thoughts based on random events in your life, and the chance meetings with people have occurred in a sequence that's completely unique to you. No one else has had the same life story that you're creating. Equally, no human in the future can replicate your life. Have you ever considered how unique your life is? Should one of our most important tasks be to contemplate our existence? If you step away from patterned thought, emotion, and the daily details of your life, do you ever voice what your life means to you?

What if all of us are already on a quest to find our own personal meaning for why we were born and why we will age and die, but we don't recognize the journey because we're caught up in the chatter and immediacy of our current situations and the overlay of our frenetic external world?

Could it be through recognition that we're searching for meaning that we take the long view of our lives and of mankind in general? Could it be in searching for meaning, even if we feel that we haven't yet found it, that the process helps us gain a perspective to surmount difficult times? Could it be that finding meaning in life is not an arrival point, but is instead a progressive revelation gleaned from not only the exalted but even the most mundane and unexpected of sources?

We have a rich history of the search for meaning over the thousands of years of the oral-tradition communication of our ancestors, which was later enhanced by bards whose only livelihood was storytelling. As they traveled from town to town, these storytellers delivered entertaining accounts of the sagas and legends of each culture and of heroes and heroic events. Around 30,000 years ago, representative language began to gradually overtake oral traditions in importance. Painstakingly precise, labor-intensive, and slowly completed methods of "written" communication such as cave paintings, hieroglyphics, and symbols inscribed on papyrus recorded events in a reliable, more permanent manner. Written language gained momentum around 1440 with the invention of the Gutenberg press, which allowed previously hand-copied manuscripts to be mass produced at an "affordable" cost, although access to these texts was available only to a relative handful of humanity at the time. In our lifetimes the advent of electronic communication has revolutionized the volume and accessibility of the human record. We can now review the records of human achievement and musings on the nature of man from as far back as has ever been recorded. Even more amazing is that Internet access to this record is now potentially at the fingertips of every person on the planet.

An Internet search on "the meaning of life" revealed 26 million hits that provide definitions, descriptions, and the historical record of the quest for meaning in life. This search explored the views of science, religion, philosophy, and beyond, including thoughts from individuals such as the following:

> *I go to seek a Great Perhaps.*
>
> —François Rabelais

> *The Ultimate Answer to Life, The Universe and Everything is . . . 42!*
>
> —Douglas Adams, *The Hitchhiker's Guide to the Galaxy*

> *Life has no meaning. Each of us has meaning and we bring it to life. It is a waste to be asking the question when you are the answer.*
>
> —Joseph Campbell

What is the meaning you bring to life? Do you grapple with or avoid the subject? What thoughts (or avoidance of thoughts) on the meaning of life limit some of us from focusing in an optimistic manner on our personal and societal trajectories? The more time spent reading philosophers like Socrates or Kant, the perspectives of recent authors like Joseph Campbell, and even such unlikely genres as science fiction, such as Roddenberry, Bradbury, Heinlein, and Card, the more potential for examined thought. We can also expand our insights by speaking in depth to other people. We can mine for the potential learning points in even the most commonplace and, on the surface, simple encounters.

Through consideration of what others have determined as important to their notion of existence, you can be challenged to consider whether their thoughts are in line with your own conclusions, whether their speculations are harmonious and can be added intact or melded to your own, or whether they should be rejected outright if antithetical or disharmonious to your conclusions. However, to speak only with those with whom we agree or to read only those opinions we agree with can stymie creative thought. As Alexander von Humboldt, one of history's brightest individuals, stated in 1828: "Without a diversity of opinion, the discovery of truth is impossible." It is the expansiveness achieved by new avenues of thought or fresh perspectives from other sources that opens us to new ideas. For me to enjoy cogitating on the particulars of a book, a premise heard, the theme of a movie, or a discussion, I need only be made to think in a different manner. Some of my most examined thoughts were gleaned from what some might consider poorly written books, shoddily acted movies, or outrageous premises within a movie or book.

Authors take a chance when they propose pretty much anything—particularly something controversial—that they will be flogged for their audacity by naysayers. (Fortunately, we have moved away from hemlock as a means of silencing those with whom we disagree (see Resources – Topics of Interest – Socrates). Readers, especially those who are naysayers, can punch holes in any author's character, personal life, or beliefs disparate to their own. However, such criticisms of the author or the narrative do not negate the possibility that the author's ideas may be of interest and thus worthy of at least a glancing consideration. Can we, as imperfect beings, accomplish some perfect acts? As imperfect beings can we have some "perfect" ideas?

A naysayer is generally viewed as a person who is negative, particularly about the ideas, feelings, or thoughts of others. Here's an example: "Despite improvements in the weather, one naysayer tried to cast gloom by predicting that winter would never end."

Naysayers are an extremely important portion of our human race, dedicated to making other people feel naïve or outright stupid, because without them the rest of us might go off the deep end having fun, trusting, and believing. Maybe we need all the dissenting opinions of our human cohort. Perhaps we can draw on art's great painters for a philosophical perspective. Close up, a Monet is indistinct with the juxtaposition of apparently incongruent hues of color and random brushstrokes. The secret is to view his impressionistic labors from a distance. All the brushstrokes and random color, viewed from that perspective, reveal the great beauty of the scene. In a Monet-like visualization of our world, the abundance of juxtaposing opinions creates a rich balance of thought and belief.

Okay, so maybe without naysayers, some unexamined yaysayers would float off into "la-la land" or be manipulated by "gurus of good" who are in actuality unenlightened or even of malintent. However, some naysayers seem to get a little out of hand. Is it just me, or do naysayers in general seem to voice their opinions more often and more loudly than others? Also, are naysayers so convinced of their absolute lock on rational, reasoned truth that there's no possibility of a dissenting opinion having merit? When a naysayer disagrees with a portion or all of an author's thoughts, we are presented with merely one opinion versus another. A perspective attributed to Mark Twain provides that "It ain't what you don't know that gets you into trouble. It's what you know for sure that just ain't so." What if we read the books or entertained the ideas we consider most controversial? Whether we're of the naysayer or yaysayer persuasion, would it be more conducive to reasoned thought to personally read the entirety of a book, commentary, or treatise before rendering an opinion?

Hmm. Cognitive behavioral therapists contend that some individuals have cognitive distortions that govern their negative thoughts. Could it be possible that the groupthink in which we now find ourselves regarding the health of the planet, intolerance of disparate thought, and a list of assorted complaints and grievances too large to be counted, is generated and perpetuated by cognitive distortions? All-or-none thinking can result in discarding a good idea if it's related to a broader concept considered flawed. Similarly, a valid concept can be discarded due to a perception that its human proponent is flawed. An insightful or metaphysical perspective may similarly be rejected if it cannot be proven by physical means.

By the way, when you consider buying a book it might be a good idea to read both positive and negative reviews. I enjoy the dissenting opinions and appreciate the impartial sites that publish both perspectives. There is much wisdom to be gleaned from readers who thoughtfully disagree and thereby give well-crafted caveats or intriguing additional areas of thought to books that are overall positively reviewed. Perhaps we need a term for reasoned yaysayers and naysayers such as "egalitarian contemplators." The term "egalitarian" in reference to people means that all are equal and that each human deserves equal rights and opportunities (even those with whom we disagree). A contemplator is one who considers carefully and at length before acting or speaking. A contemplator's process is to carefully ponder as he or she works through a problem, considering all sides of an issue. The truly enlightened contemplator also considers the long-range consequences of short-range thoughts and actions. My definition of an egalitarian contemplator combines the definitions of the two terms and describes those who look beyond the obvious, do not mount personal attacks, and eschew their own self-interest or narrow personal interpretation to instead give a broader reasoned look at the whole of an idea.

In this chapter, you'll be introduced to an assortment of other peoples' ideas about the meaning of life and beyond. Their premises, storylines, and conjectures might feel foreign, inspiring, comfortably familiar, or uncomfortable and outrageous to you.

You might want to try on your egalitarian contemplator hat. I get a visual of the laurel wreaths worn by the Roman Senate; what do you think? Interviewee R.L., who requested that I share her transgender experience, detailed her life as a man, her decision to assume her female role, the rejection of her decision by her family of origin, and the marked difference in her perceptions of the world as she has started on hormonal replacement. R.L. spoke of a man with whom she has interacted on her blog who adamantly disagrees with her life decisions. R.L. and her fellow blogger evidently go head to head disagreeing with each other, but at the end of the day each of them feels that they have been heard by the other even if they agree to disagree. Each of them would immediately qualify as being Egalitarian Contemplators. They disagree with reasoned arguments and are respectful of the person with whom they debate.

Let's apply the principles of an Egalitarian Contemplator to a a game of Question the Assumed. You might be up for a wild ride as you challenge the following thoughts:

- My mind and body are separate.
- Emotion is within the purview of the mind and therefore distinct from my body.
- The thoughts that I have are who I am.
- The trajectory of my life cannot be changed.
- Adversity happens *to* me, not *for* me.
- The brain is an integrated whole.
- I am separate from everyone.
- How I live my life affects only me.
- The health of the planet and the health of humans are not integrally linked.
- What I do is too small to make a difference to the world at large.

Through the 3,000–5,000 years of the study of yoga, Eastern philosophy viewed the human body and mind to be an integrated whole (Resources – Scientific, Philosophical or Psychological Concepts – Yoga). Western thought was on that order until the 17th century, when philosopher René Descartes set the stage for the modern scientific era by proposing that the body and mind are separate rather than a unified whole. Subsequently, the body and brain became the subject of science, and the mind and emotions were relegated to the sphere of metaphysical and spiritual conjecture. Recently, through the application of advanced science, this philosophical bifurcation of the nature of man has come under question.

Wow, that only took about 300 years?! This notion of the body/mind dichotomy was just Descartes' opinion. Why did the opinion of a long-dead layperson become a "law" that medicine has continued to cling to for hundreds of years? Might it be a good idea to take a fresh look at every tightly held opinion, no matter what the discipline, at least once a century? Better yet, now that information is exploding via digital means, maybe even every ten years?

Question: Could it be that the mind and body are not separate and that emotions thought to be within the mind are converted in the brain to chemical messengers that travel all over the body?

Today, when novel or innovative theories are introduced, skeptics typically look first at the author's relevant credentials. The credentials of Dr. Candace Pert (1946–2013) are quite impressive: Internationally recognized as a neuroscientist and pharmacologist who has published more than 250 research articles, she made her first major discovery in the 1970s while a graduate student. Dr. Pert discovered the opiate receptor on human cells and thus took a major step in the study of the brain. Since we had receptors on our cells for morphine, a manufactured opiate used to alleviate pain, it stood to reason that our bodies manufactured our own opiate-like substances, otherwise the cell would not have a specific place for an opiate (like morphine or heroin) to act. Using this line of reasoning, and backtracking, it was found that when the human body experiences pain, our own brains do indeed produce pain-relieving substances called endorphins and enkephalins. These endogenous (made by the body) opiate-like substances are the basis for the "runner's high" you've likely heard of, the feeling of exhilaration experienced by some individuals engaged in strenuous, often painful running. The decrease in pain and in some the euphoria is associated with the release of endorphins by the brain.

Shortly after discovering the opiate receptor, Dr. Pert broke an academic gender barrier by becoming Chief of the Section on Brain Biochemistry (Clinical Neuroscience Branch) at the National Institute of Mental Health (NIMH). Later, she held a research professorship in the Department of Physiology and Biophysics at Georgetown University School of Medicine in Washington, D.C. I stress Dr. Pert's credentials to validate the scientific viewpoint underlying her theoretical perspectives. She had an amazingly inquisitive mind, which led to her discovery of a possible means of preventing neurodegeneration through Peptide T. The movie *Dallas Buyers Club* had to do with Peptide T, an HIV entry inhibitor studied for enhanced cognition and memory, which showed promise in treating the neurodegeneration of autism and Alzheimer's disease. (For further documentation of Dr. Pert's remarkable career, see the Resources – Topics of Interest section.)

Dr. Pert's research led her to believe that emotions have a direct effect on a person's physical health. She explored the physiology underlying emotions, which suggested that specific molecules from the brain provided the link for integrating emotional communication between the brain and the body. One example used was the immediate facial blushing seen in some people who experience embarrassment. Neuro-receptors found in the autonomic nervous system connect all organs, tissues, skin, endocrine organs, and more. Dr. Pert found that receptors for the neuropeptides of emotion are found not only as expected in the brain and autonomic nervous system but also in the gastrointestinal system. There are far more serotonin receptors in our guts than our brains. The lack of serotonin is the theoretic basis for one of the classes of antidepressants currently in use. Further, Dr. Pert contended that emotions create the strongest memories, which can persist for years in the body, and that unexpressed emotion can cause illness. She proposed a new field, called psychoneuroimmunology, to evaluate the connection of body and mind. Flying in the face of some long-dead philosophers, Pert, a modern-day researcher, was subjected to scrutiny and denigration for proposing that we would be well served to view the body and mind as an integrated whole.

Hmm. Doesn't it seem that science would be characterized by curiosity regarding new ideas? Doesn't any discipline descend into dogma when it clings to established opinion and rejects new ideas that are proposed? Dogma refers to tightly held beliefs that are accepted without a critical assessment by a group of like-minded individuals. Why are original ideas (like the earth being round, the earth not being the center of the universe, the germ theory, and myriad other ideas) initially scorned as preposterous or even heresy? Rather than blindly accepting dogma, how about a collegial "Well, sure, fellow inquirer, let's have a look at that crazy new idea? You might just have something there!" The precedent of condescending and sometimes vicious rejection could be changed to unveiled enthusiasm, genuine smiles, and occasional attaboys (or attagirls). On the other hand, if the idea later appears to lack merit, fellow inquirers could say, "Oops, that didn't pan out, but I admire your Martian-level thinking skills that came up with the idea, and your courage for trying something totally new. But, like the theory that the earth is round, new ideas initially deemed incorrect might ultimately change the way we perceive our world.

Question: Can we write the text of our lives is such a way as to benefit even from negative experiences?

The "Law of Attraction," espoused by a number of authors and vocally opposed by others, suggests that positive visualization of a desired situation will result in a positive outcome. For example, visualize getting into medical school and your chances of acceptance improve. On the other hand, focusing on what you fear, not getting into medical school, is also very likely to be successful—in that you won't be accepted. The theory is that the universe brings to you what you "seek," that is, what your attention is on, whether it's positive or negative. (Naysayers, stop gnashing your teeth or you might get TMJ—it's all opinion and conjecture, metaphysical, not a scientific postulate.)

Mike Dooley, in his book *Infinite Possibilities*, suggests that we might exist in some form before our human journey begins. As a reader, my opinion was that he was suggesting something akin to a pre-incarnation, basically the essence of us, which desires to experience being human. Our mission is to feel all the human emotions, to experience all that our senses allow, even the problematic portions of what we can only encounter if we become human. It seemed that Dooley took the thought a step further, suggesting that when we come into this plane of existence we choose the circumstances of our lives and the people we interact with. As I recall, Dooley doesn't propose that we are preordained to certain action, just that we set circumstances in our pre-journey and that we then have free will to react to the circumstances as we enter into our current life.

After reading various sources regarding the Law of Attraction, I had the opportunity to interview Josh, then age thirty-eight, who at twenty-one was the victim of a car crash due to faulty tires. As a result, he lost all movement and sensation from the lower chest down. When I met him, Josh was sitting in his wheelchair in my yoga class. Josh performed what his broken body would allow. His spirit, however, was not broken, and his outlook was sunny and inquisitive. His injury was a non-issue to him and therefore to the rest of us in the class. I tried to imagine whether Josh's pre-incarnated self chose to be here for what he could learn from this difficult life odyssey and whether he chose to serve as an inspiration to others. If so, by overcoming adversity Josh has succeeded in his mission to achieve great strength of character and courage even in the face of dire circumstances. Josh's curiosity and joy in life would have fulfilled his pre-incarnate wish to serve as a role model to those of us who have so much more but perceive so much less. Like each of us, Josh and you are the sum of who you are based on all the good and bad that has happened to you. You might not have had major challenges in your life. On the other hand, perhaps you experienced the loss of a parent when you were a child, have been the victim of abuse, were given up for adoption, or were victimized. You might have made some poor choices such as choosing to be a perpetrator of spousal abuse or killing another driver when you chose to drive while intoxicated. These incidents, whether we are perpetrator or victim, do not have to be the defining moment of our lives.

If you are victimized by a perpetrator, you can choose to forgive or not to forgive. This doesn't give the offending agent a bye; such perpetrators have to live with their deserved consequences. Having experienced adversity or harm, each of us has a choice. We can succumb to our negative emotional responses or we can use the event as a catalyst for personal growth. Following this line of thought: Could you have chosen to have an abusive spouse? What would be the upside in that? Maybe as a result of that abusive spouse you had your awesome children or became a counselor for abused or battered individuals or became a volunteer in a shelter. And maybe on your way to volunteer at the shelter your car broke down and the Good Samaritan who stopped to help you became the actual love of your life. In other words, it's not so much what happens *to* you but what happens *from* you as a result of your perception of an event or events.

Interviewee Kathryn stated, "At first, when I read this outrageous contention (The Law of Attraction), I was very angry. Why would I have chosen to have an abusive spouse? But after a while, I thought, "*what if I did choose such a difficult role?* If, before I got to Earth, I set up this relationship, what did I want to learn? What good has come as a result? At my age, I was bemoaning wasting half my life in this relationship. But if every day of my life can have purpose, what have I gained? If I choose to move forward, where do I head now? If I can't see gain from my experience thus far, how can I change the script in order to gain now or in the future? I no longer feel sad for the losses. I'm not even angry anymore. I don't need to forgive. It became a non-issue because if I chose my circumstances, my challenge was not to waste my time honing my victim skills. Anger, self-abuse, and martyrdom are not part of a great résumé for an afterlife if there is an afterlife. My challenge is, and was, much more rewarding. I can mine the experiences, good or bad, to enhance the essence of who I am."

Kathryn became energized. She no longer felt victimized and was thus able to shuck off her hair shirt of anger and outrage in order to move her life forward in a more fulfilling way. She and others voiced that whether or not they wrote the initial negative script, they could choose whether to become a victim—that it was up to them to write the rest of the book of their lives.

Question: Do our thoughts have energy? Could the energy we generate impact others?

In his book *Power vs. Force,* David Hawkins, M.D., Ph.D., proposed that emotion, thought, and action can be calibrated. He posited that emotions like shame, at 20, fear, at 100, or anger, which he calibrated at 150, fall into what he considers the realm of Force. Emotions that calibrate at 200 or above, such as reason, at 400, and love, at 500, he considered to be in the realm of Power. Hawkins details his definitions of Force and Power in his book. Key concepts include the characterization of Force as automatically creating a counterforce, its effect being to polarize rather than unify. Hawkins described Power using the analogy of gravity, a standing field that affects all objects within gravitational range. He associated

Force with judgment, which makes us feel poorly about ourselves, and Power as compassionate and affirming to ourselves and others. Hawkins suggests that throughout human existence we have collectively been calibrated to be in the realm of Force. Only recently, he proposes, has aggregate human calibration entered the state of Power, that is, above 200. Hawkins's proposal is that a single individual whose emotions and thoughts are calibrating at levels higher than 200 can counterbalance many people who have negative, lower caliber emotions (for instance shame at 20 and fear at 100).

I am not trying to convince you of the validity of Dr. Hawkins's methods or contentions. From the number and passion of Internet supporters, denigrators, and book reviewers, it's evident that much controversy surrounds his theory and the unique calibration tool he used to arrive at his conclusions. Commentators and editorialists who believe or don't believe something merely state their opinions in challenging or supporting the opinions of others. Opinion is not the "stuff of proof." A person who is the loudest and most vitriolic doesn't necessarily win; he or she merely drowns out more reasoned negative or positive individual evaluations. Whether you believe or dispute any of Hawkins's contentions, there's little doubt from his writing that he was a unique, reflective thinker. Even considering that his beliefs could be true generates novel ideas for contemplation.

Are Hawkins's suggestions metaphysical, physical, provable, or not provable? Was he a charlatan or a muse, humble or arrogant, egalitarian, or an elitist? I don't know. I never met the man. There is much to Hawkins's book that an individual could explore for his or her own inquiry. Maybe the naysayers are right; but if you don't examine Hawkins's ideas for yourself, the naysayers will have swayed your opinion based on their opinion and not necessarily on fact. Each of us can accept or reject any or all of Hawkins's thousands of thoughts and opinions, his methods, and his conclusions, but I'm pretty sure you would agree that his are uniquely unprecedented and thereby worthy of at least a cursory glance.

Party planner mode: What resonated for me was Hawkins's contention that we are individually affected by our calibration level, but even cooler to me is whether, as Hawkins contends, my calibration could affect the rest of humanity.

You must admit this is a way-cool idea. What if you arose in the morning with the thought "Today I will resonate at greater that 200 all day. If I have a run-in with a non-gerbil-owning jerk of a driver, I'll think of him only as a momentary challenge. I will re-equilibrate my initial negative response of 150 (anger), then go a step further and actually wish him well. Hmm, not sure of that calibration. I definitely do not love him (500). How about acceptance? 350. Yep, that's it, that's what I'm shooting for! Since the scale is logarithmic, in so doing I will not only offset his unexamined and slightly jerky ways but for that moment might offset the calibration of a whole bunch of naysayers!

I see many opportunities for party pleasantries; for instance, the above exercise could become a terrifically fun office game. Everyone is challenged to hit their highest calibration, and any office crewman resonating at less than 200 is placed into an office "time out" until they can recalibrate themselves.

I am chagrined that Hawkins didn't calibrate humor on his scale, because I have to think it would rate really high. My definition of humor is benign, tongue-in-cheek, but not mean-spirited recognition of human eccentricities, but particularly of one's own folly, faults, and foibles in a manner that is:

- Both therapeutic for the purveyor and healing for the recipient; and
- Delivered in such manner that the resultant shared laughter can engender a feeling of collegial goodwill.

Author's note: Beware of the websites commenting on Hawkins's books and ideas; watch for veracity and intent. It's best to read his book directly if you're interested. Some sites rate many, many things—events, religions, philosophies—that Hawkins did not rate in his book, and delete others that he did include.

Question: Could metaphysical thoughts arise from the right side of the brain, which many people do not recognize or develop?

Jill Bolte Taylor, Ph.D., a neuroanatomist who trained at Harvard, was inspired to attain her degree to better understand her brother's schizophrenia. Dr. Taylor was an advocate for mental illness diagnosis and treatment through her work with N.A.M.I., the National Alliance on Mental Illness. Her life journey took a very unexpected turn when she suffered a severe stroke.

After a long recovery, Dr. Taylor wrote a book about her experience entitled *My Stroke of Insight: A Brain Scientist's Personal Journey.* I found her book inspiring. She shared her experience of losing her brain function as she progressively bled into her brain due a broken blood vessel. Dr. Taylor realized how valuable her journey was to help all of us understand, communicate with, and care for stroke victims.

An example of her practical advice given in the book was her admonition to caregivers to not speak loudly but much more slowly to someone who has had a stroke. Dr. Taylor noted that some people would raise their voice as if she were deaf when she didn't understand what they were saying. She said that her hearing was fine, but she could only process one word at a time, and had the medical staff and family spoken more slowly rather than loudly, her brain could have processed each word in order to understand them.

Dr. Taylor's practical and hopeful message about stroke recovery is a must read for all medical personnel and family members of those who have had a stroke. She revealed her story with the suspense and wonder of a scientist. Dr. Taylor also delved into the metaphysical aspect of her thoughts, which became more apparent when her more linear-thinking scientific left-brain went "offline" due to her stroke. She lost most left-brain functions including the ability to walk, talk, read, or write. As her left-brain functions deteriorated, Dr. Taylor became aware that her right brain possessed the capacity to think in pictures. This opened her to a much more expansive reality, and allowed her to see the world and herself in a different manner. She gives us a look at the spiritual right side of her brain, which is usually balanced or in some people overridden by the more analytic left side. As a result, Dr. Taylor expressed her belief that the right brain connects us to the rest of humanity. In 2008, Dr. Taylor gave a presentation at the TED Conference in Monterey, California, which remains one of the most watched TED talks ever recorded. References to her book and TED talks are included in the resources.

[Author's note: The reason that I included Dr. Taylor's work is that, like Dr. Pert, she identifies a scientific, anatomic basis for the the metaphysical. Her perspective provides scientific validity for what has previously been called mystical, metaphysical, or pseudoscience. Reality can be discovered through use of either the right or left brain. However, since we have both, should we seek to balance the two?]

Question: Are we part of a living earth? Does our survival depend on how we interact with our home planet?

In her book *The Invention of Nature: Alexander von Humboldt's New World,* Andrea Wulf does a masterful job reintroducing one of the world's most amazing scientists, whom she referred to as a polymath—a person of wide-ranging knowledge or learning. Humboldt's complexity of thought and dedication to the grandeur of the earth and the strikingly obvious interconnection of living species sparked the ecological movement, which directly inspired Henry David Thoreau, George Perkins Marsh, John Muir, Charles Darwin, and others. Alexander von Humboldt recognized the Gaia concept before it was named. The Gaia concept, formulated by chemist James Lovelock and microbiologist Lynn Margulis in the 1970s, proposed that living organisms interact with their surroundings to form a cooperative self-regulating system that helps maintain life on the planet. Gaia as a philosophical approach considers each individual life form to be a part of a living planetary whole called Gaia.

Question: Are we connected to each other?

I share the opinion of some that many of the Ted Talks at www.ted.com are among the most valuable tools available to improve the human condition. The TED mission is to "spread ideas." I wish it were a mainstream television program. I've never seen a TED Talk that I haven't enjoyed, but some of my favorites are included in the resources.

We humans used to have the burden and the boon of anonymity, but with the advent of the digital age, the stuff of our lives will be forever recorded and available. What you say or do now might in five, fifty, or 500 years be looked to with reverence as to the particulars of your life or of your unique thoughts. That's all well and good, but you probably won't know about it, although it's possible that you might if your connectome has been preserved or that there actually is an afterlife. But what's most important is what you do with the only time you have—this moment.

Using tools like CBT to analyze your thoughts, exploring the mind-body continuum both from the scientific and the metaphysical perspectives, thinking about suppositions such as the Law of Attraction, exploring the potential impact of emotion on you and your fellow humans, looking at an injured scientist's perspective on the linear left brain and the expansive right brain, and having your thought processes moved a skosh toward where they've most likely never been, might help you relook at living, aging, and dying. Even if you're pleased with your general trajectory, any of these authors' ideas might trigger ideas to improve your life.

Chapter 9

Getting Started—Growing Up

Hello, this is MN26X again. We Martians are convinced of the efficacy of our "manual-driven" life, but our society has recently been in a bit of flux—a few too many solar flares, a couple of comets crashing, and our water pipes have frozen. I know your human society has been a bit destabilized too, but I am convinced that you will adapt beautifully when you get to your "sea legs," as my fellow Martians are also struggling to do. Feeling a bit unsettled with the changes in our lifestyle, $MN26X^2$, my eldest snigbot, went completely off protocol when he wrote to me of his concerns. I thought sharing Junior's perspective might be helpful to you human parents. What if your child handed you the following note? (I have adapted it for human use.)

Dear Mom and Dad,

I really want you to know that I need you for my everyday food, clothing, and shelter, but most of all I need your love and emotional support. I do have some requests though. Please teach me to laugh more by laughing more yourselves. Show me the folly and grandeur of the Martian (oops—I meant to change that to "human") condition, and thereby model equanimity when we encounter irritating, non-gerbil-owning space pilots. I'd appreciate it if you'd teach me to survive in the real world, where I will not be a superhero or a princess. In the real world, I'll be treated as just another person, with no special rights, and in fact will be dealt with harshly by other children and adults who were trained as superheroes and princesses and as a result feel entitled, have not developed empathy, and are often unkind.

I'd appreciate it if you would just sit and listen to me without judgment. You know, a wise Martian (dang it, I meant "human") once said, "there isn't quality of time without quantity of time." Even when your time is limited, if you take a breath, relax, and don't rush through our shared "task time," like grocery buying, we can actually have fun together and accomplish the needed chores. Ask me to help you get things done so that I feel I've contributed. Please don't spend so much time distracted from me. When you're on the phone, texting, or emailing, you're not looking directly at me. I feel abandoned at worst and that I'm an afterthought at best.

Remember that I'm learning from you every minute of every day, so when you model kindness and appreciation for the efforts of the grocery checkers or fast-food servers you teach me to see them as fellow humans and value their efforts on our behalf.

(This is MN26X again. I remembered to change Martian to human that time . . . although we have replicators for our food—guess where Star Trek got their ideas?!)

Expect more of me. Teach me to respect boundaries. Help me to learn the value of work for both myself and society as a whole. Take a breath when I mess up, because I'm a work in progress. It's hard to wait eighteen years to see if you've succeeded in helping me become a mentally, physically, and emotionally healthy adult who can stand up to adversity. Notice the little things I do each day that reaffirm how much I love you and that your efforts are paying off. Please care enough to read about me through books on parenting, child psychology, and the way my brain is developing. Even though I am really young, ask me about my goals and the specifics of what I desire to do or to become. Read to me as well about real people and heroic action, not unattainable superpowers, fantasies, or alien forces that humans have no ability to overcome. Read to me, not just to get me to sleep but during the day, when we can discuss what is meaningful about the book.

Give me choices you can live with so I can make my own decisions. Please treat me with respect but don't defer to me. I need to learn that my opinion is mostly important to me and not an edict for other people's behavior toward me. Teach me to respect and venerate age because one day you, and ultimately I too, will grow old. Maybe the way to do that is to get me to my extended family as often as possible, especially for weeks at a time in the summers. It would give you a needed break and is a lot cheaper than summer camp. If you seek out older mentors for me whom you treasure you will thereby teach me to treasure them as well.

Tell me stories, maybe in the car while driving, of your childhood and the memories that you have of significant people in your lives as children. Tell me of your struggles with bullies or perceived or real parental injustices. Solicit my problem-solving skills for how I would have handled the situation, and thereby activate my critical-thinking skills and resiliency in case I'm ever in a similar circumstance. Prepare me for loud and aggressive persons who might say unkind things. Teach me to handle fire drills, family disasters, and even crime drills. It's unlikely that any of these events will occur; however, by teaching me that they can happen and giving me the critical-thinking tools to overcome them, I become more resilient to deal with the real world.

Please teach me the value of running through the finish line, to enjoy each age to the fullest, and to look forward to the next age with enthusiasm, wonder, and curiosity.

With affection,
Your Snigbot, MN26X²

Growing up—Childhood

What if we parents spent time "reading the manual" about the amazing maturation that transpires in the brains, emotions, and learning capacities of our children? Better yet, what if we then applied our critical thinking to those recent scientific advances to create our own manual for each of our unique children?

The brainwaves of a baby are primarily Delta waves, which are measured at 0.5–4.0 Hz and are characteristic of the unconscious mind. The Delta wave is the slowest and is associated with sleep, which is one of the reasons babies sleep so much.

A toddler, at around age two years, begins to demonstrate both Delta and Theta waves. Theta waves resonate at 4.0–8.0 Hz and characterize the imaginative and emotional mind. The toddler wakes up and becomes independent and very physically active.

A typical six-year-old is characterized by a third form of brainwave. These Alpha waves (8–12 Hz) are associated with calm consciousness. The six- to eleven-year-old is typically the calm child before the storm of adolescence.

A twelve-year-old usually begins to display Beta waves (12–75 Hz), associated with active consciousness, which has historically been thought to complete the adult complement of brainwaves.

This addition and the second apoptosis account for the "new person" in your midst.

Researchers have recently begun to focus on yet another waveform called Gamma waves (38–90 Hz). These are the fastest brainwaves, and relate to simultaneous processing of information from different brain areas. These waves had previously not been recognized to be anything other than background noise, because our brainwaves were not supposed to be able to fire that fast and were undetectable as waves by standard EEGs.

According to a recent article about Gamma waves, research focused on monks who meditated on compassion identified the highest levels of Gamma waves seen in humans. Beginner meditators displayed very little Gamma activity, but as they exercised their meditation skills they were able to increase the incidence of Gamma waves (Resources – Web – Dobbs).

> At what age do you think Gamma waves become detectable? Music from the game show Jeopardy is heard in the background. Gamma waves have been detected in children! Yes, but even cooler, Gamma waves have been detected in toddlers as young as eighteen months. Hmm. I wonder if Gamma waves originate in the right brain and connect us with what has been considered to be the metaphysical. Perhaps this perspective supports meditation as a means to exercise right-brain function.

Reading about the actual neurologic processes occurring in the brains of children can help parents to better understand developmental milestones and the needs of the various ages. It's been said that children exposed to music, art, dance, and foreign languages by age six develop a "placeholder" that holds channels open for more formalized studies of these subjects in adulthood. In an article by Steele, et al., published in the *Journal of Neuroscience*, there was felt to be a sensitive period in development during which training may have greater effects on the brain's structure than training in later life.

The authors posited that training in music, for instance, before the age of seven alters the brain's white matter connections and that these connections might serve as a "scaffold" on which later training can build. Hensch noted that training during periods of development changed young brains in various areas including auditory and visual regions (Resources – References – Web Sources – Hensch).

Maybe creating these "placeholders" provides a testimonial to the saying that "neurons that fire together wire together," thereby making it easier to pick back up on the use of these neurons needed for music or language if one wishes to pursue such complexities at an older age (Resources – References – Web – Hebbian).

As discussed earlier, the brains of two-year-olds and young teens undergo a pruning process called apoptosis. Maybe the circuit patterns in the brain that haven't been utilized by age seven are selectively pruned away as superfluous. The above research would suggest that creative skills such as music, art, and language might be particularly vulnerable if not stimulated at an early age. If adults in calm meditation have increased Gamma waves, do we set up a pruning of children's creativity, curiosity, and ability to concentrate by not allowing for quiet, unstructured time to encourage their Gamma-wave development?

Studies conducted by April Benasich, professor of neuroscience at Rutgers University, found that children with better attention spans also had higher gamma power. Dr. Benasich's research into the gamma activity of adult brains revealed these waves to be the bond that links thoughts and memories to perceptions.

https://www.sciencedaily.com/releases/2008/10/081021120945.htm

Do we overschedule and overstimulate immature brains with the frenetic pace we adults keep, at an age when children can't process the megabits of data thus generated for their baby computer-brain processors? It's almost a badge of honor for us adults to be overscheduled at the expense of restorative sleep. What about children, whose brain circuitry is immature, who historically were put down to sleep by 7:00 or 8:00 in the evening and allowed to wake up in the mornings by their own biologic circadian clocks? From an article entitled "How Much Sleep Do Babies and Kids Need?" the recommended sleep for infants was up to 17 hours and for toddlers and preschool age children a minimum of 10 or 11 hours. Older children were felt to need 9–11 hours, with teens through age seventeen requiring 8 or 9 hours optimally. Adults, who should get 7–9 hours' sleep per night, in today's world are often lucky to get 6–7 hours of interrupted sleep.

As we begin to realize the complexities of brain development in children, are we inadvertently doing harm? Teaching our children is important; however, would toddlers and preschoolers be better served if they were also allowed to learn about their world through their own exploration rather than constantly being directed by our teaching?

Could the makers of flashy packaged and marketed games and videos, who seduce us with the message that their product is good for children, actually be selling items that if used in excess are detrimental to a child's neurologic development? What are the unintended consequences of overutilized electronic stimulation? Will we find in future studies that we're short-circuiting brain pathways that children need for the development of imagination and critical thinking? Can they learn mechanical principles (like leverage, inertia, or torque) from digital or electronic toys and games? Do we set children up for attention deficit hyperactivity disorder (ADHD) if they're not encouraged to entertain themselves? One teacher interviewee said that a classroom can't compete when children "grow addicted" to flamboyant, colorful, eight-second-or-less increments of electronic stimulation.

What if we encouraged quiet, reflective time without external stimulus for our children and ourselves? What if we didn't celebrate basic learning experiences by applauding everything a baby or child does? If we allowed self-discovery and self-reward, could children internalize their self-esteem rather than look to others for validation? What if there's a symbiotic need for all age groups to bond with and learn from each other? What if we adults, instead of needing to teach our children, decided at least once a day to assess what our children have to teach us—to remind us of the unfiltered joy and curiosity we gave up as we exited childhood?

On the other hand, do we do a disservice to our children if they're not allowed, in some measure, to progress through Abraham Maslow's human developmental levels? Obviously, their basic needs must be met, but could helping children learn of the struggles necessary to attain those needs be important? Can we humans develop the infrastructure of understanding needed to attain the higher-order functions of appreciation, altruism, and self-actualization if we have no grasp of the foundational efforts needed for survival? In modern society children are not often aware that others are providing all their elemental needs—food, shelter, and clothing. Without such awareness, can they feel gratitude? What if we began to treat children as children, not as friends or peers? What if our children need us to establish a family system that listens to them, does not exalt them, loves them with all our heart, but still prepares them to deal with reality?

Martin Seligman, Ph.D., and others at the University of Massachusetts have launched the study of "positive psychology." Rather than exploring a disease model, these researchers have focused on what leads to happiness in life, as well as physical and emotional wellness. These researchers suggest that being grateful makes you happy. Their studies have revealed that daily discussion of gratitude can positively impact attentiveness as well as duration and quality of sleep, among other beneficial effects. Grateful people are found to have less stress and depression.

https://www.umassd.edu/counseling/forparents/reccomended readings/theimportanceofgratitude/

Because of recent history's precipitous changes in family structure, elders have fallen from grace. Where elders had previously earned their high level of respect within the family hierarchy, children have usurped that position. The legitimate power of experience and achievement has been displaced by the power given over to children. Are children given excessive control within the family structure when their wishes take precedence over those of adults? Given power that they haven't earned and don't know how to wield, could it be that children don't learn the adult life skills necessary to survive in the real world? Frequently, children are not expected to expend effort to the benefit of the function of the family. If they're not needed for chores or polite behaviors, do they feel superfluous and unnecessary?

E.N., age eighty-four, remembers that she and her sisters and brothers were expected to do chores and received the wings of the chicken at dinner as the adults ate the meatier parts. When asked if she resented it, she said that it had never occurred to her, that since the adults were doing the harder work for the family, it only made sense to her that the parents' needs would take precedence over those of the children. E.N. said that she would never have interrupted adult conversation or addressed an older person by anything other than Mr., Ms., or Mrs., because to use their elders' first names would have been considered rude. E.N. said that children were to be seen and not heard, an expectation that encouraged the development of listening skills.

According to the elementary schoolteacher interviewee, children learn to interrupt adults in their families, which makes her job of teaching much more difficult. Children in her classroom often have no prior understanding of appropriate social hierarchies, leading to difficulties with the teacher-student relationship.

Are we parents doing a disservice by over-praising, applauding, and providing excessive verbal validation for actions not warranting such attention? Do we thus preempt the development of internal validation? Children reared as the "star" of the family often feel that their individual wishes are of greater importance than those of their peers or teachers. We try to do the right thing by accepting the current trend of highly involved parenting. We tend to look back on our own childhoods for what we did not get or had to suffer through, thinking *we can't let that bad stuff happen to our kids.* What if the struggles and the adversity that we as children and young adults endured forged the resolve of our spirit to become who we are now privileged to be? Sound outrageous? Arguably yes, but the sad reality is that something we're doing in our parenting has gone awry. Consider also the role of grandparents. Perhaps with the breakup of the traditional extended family unit, grandparents have become overindulgent gift givers rather than respected elders with legitimate dignity. Should grandparents be charged with sharing knowledge and life experiences with their second-generation progeny and expecting appropriate behaviors and actions?

The request by Snigbot $MN26X^2$ that his parents prepare him for loud and aggressive persons who might say unkind things brings to mind a story from interviewee T.M., who said that on her innocent three-year-old's first day of preschool another child called her stupid. T.M.'s daughter was devastated. In the concrete thinking of a three-year-old she believed the cruel words to be true. The child had no fallback and therefore no resiliency to weather the verbal attack. Said the mom, "It never dawned on me that another three-year-old would be so unkind or that it would do such lasting damage." The mother said, "I wish I had told my daughter that she might meet some children who are cruel but not to take it personally and to be sure to discuss the event with the teacher and me." T.M. learned to prep her children for potentially challenging situations so that they, at a minimum, weren't bowled over by unexpected, not previously experienced, negative encounters.

Growing Up—Teens

"Growing up" is an interesting concept. By convention, we think of growing up as something children and teens do, and we consider them to be a grownup when they reach adulthood, around age eighteen. By this definition, the process of growth stops, which in a way is true regarding the size of someone's body, but not necessarily true of the mind. Recent research has determined that the brain continues to mature beyond the teen years. The prefrontal cortex, which begins to develop around the onset of puberty, does not complete its development until age twenty-five. This section of the brain controls impulse inhibition, goal planning, and organization. The brain's reward system also becomes highly active around the start of puberty, receding to a normal adult level around twenty-five (Resources – References – Web Sources – At What Age Does the Brain Stop Developing?).

Wow! No wonder teens, particularly, make some untoward decisions. They have an immature prefrontal cortex that tries to make sense of the world in order to make rational decisions. In fact, that vital part of the brain's decision-making capacity may be a decade away from being fully online. That's not too bad until you factor in that the limbic system (the brain's reward circuitry) kicks into overdrive at that age. According to excerpts from a National

Institutes of Health (NIH) article regarding the brain's propensity toward addiction, the limbic system is activated by healthy, life-sustaining activities such as eating and socializing, but is also activated by drugs of abuse . . . and is responsible for our perception of other emotions, both positive and negative, which explains the mood-altering properties of many drugs.

https://www.drugabuse.gov/publications/drugs-brains-behavior-science-addiction/drugs-brain

According to Casey, Jones, and Hareb, the implication in their research model is that the adolescent is capable of making rational decisions, but in emotionally charged situations the more mature limbic system will win over the prefrontal control system.

https://www.ncbi.nlm.nih.gov/pmc/articles/PMC2475802/

"Charlie," sixteen years old, stated that she has known since the age of three, after seeing the movie performance of *The Phantom of the Opera,* that she was going "to be a performer—vocal, acting, and dance." Charlie has dedicated her young life to accruing the skills of the trade needed to attain her goals. At fifteen, although the school was hundreds of miles from her home state, she decided to attend a performance charter school, and set about applying for admission. At the time of her interview for this book, she was awaiting the results of her audition to see if she'd be accepted. Her strategy is to attend the school during her junior and senior years of high school and to spend the intervening summers getting her cosmetology training. She formulated this plan so that once she graduates she'll be able to support herself as a hairdresser while working toward her "break" into the theater ranks in New York or Los Angeles. So began one of the most intriguing of the hundred-plus interviews that have helped enrich this book.

Charlie's was a unique interview in that no other person polled had been as clear of his or her life trajectory at such an early age. To attain such clarity by sixteen was unprecedented among those interviewed, but hers was actually a path charted from age three. Some young people are referenced as being mature because of their manner of speech or general attitude of calm. However, as sixteen-year-old Charlie spoke with such assurance of her future successful outcome and of her well-reasoned practical plans, I felt as if I were interviewing someone in her thirties or forties. Charlie sees herself in middle age as "a star with a Broadway show, good finances, love, married, a kid on the way . . . successful and happy." She stated that she is "not happy now . . . too mundane. I want excitement and value. I can't wait to get a job, to live my life." One of her quotable quotes is "I want to grow up some, but not give up."

Reflecting on Charlie's take-charge attitude as I look back on my own adolescence, I wish I'd considered all my possibilities in life. I never thought to ask the searching questions that would have led to me to explore my options. Maybe if I'd had a mentor, he or she would have admonished me to identify my dreams, then argue for their successful completion rather than argue for self-imposed limitations. Here are some questions I wish I had asked of myself:

What do I wish to do?

Who do I wish to be?

Is there something I enjoy now, or think that I would, but haven't yet had the opportunity to explore? Have I considered all my possibilities, such as singing, dancing, learning karate, trekking the Appalachian Trail, traveling to Europe, becoming a doctor, discovering art or writing, learning to play piano or guitar . . .?

What's my plan for the next five years? The next ten? For example: In the next five years, I plan to take piano lessons and have my own band; in the next ten years I want to go to college and major in engineering, or I want to become a welder so I can work on skyscrapers in Hong Kong.

Since I will likely live to be eighty, ninety, or beyond, what would I want to see or experience or accomplish in my life?

Just like reading a novel or a biography of some historical person, what if I could write the script of my life? Do I want to remain who I am now, or would I visualize someone different?

Am I willing to make a plan and, if need be, ask for help accomplishing what I wish to have happen?

Chapter 10

Keep Growing—Adulthood

Our brains continue to develop well beyond our childhood years. Okay, so instead of approximately eighteen as the age when human brains stop growing, we can for sure say we're grown up by our mid-twenties—well, not exactly. Scientists are finding that our brains can continue to grow throughout adulthood. Mario D. Garrett, Ph.D., in his web article "Brain Plasticity in Older Adults," suggests that the adult brain can continue to grow at any age through a process known as neurogenesis, the formation of new brain cells. The brain of an older individual retains the ability to increase brain cells in a portion of the brain that's being used more and to form new connections between brain cells. In a study of cabdrivers whose brains were evaluated while they were learning thousands of routes through the streets of London, the part of their brains where geographic knowledge is stored increased in size.

Similarly, French scientist Dr. Sandrine Thuret notes in a fascinating TED talk the good news that the brain, which had been thought not to have the capacity of continued growth during adulthood, in fact reveals areas that produce new cells every day. This growth is particularly identified in the area of the brain known as the hippocampus, which is involved in memory. The bad news for us workaholics is that the process is negatively impacted by stress.

https://www.ted.com/talks/sandrine_thuret_you_can_grow_new_brain_cells_here_s_how

Wait a minute: Are you saying that those of us in our middle and elder years might still be considered to be growing up? Synonyms for "growing up" include, among other terms, aging, advancing, emerging, in process, in progress, and maturing. Thus "growing up" is synonymous with aging, developing, and emerging. In fact, we humans are in process, in progress, and maturing at every age we achieve. So, if we are to rewrite growing up, we might want to think about it in terms of children, teens, young adults, middle, and elder adults.

Growing Up—Young Adult

The following is a story related by M.T. of a movie she watched years ago. She can't remember the name of it, and has been unable to find such a plotline on the Internet to get the facts and to give credit where credit is due. Nonetheless, she paraphrased and embellished the plot as follows: "A group of friends start out on a road trip, heading to California. As they drive, one suggests that they stop to see a roadside marker, which leads to a random encounter with someone who suggests a diversion to another interesting site. Along the way, more and more unscheduled encounters occur. At various times, each of the original travelers silently registers some personal concerns about the circuitous nature of their trajectory but doesn't wish to be the party pooper to suggest that the group get back on track to California. Ultimately they end up in Omaha and are puzzled as to how they came to be so far from California." Since hearing the above storyline, I've used the phrase "How did I (or we) end up in Omaha?" whenever I'm puzzled as to how I ended up so far from my originally planned destination.

The metaphor is particularly applicable when an outcome seems far from the original intent. A college education used to be a step toward a lifetime of monetary success. Loving parents saved money to pay for college for their children, sometimes from the moment the children were born. Young people whose parents couldn't afford the tuition worked hard for scholarships and took out loans to invest in their own future success. Our original intention was to improve the lives of our children through education, but have we ended up in Omaha?

At an average cost of $28,000 per year, the total tuition for a four-year public college is now approximately $112,000. Private colleges, on average, cost $59,000 per year, a total four-year cost of over $236,000. Both numbers continue to rise (Resources – References – Web – Onink).

College is great, but so is trade school. Electricians, plumbers, welders, and carpenters sometimes make a higher income than college graduates who are unable to get positions in their chosen areas of study. These trades generally require fewer years devoted to study. Because of income earned during apprenticeships, the training for such trades may result in minimal debt to repay or possibly none. It's interesting, however, that some of those trained in a trade feel less of themselves because they don't have that "mandatory-to-life-success" diploma in hand that would prove their worth.

Interviewee Dan, a fifty-one-year-old plumber, prefaced his interview with "Well, you know that I don't have a college education." He self-denigrated his ability to participate as an interviewee because of an internally perceived lack of credentials. On the other hand, other "laborers" who completed relatively short training to attain their respective lucrative fields of employment expressed the sentiment that those who go to college may be "a bit crazy." These laborers recognize that a college student not only defers immediate substantial monetary reimbursement for four to five years but might also go into tremendous debt to attend college. All too frequently, a college degree alone doesn't lead to a high-paying job.

Well-meaning parents strap themselves financially and defer saving for their own retirement as they adhere to a construct of "good parents must pay for higher education" for the beloved young adult. Should young students whose prefrontal cortices are not fully mature and whose parents cannot underwrite their college educations be forced take out loans themselves? Could it be that subliminally communicated messages from lenders, colleges being overly optimistic about employment possibilities for graduates, or the unexamined or unrealistic expectations of the students themselves cause them to think that they don't need to worry about loan repayment? Many perceive that they'll make so much money post-graduation that they'll quickly be able repay the debt. On graduation that is frequently not possible.

A chance interview with an obviously very bright waitress, Ann, revealed that she, a twenty-seven-year-old, is working two unskilled jobs to repay her college loans. Ann said that neither position is in the field she studied in college. Because potential employers don't consider her skilled enough for entry into graphic design employment with just a bachelor's degree, Ann has been unable to get a job in the highly competitive market where she lives. There are also a number of students who flunk out or quit college but have accrued a significant debt, borne by themselves or their parents, with truly nothing to show for their investments.

A.N., a successful forty-five-year-old family practice physician, said that his three teenage children will be attending college within five, seven, and nine years respectively. He said he wouldn't have his own college and medical school debt paid off by then, so he'll be adding their college debts to his own. "In fact," he said, "I'm not sure I'll be able to retire in twenty years because of the accumulated debt I'll still owe by then."

Robert, a forty-eight-year-old graduate-school-educated writer, said he never realized that his educational debt would be so difficult to repay. He has spent the last fifteen years thinking one of his books would become a bestseller and that the million-dollar script would easily pay back what he owes. He is not only discouraged that this anticipated reward for his efforts and sacrifice will never happen but also now has a deep sense of melancholy as to what havoc the debt has wrought upon his life. He said, "I feel as if my life is like a tree that's had to grow up around this tremendous obstacle of debt and has, as a result, become stunted and distorted. Even if I sell the million-dollar script, the tree will always be twisted." Robert does contract work rather than having a corporate position with a regular salary and benefits because if he takes a corporate job, his wages will be garnished. Together for ten years with a woman whom he loves, he stated that he'll never marry her, for to do so would be to transfer the burden of his student debt, incurred twenty years ago, onto her shoulders as well. Worse yet, without marriage he doesn't want to have a child. Robert said, "If we're married and I die, the debt would pass solely to my wife."

The prevailing cultural thought has been that young people need to go immediately from high school to college because they might otherwise never go. Bearing in mind that neurologic maturity may be delayed in some individuals, parents and young twenty-somethings might wish to delay college a few years. Perhaps in the future people can gain education in the humanities and other disciplines through alternative educational models. Innovative colleges are offering opportunities even for those in their eighties or nineties to participate in college curricula. One interviewee proudly spoke of her ninety-three-year-old aunt who still regularly takes courses at a local college. What a great idea this is for cross-generational interaction.

Growing Up—The Middle Years

Many older-age students who didn't fare well the first time they attended college, or who never went in the first place because of poor high school performances, are now coming back into colleges and graduate courses. Because they're more mature neurologically and experientially, they're taking advantage of their brain plasticity to do very well in classes.

Interviewee E.R., now forty-seven, has just graduated first in his class in physical therapy assistant training. His fears that he would be as poor a student as he was in high school and would be shunned because of his comparatively advanced age never materialized. In fact, his twenty-something classmates looked to him for life wisdom and advice. Maybe the lesson for adults is to avoid limiting their aspirations because of prior school or job failures.

But what if you don't want to go the route of higher education in the first place, or if you wish a hiatus until you find a passion worth going into debt to achieve? In his amusing and informative article for the *Psychology Today* blog, "Ten Underrated Jobs," author Marty Nemko concluded that jobs that are lower paying but that require fewer, less stressful work hours may be a better choice for a better life. He presents his insightful perspective on such jobs as being an Uber driver or a barista who serves up coffee and has a simpler, less stressful work life.

How about if those people who are mature enough, who have a solid idea of their life trajectory, head off directly into college and graduate school? Within that, however, how about asking colleges and graduate schools to negotiate lower fees in the first place, to offer lower rates of interest for college loans, and to defer the initial payback until any additional graduate work is completed and a commiserate level of employment in their area of study is accomplished? Before going to college "because everyone does," as young adults or adults, how about considering the following questions?

How important is a high-paying job to you? What salary would you like to earn? What specifically would you buy with your earnings? What are you willing to sacrifice for the high pay in terms of years spent, labor expended, deferring the pleasures of a carefree life, and monetary investment?

Would you prefer to go to college now or at a later date? What is your projected area of study? Do you know what it will cost for you to go to the college of your choice? Are you willing to work hard academically in high school to earn a scholarship? Would you be willing to earn all or a part of the money needed for your extended education so your parents can be responsible for their own debts? Would you be willing to work at needed campus jobs rather than pay tuition, as they do at the College of the Ozarks and similar schools, so you don't accrue debt?

What is your passion right now? Have you been discouraged from the pursuit of this passion because you "can't earn a living at it"? If so, be sure to watch the Ted Talk by Sir Ken Robinson, the number-one-watched Ted Talk ever, who humorously and passionately discusses our educational system and the little girl "with ADHD" who would never make a living as a dancer, but in fact became a prima ballerina and multimillionaire (Resources – References – Web – Robinson).

Would you like to live a year abroad? Would you be willing to work to save money for the trip and work to support yourself during the year? Would you consider a year of school during which you learn entry-level drafting skills, or skills as a medical assistant or web designer or in machine repair or welding? Could this experience be used as to help you decide whether to study these trades more extensively in order to make one of them a career? Or could the skills attained be used for jobs to underwrite costs if you later decide to go to college or pursue a professional career? Would you be willing to solicit unpaid or low-paying internships in your areas of interest? Would you do a year of service in this country or another as an English tutor or assisting in Habitat For Humanity-type projects? These are just a few of the questions you could pose to yourself as a teen or twenty-something; the answers might enlighten, delight, challenge, and spark the creative juices to make your life path extraordinarily fulfilling.

Do we need to relook at a curriculum relevant to today's job market, not one that continues to support the needs of an obsolete industrial revolution model? Could one reason for the alarming high school dropout rate be the lack of relevance to teens' lives? By the way, much educational theory, neurologic development, and child-psychology expertise is not integrated into the curricula of elementary, junior, and senior high schools.

Sometimes unrecognized or ignored learning disorders that were not as obvious in lower grades due to the academic structure become manifest at higher, less directed levels of schooling.

Interviewee Marta, now sixty-two, had two types of dyslexia that were unrecognized and unaccommodated such that she could not read or write well despite an obviously high IQ. She said she never married or had children because she thought she couldn't possibly live very long, since she couldn't take care of herself in a world of readers. Not until the advent of computers and the proficiency she achieved with them did she ultimately get her life and career on track.

Among young women interviewees in the twenty-eight to thirty-five age range who have deferred marriage and children to advance their careers, there's a common note of near panic in their voices as they describe concern with their ticking biologic clocks. One woman, now thirty-two, who has completed fourteen years of post-high school educational commitment, bemoaned her need to find a potential mate. She felt that she should know him for at least two years before marriage, then be married for a year, and then get pregnant. She was very concerned because by then she would be over thirty-five, entering a period of higher pregnancy complication risk.

Children can be a wonderful addition to your life, may give meaning to your existence, and be well worth any sacrifice you make, but eventually they'll be adults and have lives of their own that might not necessarily intersect with you as you age and they are far away. Any young woman with child-bearing angst might be well served to reflect upon whether she's feeling pressure from family, society, or her own biological clock. Did you from an early age dream about having a child? Have you had a lot of experience with caring for a child? If the total amount of time you've spent taking care of a child for whom you are directly responsible is less than a hundred hours, you might want to do a bit more research. Raising a child requires an extensive investment of time for twenty-five-plus years during which you defer your own interests. Do you have any idea how much of a sacrifice you will make in terms of your own free time and finances? These personal resources will not go toward your passions but rather be utilized for the child's welfare. Are you willing to put a child's welfare ahead of your career path, or do you feel you can do it all? If you never wanted a child until your late twenties, you might be at the mercy of your genetic directive to procreate for the survival of the species, rather than of your well-thought-out personal life plan.

Perhaps you've noticed that the human species is doing very well. As of 2016, the number of humans living on the planet was estimated at over 7 billion. Remember, folks, it took almost 200,000 years to get to 1 billion, 127 years to get to 2 billion, and now we're adding a billion about every ten years. The United Nations now estimates the number will rise to 11.2 billion by the year 2100, but the U.N. may be underestimating population growth. Interestingly, though, while many projections estimated a world population of 9 billion by the year 2100, one website placed that estimate at 17 billion. Children born in 2017 will likely live until the year 2100.

What will their world look like? (For a continuous real-time tally of the world's population as it occurs with births, deaths, pollution, and the like, see Resources – References – Web Sources – Poodwaddle World Clock: http://www.poodwaddle.com/worldclock/)

Are you willing to put in the effort and sacrifice necessary to raise a child who will ultimately benefit the earth and humanity? Have you ever figured the cost to the environment of each new person who arrives on the planet? Not finding an inclusive figure for the cost to the planet for a single human makes for some interesting speculation and computation. The average life expectancy in the United States is currently seventy-nine years, which combines male and female projections. That equates to approximately 4,119 weeks or 28,835 days.

The average US food consumption per day is 5.46 pounds or 2,700 calories. Annually, that would equal 1,993 pounds of food per person. Over a lifetime of seventy-nine years, the average US citizen would consume approximately 78.7 tons of food (Resources – References – Web – How Many Pounds . . .).

Each person in the U.S. consumes about 55.6 pounds of beef, 50.8 pounds of pork, and 93 pounds of chicken annually (Resources – References – Web – Per Capita Consumption . . .). Over a lifetime of seventy-nine years, the average citizen would consume approximately 2.2 tons of beef, 2 tons of pork, and 3.7 tons of chicken. Meat consumption has major secondary environmental implications related to grain production to feed the animals and to animal waste. According to a 2006 report published by the United Nations Food and Agriculture Organization, livestock fecal load generates 18 percent of greenhouse gasses. That's more greenhouse gas than is generated by the transportation sector (cars, trucks, trains, and buses combined).

What about you or your potential child? The average human produces about 11 ounces of feces per day. Over a lifetime of seventy-nine years (U.S.), that's almost 20,000 pounds of poop.

The average adult also produces about six cups of urine per day, or about 8,000 to 16,000 gallons over a lifetime.

What about the aggregate human fecal load? According to his book *The Scoop on Poop,* Dan Chiras states that our 7 billion humans "excrete an estimated 1.12 trillion pounds of feces per year . . . and 3.1 trillion liters of urine per year." Even poop-related diapers have a significant impact. The Real Diapers website estimates that the U.S. uses 27.4 billion disposable diapers per year.

What about the number of chemicals utilized on "behalf" of each human, i.e., the chemicals used as fertilizer for food, the chemicals we use on our lawns and in our households, and those used in the disposable diapers?

RealDiapers.org notes that some disposable diapers contain dioxin, which according to the EPA is the most toxic of all cancer-linked chemicals. Dioxin is a byproduct of paper bleaching. Some disposable diapers also contain the chemical tributyltin, which is known to cause hormonal problems in both animals and humans.

http://realdiapers.org/diaper-facts

Every day the average person produces 4.6 pounds of garbage that goes into landfills. That's about 1,674 pounds per year or 66 tons in a lifetime. It may be a balm to your psyche to say that you recycle, but what if you didn't consume so much in the first place? Guess what? Disposable diapers are the third largest consumer item in landfills, and represent about 4 percent of solid waste. In a house with a child in diapers, disposables make up 50 percent of household waste.

As to recycling, there's a significant energy cost to recycle the materials into more consumables, and another concern is how much of what's sent to recycling is actually put into landfills instead?

What about consumables? Each of us gets a new computer and cell phone every two to three years, each of which requires rare earth elements and plastic and produces manufacturing waste.

If the current trends continue, we would consume around thirty phones and computers per lifetime.

Based on the longevity of cars today (about ten years), it's estimated that the average US citizen will own about six cars in a lifetime. Each must be manufactured. The metal needed to make it is mined using fossil fuel and producing waste at a cost to the earth (the earthmovers to do the mining must be manufactured and shipped to the mining site), then the metals for the cars must be shipped, using fossil fuels, to the assembly plant where they are assembled by machines (that also must be manufactured and shipped to the plant that is producing the car) into car parts and the assembled auto.

The average per capita consumption of gasoline in the U.S. is 392 gallons or about 31,000 gallons per lifetime (Resources – References – Web – Average U.S. Gasoline . . .).

How many homes will an individual own? Do we all need new appliances, updated cabinetry, and granite countertops?

From the above, very abbreviated, synopsis of each human's cost to the environment, the load levied against the earth is staggering in amount and complexity. I hope that some fire-in-the-belly readers will pursue this line of reasoning to give all of us some idea of the debt that each of us as an individual owes back to the earth in reparation. We seem to have applied the ostrich philosophy to population density and to the damage done to soils stripped of nutrients and replenished by petroleum-based chemicals and fertilizers, as well as the staggering amount of food required to feed our billions. We can figure these issues out, but only if we recognize that it might be us, as metaphorical mastodons, being driven off the cliff if we continue to blindly follow our current habits.

How about if those of us concerned about these issues figure out what can be done to remediate what we've done to the planet, each other, and ourselves? Let's resonate at a high level with our can-do attitude, our courage, and our willingness to put in the hard work to make the solutions happen and thereby tip the earth and the people inhabiting it toward a higher, more conscious awareness that we are interconnected, whether we're aware of it or not.

Growing Up—Elders

Despite some examples of a healthy, vital retirement, many people in assisted living and nursing homes look as if they're sitting and waiting to die. Some appear to be in abject misery or seem completely vacant, and refuse to participate in activities that could give meaning to their last few years. What if we refuse to be warehoused and instead continue to be a vital force for our own good and the good of the whole?

Even though many elders face the possibility, many have not and will not acquire dementia. With its neuroplasticity, the brain can continue to grow and learn. Could dementia be avoided or substantially delayed if we made it our obligation and joy to continue to actively learn, to challenge ourselves by either staying on the job or volunteering? Can we stave off dementia with positive psychology, decreasing our stress load, and resonating at higher levels of our most powerful emotions? Motivated elders in their seventies and eighties are going back to school, forming new companies, and organizing charitable organizations to benefit the rest of humanity. What if those of us who need the extra help of assisted care continue to be engaged in life, in reading, painting, dancing, volunteering, and mentoring?

Joan, age ninety-six and three quarters, a vital woman who has served as a mentor to many, granted an interview in which she spoke of a teenage dream to become a fashion designer. When asked why she had not, she said, "Life gets in the way of life." Joan stated, "I am a recovering alcoholic." She said that she had never recognized her alcoholism until someone finally told her somewhere in her sixties, "I had the disease." Joan joined Alcoholics Anonymous (AA), worked with her sponsor, and subsequently sponsored an untold number of others who were trying to recover. Joan said that AA has been one of the pursuits that have given meaning to her life. She said that the unexpected upside is that now that she's in her nineties, many of those she sponsored keep in close contact. Two of them come to see her for lunch and to "talk" each week. When asked about growing up, she said that, at age ninety-seven, she feels that growing should be synonymous with being curious. She said, "If you remain curious, you adapt and learn." When asked about the role of mentors, she replied, "They ask the questions that need to be asked. You have to do the thinking."

Chapter 11

Challenges of Aging

When reflecting on aging and dying, you might default to your old pattern of "That's too heavy a burden to think about; maybe it will go away if I ignore it." On the other hand, you could apply your critical thinking skills and begin to form a habit of positive reflection. The head-in-the-sand behavior might work for ostriches, but it's not a great plan for humans. If you decide not to think about aging or dying you are making a choice. You thereby answer no as to whether you make an action plan for the last one third of your life. As to not needing to plan because you won't likely live that long, there's good news and bad news. Most people, despite everything they fear, will live longer than they think. Relook at the actuarial tables in the resources section. If you are 40 now, you'll likely live another 38.5 years to age 78.5. For those 50-year-olds, you might well be around another 29.5 years, reaching 79.5 years, and at age 60 you can get betting odds that you'll live to be 81.4. Notice that the longer you make it, the longer you can expect to make it. (See discussion in chapter 3.)

If you are toward the end of the Young age group, i.e., the latter first trimester of In Utero II, the following discussion is important to you if you wish to understand your own middle-aged parents or want to check out the trajectory you might wish to chart for yourself as you enter middle age. If, however, you are in your middle years, there are pressing issues to consider right now. Of those, whether and how to retire are two of the top priorities.

Compared to the thousands of years of human history, "retirement" would have to be considered a new human construct. Used as a verb, to construct is to build, as in building a foundation, wall, or roof of a house. Used as a noun, for purposes of this book, a construct is an idea based on assumptions that may or may not be valid. Some human needs such as food, shelter, and familial relationships are foundational and have been proven important based on human historical precedent. The more recent scaffolds on which we are building, like the changes in family structure and proximity, digital communication, and retirement have not necessarily passed the test of legitimacy of long historical precedent.

Say what?!

I'm a bit concerned that retirement, which hasn't been around very long as an expectation as we currently think of it, might be unsustainable. That might not be such a bad thing. Remember: "Don't shoot the messenger." I'm just trying to get a dialogue going here. When it was revealed that there were no retirees depicted in cave paintings, we were presented a resoundingly irrefutable argument that retirement is a new form of behavior for humans. To have lolled around in retirement garb and retirement mental processing would have led to a very short time in retirement, as some passing saber-toothed cat decided to dine upon you. In exploring the concept of retirement, I followed my usual progression:

[Hmm. In this case . . . retirement. I hit a thread of inquiry and came up with my own ideas, putting pen to paper as a placeholder so that I could subsequently know what thoughts were purely my own; then I began to research whether other people's thoughts on the subject were similar. So, looking back in time, how did we get such an ugly sounding term as "retirement," and what exactly does it mean?]

The inquiry was as follows: Where and with whom did the concept of retirement start? I always try to guess the answer. In this case, tires belong to cars, so to "re-tire" could possibly mean putting new tires on a car. Following that logic, it seemed likely to me that the concept of retirement had something to do with the auto industry. Could it have been that when someone became older and was no longer physically able to perform on an automobile assembly line, that he was given a gold watch and escorted to the door marked "Exit Only"? Having used my imagination, I then began to research the topic of retirement.

Generally we define retirement as leaving the career in which we have been employed at about age sixty-five. As to the origin of the word, there's very little of substance on the Internet. It may have been related to the French *retirir,* which meant to withdraw, as in to withdraw to bed. However, this explanation seems woefully lacking because it was not at that time related to any sort of retirement from work. I also doubt that the word "retirement" is of French origin since it's quite unattractive to the ear, that is, no sexy-French-gusto pronunciation.

The concept of retirement appears to have started in the year 1883 with German Chancellor Otto von Bismarck. It seems he wanted to recruit younger, less expensive laborers from surrounding countries. To free up positions, he proposed giving a pension to older workers to expedite their exits from the workforce. One astute observer pointed out that it was a pretty good deal for Bismarck in that the average life expectancy at that time wasn't a whole lot beyond sixty-five anyway, so he wouldn't have been out a lot of money. Reflecting on the fact that retirement was created as a business proposition in the 1800s, is it possible that we should reconsider the entire concept by asking questions such as:

What is retirement? What are the mission and vision? What is the plan?

Is retirement good, bad, or both?

Did anyone apply "Law of Unintended Consequences" scrutiny to this ostensibly great notion? Not working might have been an excellent idea if you didn't like your job, but what if you really liked working? What if work gives meaning to life and therefore some people don't want to quit?

Wow, who came up with the mandatory retirement age? Isn't that rather draconian? What were you supposed to do for the remaining time you had on Earth? Did this new human construct add to the angst of aging because it was an end with no defined beginning on the other side?

Have we grown tired of the term "retired"? Could we consider a new term for this vaguely defined condition of human development known as "ceasing to work"?

What if we defined retirement in terms of what it could be? Could this ofttimes pejoratively considered term thereby become less problematic for those not currently retired? In casting about for a better term, a collaborative discussion with interviewee O.G. netted the expression "re-emergence" as a potential replacement. This seemed to fit better with stopping one activity, i.e., one's job, but starting another. How about considering that you're retiring one persona and creating a new one. Hmm. How do you like the term "reinvention"? As an example, "I retired from welding, and have reinvented myself as a writer or commercial fisherman or actor."

I'm enthralled with the topic, what about you? Did you ready yourself for this, your next phase of life (in great detail, not just a 401k tax plan) while still in the preceding phase? If so, great, skip the following. (Youth please note: if you put your planning hat on and wish to make a preemptive strike at getting your middle-years' celebration going, read on.)

Another thought from interviewee "Toto," a financial planner, was that we substitute the word "redirection." Since redirection is easier to say and implies taking a different or parallel path rather than reinventing oneself, this might be the better replacement for the concept previously known as retirement. Consider N.N., fifty-three, who took up the guitar approximately ten years ago. Over his working life, Nick has had several jobs that were quite varied. By choosing to learn to play the guitar, committing the time necessary for its mastery, and developing relationships with other musicians, N.N. looks forward to retirement as an opportunity to expand his musical exploration. If the research is correct about the value of music to brain health, Nick might be staving off dementia as well.

What passions would you like to develop now, well in advance of retirement, that will sustain and fulfill you during the greatest trimester of your life? The message of this rewrite chapter, as is the goal of this book, is to get your celebration started. So, what do you think?

- What does retirement mean to you?
- Do you wish to retire?
- What would you desire from your retirement?
- How will you accomplish your goals?

I pledge that I didn't read the following article until I came up with my own thoughts on retirement first and then began to research what other people were thinking. I found myself in a karass of people who are also analyzing this life phase. The term "karass" was coined by Kurt Vonnegut in his 1963 book *Cat's Cradle.* Karass has been defined in several ways; for this discussion, it's a group of people on the same mission (in this case pursuing a thread of inquiry into the concept of retirement), but not necessarily aware of each other.

There can be parallel "original" thoughts as I found when I discovered Arianna Huffington's delightful and insightful article "It's Time to Retire Our Definition of Retirement," in which she expresses an overall message regarding retirement that is positive and inspiring. She also proposed that we should develop an alternative term for "retirement." I hope Ms. Huffington reads this chapter at some point and weighs in on whether she thinks one of the terms—re-emergence, reinvention, or redirection—would work. As they say in business, we need to re-brand retirement not only to find a better term but also to redefine the concept. As I had proposed not only a new word but also a new definition of retirement, so too had Ms. Huffington. I define "redirection" as a landmark in human life generally occurring at approximately age sixty-five, at which time the individual chooses to redirect his or her life path.

Even though Huffington is generally optimistic about the potential adventures of such redirection, she is realistic about the attendant financial needs. She cites the Employment Benefit Research figures showing that at least ten times a current salary level is needed to continue the standard of living for an employed individual. Another sobering statistic involves those young adults who are not leaving the parental home. Evidently, one in seven middle-aged American workers is now providing financial support to both an elder parent and an adult child (Resources – References – Huffington). [*Note from the worm wrangler: Don't go all gloom and doom here if this is a little scary.*]

The sobering financial reality must be looked at squarely, objectively, and with an attitude of "can do"; otherwise we descend into fear, helplessness, and hopelessness. With enough good minds working on the subject of retirement, I'm convinced we can figure this out; that is, if we start addressing retirement's financial realities. Right now, too few people are putting enough planning into retirement, especially financial planning. What are the opportunities?

1. Could it be that families can reproduce the structure of multiple generations living in close proximity or in the same house, either through small "f" or large "F" families to the financial benefit of all?

2. Could we apply business principles by leveraging the buying power of large families for purchasing food, shelter, or clothing?

3. Are parents doing a disservice to their adult children when they financially and emotionally enable them to extend their adolescence?

4. Could families benefit by discussing a business plan, maybe even starting a family business and writing down mission and vision statements to get them started?

5. Fundamentally, should families be able to answer the question "What is the Plan"?

More people in their middle and elder years are now approaching aging and retirement in positive and creative ways by founding new companies, particularly ones that are aimed at benefiting aging populations. A Google search of "retirement age entrepreneurs" netted 2,080,000 results. Those who are starting new businesses at age fifty-five and above make up the fastest-growing age group of entrepreneurs. These redirecting individuals are tapping into their core age group to fund their businesses and to market their products.

We now see more and more books and essays on the plight and potential solutions to issues of retirement, redirection, or as one author coined it, "unretirement." Some are pessimistic, some optimistic, but all opinions are important in the dialogue regarding our attitudes and action plans. I'll leave this one up to you. I encourage you to look at some of the accounts of new ventures when searching retirement-age entrepreneurs. The message from many in the karass of inquiring minds is the same: There are millions of creative, motivated people with remarkable talent whose experience is being lost to a society that needs all the help it can get. Put your noodle to this one. What are some of your thoughts? Join me in chapter 14 as I share some of my ideas.

After retirement, the next most pressing issue we must address in our middle years is probably the dread specter of Alzheimer's disease and the other dementias that rob us and our loved ones of our memories and our lives. Here's what I suggest might be an upside to not retiring: One of the vanguards of decreasing your chances of Alzheimer's is social engagement and continuing to actively use your mind, both of which are served by continuing to be employed. So, it might suck to have to keep working, but maybe it could be an aid in staving off Alzheimer's, which by the way can be detected as early as thirty years before the disease is diagnosed. Yep, fifty- and sixty-year-olds, stay vigilant. Seriously, any straw that we can grasp is important to getting our greatest health menace controlled, reversed, and ultimately prevented.

Wait a minute, you might say, I thought you wanted me to celebrate my middle years; why depress me by making me think of something that makes me shudder in fear for me and those I love? Well, here's the deal: We have a problem. We're all afraid of Alzheimer's. When you forget someone's name, can't find a word you need, or have the following scenario occur—enter a room to retrieve something, and leave, only to realize what you retrieved was not what you went after in the first place—does it enter your head to think *Oh, no, is this how it starts?* Since we all fear losing our mental faculties, any small memory issue makes us apprehensive of the possibility of developing Alzheimer's. Fear is a major impediment to enjoying our whole life continuum, so let's figure this one out. Let's identify the problem and then make an action plan to solve this sucker!

"Alzheimer's disease is (described as) an irreversible, progressive brain disorder that slowly destroys memory and thinking skills and eventually the ability to carry out the simplest tasks. In most people with Alzheimer's, symptoms first appear in their mid-sixties. Estimates vary, but experts suggest that more than 5 million Americans may have Alzheimer's, which is the most common cause of dementia among older adults. Dementia is the loss of cognitive functioning—thinking, remembering, and reasoning—and behavioral abilities to such an extent that it interferes with a person's daily life and activities. Dementia ranges in severity from the mildest stage, when it is just beginning to affect a person's functioning, to the most severe stage, when the person must depend completely on others for basic activities of daily living."

(https://www.nia.nih.gov/alzheimers/. . ./alzheimers-disease-f).

Recent advances, however, challenge some of these "facts." Alzheimer's disease is not necessarily irreversible. A vaccine may enter clinical trials within the next three to five years. Early research also indicates a potential tie between the herpes virus and Lyme disease bacteria and Alzheimer's, which may lead to new forms of treatment. Many diseases originally thought incurable have subsequently been conquered. (By the way, the unsung heroes also known as researchers should be lauded. Go find one and hug her or him).

Here are the facts:

1. Alzheimer's disease is named after Dr. Alois Alzheimer, who discovered it in 1906.

2. One hundred ten years after the disease was discovered, we've made almost no progress toward the prevention, and none toward the reversal, of Alzheimer's. That's 110 years!

3. From 2000 to 2010, the percentage of deaths in the U.S. from cancer, HIV/AIDS, and cardiovascular diseases declined substantially, while deaths of people with Alzheimer's increased dramatically.

4. Alzheimer's disease is currently ranked as the sixth leading cause of death in the United States, but recent estimates indicate that the disorder may rank third, just behind heart disease and cancer, as a cause of death for older people.

5. Think about it. One in every three seniors dies with, although not necessarily directly from, Alzheimer's or another form of dementia. You might not be a senior yet, but you're going to be.

6. Over the next decade, cases of Alzheimer's are projected to increase by 40 percent, barring a medical breakthrough.

7. If research dollars remain unavailable, Alzheimer's will affect nearly 14 million seniors by the year 2050, nearly triple the number of people it affects today.

(For data sources, see Resources – Scientific, Philosophical or Psychological Concepts – Alzheimer's; specifically, a web article cited in the Resources entitled "Alzheimer's Research Spending vs. Annual Care Costs.")

In a 2013 article appearing in *USA Today,* Don Campbell identified that the National Institutes of Health was at that time spending close to seven times as much money on HIV/AIDS research as on research into Alzheimer's. Mr. Campbell was not calling for fewer dollars to be spent on HIV/AIDS but pointing out the disparity in effort and funding for research. The difference in the amount of money committed to saving the people who now suffer from Alzheimer's is even worse when you note that five times more people are affected by it than by HIV/AIDS. As an example, if $3,500 is spent per person with HIV/AIDS, only $100 would be spent per person for Alzheimer's. Consider that, just like the rest of us, every HIV/AIDS patient saved still faces a one in three risk of dying of dementia. We should not decrease spending on AIDS research but work to increase research dollars available for Alzheimer's disease for the benefit of us all (see appendix 6).

As to HIV/AIDS: Because of the complex nature of the retrovirus responsible, which was really good at changing itself to circumvent being eradicated, it was originally thought that it would take many years to cure and that it might wipe out a good portion of humanity in the meantime. The following provides testimony to the tenacity, creativity, assertiveness, and commitment of researchers and research dollars: The time period for HIV/AIDS from the point at which it was recognized as a major threat, to the discovery of an initial helpful treatment, was less than twenty years. With treatment HIV/AIDS is now more of a chronic illness like diabetes, whereas before medication became available, both diabetes and HIV/AIDS carried death sentences. After a hundred years, we still don't have effective treatments for Alzheimer's, which is progressive and fatal.

Why is there not more being done for the prevention and reversal of Alzheimer's? With so much on humanity's plate right now, curing Alzheimer's disease may be a low priority for several reasons.

1. It affects old people and they're going to die anyway.
    a. The Young: "Not my problem. I won't even live to be that old."

b. The Middle-Aged: "Sure, I'll be older in twenty to thirty years. I'll think about it some other time. Let's worry about tsunamis thousands of miles away—and, oh yeah—I have a football game to watch."

c. The Old: Too late. "I'm screwed anyway. I have no purpose for living. Can't wait to get to where I don't know anything."

2. Alzheimer's disease is not sexy; "It doesn't affect young, healthy people."

3. So much money is going out the door. "We want no new taxes" (according to both taxpayers and legislators).

Let's return to the current costs of Alzheimer's. The following data were extracted from the 2016 Alzheimer's disease facts and figures produced by the National Center for Biotechnology Information (Resources – Scientific, Philosophical or Psychological Concepts – Alzheimer's):

- Every 66 seconds someone develops dementia.
- In 2015, more than 15 million caregivers provided 18.1 billion hours of unpaid care to family and friends with dementia.
- On average, family caregivers spend $5,000 per year of their own money.
- In 2016, dementias cost the nation about $236 billion.
- In 2050, dementias are expected to cost the nation $1.1 trillion. [*Let's put that into perspective: a million seconds is 11.6 days; a billion seconds is 31.7 years; and a trillion seconds is 31,709 years.*]

Important things to consider

There are multiple types of dementia, including vascular and Lewy body, but the major type is Alzheimer's disease. There are two types of Alzheimer's. The most common form has not been linked to genetics and generally has a later age of onset, starting after sixty-five. A rare genetic form of the disease can manifest as early as age forty, but some patients develop symptoms even in their thirties. The following questions summarize the ambiguity regarding the cause of later-onset Alzheimer's, which may be a perfect storm of many interactive events, exposures, and deficiencies, the sum of which is this dread disease.

With a new case diagnosed every sixty seconds, shouldn't the focus of research be greatly expanded to pursue multiple potential causative agents until definitive agents and therapies have been identified? Disparate research initiatives should be carried out concurrently rather than one after the other. Finding the cause or causes of Alzheimer's and the related cures should be a national if not global priority. Could it be that Alzheimer's disease is not a specific diagnosis but instead is the perfect storm of many factors culminating in the production of common symptoms such as loss of cognitive abilities, abstract thinking, and memory?

Could it be that we are barking up the wrong tree by focusing on amyloid plaques and neurofibrillary tangles as the cause of Alzheimer's? Could it be that these anatomic changes are the consequence of an as yet unidentified causative agent? The vaccine noted above might not target the actual causative agent, and the study is years away from completion.

Could it be that the sadness, loneliness, and fear of aging make people vulnerable to Alzheimer's?

Could fear and stress hormones contribute to the development of Alzheimer's? Could a positive outlook, which decreases these hormones, be partially preventative?

Could there be a dietary factor that also contributes to the development of Alzheimer's? During the 18th century, disease killed more British sailors than enemy action. In his celebrated voyage of 1740–1744, George Anson lost nearly two thirds of his crew (1,300 out of 2,000) to scurvy within the first ten months of the voyage. After the solution was proposed, it took another forty years before the Royal Navy began to treat the sailors. The solution, using citrus fruits to provide needed vitamin C, resulted in the term "Limeys" to describe the navy. But if a simple dietary lack could have killed untold thousands of British sailors, could a similar dietary deficiency be a cause of Alzheimer's? I'm not proposing that Alzheimer's disease is in any way related to vitamin C, but could a combination of lack of vitamins or micronutrients be contributory? Further, could dementia somehow be related to dietary additives or adulterants?

A Gaia proponent would be very concerned about our soils, which are depleted of the natural microbiome and of the full panoply of historically present micronutrients. Could it be that replacing only three of the hundreds of nutrients (nitrogen, phosphorus, and potassium of typical fertilizers) meant to restore the soils is inadequate? Could it be that the full complement of previously plentiful micronutrients, and more important, the total interactive nature of soil composition of the past, is necessary for our foods to sustain vibrant health of body and brain?

Could toxic chemical exposures be a contributing cause of Alzheimer's disease? Any one chemical could be problematic, but the full measure of what we're exposed to every day is astounding. Rachel Carson's concerns about toxic chemicals, addressed in her book *Silent Spring,* prompted an exceedingly important movement to clean up our environment that unfortunately is now focused almost exclusively on our carbon footprint. Today, little is said about the toxic milieu we're bathed in, which was Carson's original focus. Hmm. Why have we lost the focus on pollution? For a humorous and eye-opening assessment of our current exposure to toxins, there's a very short TED Talk that speaks to the accumulation of chemicals in our bodies over our lifetimes (see Resources – References – Lee).

What about possible toxicity associated with aluminum, copper, and iron? Could any or all of them be causative or contributory factors? Controversy has swirled over whether such exposure can be proven to be a problem (for details see Resources – Scientific, Philosophical, or Psychological Concepts – Alzheimer's).

Aluminum

Four observations from a 2011 National Institutes of Health article are of particular interest:

1. Aluminum (Al) is the most abundant neurotoxic metal on earth.
2. [Since] 1911, experimental evidence has repeatedly demonstrated that chronic [aluminum] intoxication reproduces neuropathological hallmarks of [Alzheimer's disease].
3. The hypothesis that [aluminum] significantly contributes to [Alzheimer's] is built upon very solid experimental evidence and should not be dismissed.
4. Immediate steps should be taken to lessen human exposure to [aluminum], which may be the single most aggravating and avoidable factor related to [Alzheimer's disease]. Kawahara, Masahiro, and Midori Kato-Negishi. "Link between Aluminum and the Pathogenesis of Alzheimers Disease: The Integration of the Aluminum and Amyloid Cascade

Hypotheses." International Journal of Alzheimers Disease 2011 (2011): 1-17. Web.

Just because science cannot irrefutably prove something is a cause doesn't necessarily mean that it's not. Further research on potential causal links between exposures and Alzheimer's disease should be a national priority. If Alzheimer's is of concern to you, please see appendix 6 for more detail on aluminum and other metals that have been implicated. Also provided are more details on other research initiatives and statistics.

My main concern is that the dialogue needs to accelerate to the benefit of us all. No one is immune to the threat of the disease. Clearly more research is needed; accumulations of metals in the brains of people who have died of Alzheimer's would seem to be a prime target for research dollars.

Do you have an Alzheimer's avoidance action plan?

I highly recommend that you review the full articles cited above and others in the resources regarding Alzheimer's disease (Resources – Scientific, Philosophical or Psychological Concepts – Alzheimer's). It has been found that brain changes consistent with Alzheimer's can be detected as early as thirty years before the disease becomes obvious, so start now to research, formulate, and carry out an action plan:

1. Read, read, read, and then speak with friends, family, and physicians. A reasoned dialogue is a great starting point for increasing awareness of potential risks.

   As an example, Sandrine Thuret, Ph.D., states that research on intermittent fasting can lead to a 30% improvement in verbal memory over a period of just three months (Resources – Web Sources – Thuret).

2. Do everything in your power to delay or avoid Alzheimer's, including diet, exercise, social engagement, and other interventions you might discover. Fortunately, this commitment to your mental health also serves to decrease your chances of heart disease, stroke, and cancer.

3. Take twenty minutes to draft a note to your state and federal representatives regarding the need for extensive and immediate funding increases for Alzheimer's research.

Stop the Press!

This book was already copyrighted when interviewee O.G. suggested I attend a conference he had found entitled The 14th Annual Natural Supplements: An Evidence-Based Update. I'm thrilled to say that this group of dedicated researchers and clinicians may have found some of the keys to unlocking the mysteries behind the symptom complex currently known as Alzheimer's disease. I was impressed by the practical, relatively inexpensive, common-sense dietary and lifestyle recommendations and the diagnosis and treatment options for toxic exposures to chemicals and heavy metals that, according to recent research, contribute to the overall burden on the brain.

Dr. Dale Bredesen, one of the many excellent speakers at the conference, discussed the prevention of Alzheimer's disease. Dr. Bredesen gave me verbal permission (yep, I met him) to quote some of his materials and to cite his work on this topic so vital to us all. The manner in which he has evaluated and personalized the treatment for some people suffering from Alzheimer's has resulted in a reversal of some of their cognitive defects. One patient was described as a very intelligent man who began to exhibit severe cognitive decline with one mathematical parameter scoring at less than 5% of normal capacity. After fifteen months of a multipoint intervention involving, among other measures, the addressing of gut bacteria, treatment of nutritional deficits, and chelation to remediate toxic metal exposures, repeat testing revealed the mathematical parameter to be improved to greater than 90% of normal. Of course, not everyone will have such dramatic improvement. Because some people begin to show mild symptoms of dementia in their 50s, it makes sense to diagnose early and treat aggressively. However, even folks with significant deficits have evidently demonstrated some improvement.

Dr. Bredesen deserves to be lauded for his work on humanity's behalf, but he was quick to credit the pioneers with whom he trained and those current researchers he works with. Dr. Bredesen has developed a protocol for treatment of Alzheimer's disease. You can begin to explore his approach at https://www.drbredesen.com/thebredesenprotocol. Another pioneer is Dr. David Perlmutter, whose book Brain Maker: The Power of Gut Microbes to Heal and Protect Your Brain—for Life provides fascinating insight into the symbiotic relationship between our gut flora and our mind and body. Dr. Perlmutter is a neurologist and nutritionist who explores the effect of diet and the gut bacteria on our physical, mental, and emotional health.

The approach of these and other researchers and clinicians moves away from a disease model to an ongoing health model of medical intervention. Our current disease model can be compared to the old saying involving the futility of closing the stable door to keep a horse inside after the horse has left the barn. After damage has been done, treating chronic disease such as heart disease and diabetes is certainly less effective than prevention.

These pioneers may not have found all the answers, but their questioning of the status quo by striking out in a new direction is encouraging. The only potential downside to the work of these pioneers is that there's no magic bullet (or pill). We cannot abdicate our responsibility for our life choices and expect a pill that miraculously cures us of the consequences of poor lifestyle choices.

Chapter 12

Perspectives on Dying

Whether or not we live to our elder years, are diagnosed with Alzheimer's, cancer, or the like, we all have an expiration date. This date of launch from In Utero II can usually be impacted to the good with proper care of our bodies and minds, but ultimately we will die. It's our destiny from the moment we come into existence, so why not consider it a lovely end to our days on Earth? Planning can impact our lives and those of our loved ones, making the transition a time of celebration of life and relationships.

Whether you are in your young, middle, or elder years, the ideas in this chapter are applicable if you choose to make them so. I invite you to open your contemplative perspective as you read the chapter—with a caveat: No book can give you all the answers; it can only provide perspectives. Please do not read this section at all if the news of a terminal or potentially terminal illness has *just* been made for you or a loved one. As someone who has received this kind of news, it's my opinion that your first focus should be on processing the bad news in whatever manner works best for you. If you found yourself reading the previous sentence for the second time, yes, I received that type of news a long time ago. While the pain of such news is initially fresh and raw, I assure you that it can take on a very different perspective in the long view.

[If you skipped the first few chapters of this book and have started on this section, you will do yourself a disservice if you proceed without first reading at least chapter 1 to chapter 3. If you don't like my message or my style of communication in those chapters, you will for sure not like what's in this chapter. Please take some time, read the first three chapters, and preferably all the previous chapters, and then tackle this one if it seems right to do so.]

When people receive bad news, it can be overwhelming. Time to adjust to the feelings you have about a life-threatening diagnosis and its implications is vital. Consider seeking the counsel of friends or family who have been in your position, asking medical experts, and reading books on the subjects you're most concerned about. One of the books that helped me "get out of my head" and deal with the endless loop of unhelpful thoughts regarding my circumstances was written by Dr. Elisabeth Kübler-Ross. A Swiss psychiatrist, she was motivated to write her book based on her work with dying patients and her concern that there was no medical school curriculum to teach would-be physicians about the subjects of death and dying. Kübler-Ross noted that the grief process in her patients in response to a diagnosis of a potentially terminal illness included: denial, anger, bargaining, depression, and acceptance.

Kübler-Ross noted later in life that the stages are not a linear and predictable progression and she regretted writing them in a way that was misunderstood. Rather, they are a collation of five common experiences for the bereaved that can occur in any order, if at all. Elisabeth Kübler-Ross wrote many valuable books about the years she worked with terminally ill children and adults. Her messages can bring solace and understanding to those who face their own impending death or the death of a loved one (Resources – Scientific, Philosophical or Psychological Concepts – Kübler-Ross).

Whether or not you agree with any of her conclusions, Dr. Kübler-Ross did us a favor by opening a dialogue on a topic important to all. Everyone processes death differently. You might not wish to read anything, but if you do seek outside references to better understand your own or a loved one's thought processes near death, Kübler-Ross's book might help you gain an understanding of how some people have felt in similar circumstances.

When I was informed of a potentially terminal event and surgery was recommended, I fell back on my usual manner of handling problems. Tending to need time to reflect and set a course of action, I chose not to discuss the diagnosis with anyone until I'd had time to think through the implications of having an expiration date for my earthly travels. I had the option to say yes or no to the proposed surgery or to hide my head in the sand and thereby also say no to surgery. First, I researched everything I could find concerning my diagnosis, and then I spoke at length with medical providers. As the final part of the decision-making process, I checked in with my feelings regarding the go or no go decision about the surgery. Ultimately, I chose not to have it because the risks of the procedure were the same risks of what might happen to me if I didn't have it. My decision worked for me; I'm still cavorting about.

Please do not follow my course of action.

If you or a family member is faced with a similar situation, I urge you to make the best decision you can with the input of your medical team, your family, and your own researched information. After deciding not to have surgery, I made an action plan and carried it out. I always try to hedge my bets. In the worst-case scenario, what do I need to do? My children were young. I didn't want them to be left without a mother to guide them through landmark times such as entry into the various levels of school, puberty, early adulthood, marriage, and childbearing. I videotaped myself sharing thoughts on each of those phases, to be viewed when they reached that stage. I guess that's what started my fascination with a "message in a bottle": it seemed I was providing exactly that by planning ahead for future timely messages for my children. It gave me an amazing sense of peace once I'd accomplished the task. These messages went into a lockbox. I think they were ultimately lost when they became no longer applicable.

Even though family and friends didn't know of my diagnosis, I started general conversations about the end of life and made my wishes abundantly clear. Then I wrote down my wishes should I be left in a brain-damaged or vegetative state sometime in the future. I executed all the appropriate documents (wills, living wills, powers of attorney, etc.) available at the time. I say "etc." because I can't remember what specific documents were recommended back then. Finally, I planned my memorial service should I "launch," wrote out what I wanted said by the officiant, and filed it so it would be available if needed.

Afterward, I tried (I haven't always been successful) to adopt the attitude that I might live one more day or survive to age one hundred. For me, considering each day as if it were my last, has helped me keep an eye on relationships and enjoy every moment. If I were to live to one hundred, I wanted to keep my body and mind in as good shape as possible. This strategy evolved over the years influenced by the cases I read in which, despite terminal diagnoses, people did not die as or when expected. One particularly enlightening case involves the medical diagnosis, prognosis, and ultimate life of Stephen Hawking.

Dr. Hawking was diagnosed with amyotrophic lateral sclerosis (ALS) shortly after his twenty-first birthday in 1963. His life expectancy was approximately two to five years. At the time of this publication, he has beaten the odds—by almost fifty years. Despite a predicted expiration date, Dr. Hawking went on to Cambridge and became a brilliant researcher. From 1979 to 2009 he held the post of Lucasian Professor at Cambridge, a chair held by Sir Isaac Newton in 1663. Professor Hawking, who holds more than a dozen honorary degrees, is considered one of the most brilliant theoretical physicists since Einstein.

Through the years, the disease has progressively taken its toll. Dr. Hawking lost his ability to walk and talk—other than with the assistance of a computerized voice system for communication. Hawking has a family and has collaborated on authoring children's books. He continues his research into theoretical physics and hopes to make it into space someday. http://www.hawking.org.uk/

Stephen Hawking is an inspiration to us all. Someone the world would consider profoundly disabled has beaten the odds regarding his disease, and more important, has led a full and amazing life. Not everyone will be as successful in delaying death, but Hawking's courage and stamina, despite a terminal prognosis, provide an excellent example for all. You might wish to consider the following actions steps if you or a family member are facing a potentially terminal illness:

- First, do not give up your power. It's still your body and your decisions. Considering yourself the CEO of the business of your life, you can solicit opinions, but it's still your "business." You might consider a big beefy bouncer attitude.
- Are you convinced that the diagnosis and proposed medical action plan are correct? If not, a second or third opinion might be helpful. My understanding is that a mother whose child was ultimately diagnosed with Lyme disease persevered in getting many "second" opinions until organized medicine finally recognized the disease.
- Think of best-case and worst-case scenarios regarding your diagnosis, and formulate your action plans for each possibility.

You might or might not beat the odds and live a long life, but ultimately, living like you'll have only today and that you might live to be a hundred still applies. Realistically, we are all going out at some point. It's your decision whether to accept your diagnosis or go to the ends of the earth to find a medical cure, which if found provides justification for this approach. If not found, searching for a cure might rob you of peace and comfortable time with your family. Your call.

Decide if and to whom you will speak regarding the above, including family and friends. Be very selfish here; if some of your family and friends aren't helpful in general, and particularly in a crisis, they might be better avoided. Too many times these drama mourners (of and related to drama queens and kings) are all about their own pity party. The people I have observed at the time of transition are weary of the journey, and their energy is very low. In my opinion, it's a terrible disservice to sully the potential beauty and peace of their passing with ridiculous displays of selfish mourning styles.

In your middle years, when you are not in need of it, when there is no drama, when you have time to think through decisions in detail, is the most appropriate time to execute all the legal documents necessary for end-of-life planning. Your wishes about your financial and medical care will then be carried out exactly as you want them to be. You'll definitely be doing yourself a service, but possibly even a greater service to your loved ones (see appendix 6).

Decide what types of care you do not want and make plans to circumvent them. There's no better example of this than planning the measures you will allow for your end-of-life medical care. If you want heroic measures you'll receive them. If you don't want ICU time, resuscitation, and potentially being maintained in a vegetative state, you'd be well served to tell all your family, friends, and medical personnel verbally and in writing. Perhaps even better is to film your wishes with witnesses in the room to verify that you were of sound mind and not coerced. Consider legally documenting your intent while you can, (living wills, advanced directives, or powers of attorney). If you stick your head in the sand thinking the untoward diagnosis might just go away, as you near death medical personnel might have no option other than to continue a regimen that does not reflect your choices. Only about 10 percent of the general public has completed an advance directive or obtained a durable power of attorney for healthcare.

In the resources is a reference to the article "Pulling the plug: ICU 'culture' key to life or death decision" from NBC.com. Be sure to read the selected reviews on the blog. There are some well-stated pros and cons for you to consider in your decision process. The blog entries are exceptionally helpful in that they run the gamut of reactions to end-of-life care. Dr. John Luce, an emeritus professor of anesthesiology and medicine at the University of California, San Francisco, has researched and written about end-of-life care. In his own end-of-life documents, Dr. Luce has expressed that he would not want to live unless he could retain his ability to think, speak, read, and write. He would not want intervention that could not restore him to his full self.

A specific tool now available to you, called POLST (Physician Orders for Life-Sustaining Treatment), enhances your advance directive if you choose to pursue a more precise documentation of your wishes for medical care. The form, which can be completed with your doctor if you are acutely in need, allows you to be very specific about each of the treatments you would want and those you would not. https://www.deathwithdignity.org/polst/

> POLST is an end-of-life planning tool, initiated when your doctor expects you to live a year or less. It contains your instructions for medical treatments for specific health-related emergencies or conditions. The instructions are based on decisions made by you and your healthcare team

placed in your medical chart (sic). POLSTs don't restrict or eliminate treatment (sic); rather they spell out treatment levels you desire. You and your doctor jointly sign the POLST.

POLST is an innovative approach to ascertaining and communicating healthcare wishes, but it isn't meant to replace traditional end-of-life-care communication tools like advance directives or "no code" or DNR (do not resuscitate) statuses. Instead, it augments and supports other communication tools.

Whereas advance directives identify a surrogate decision maker and provide guidelines and values underlying a patient's wishes, POLSTs turn those wishes into medical actions ordered by a physician. The two are complementary in every sense.

When you fill out an advance directive, you are considering myriad future medical interventions. You can and should fill out an advance directive at any time, independent of your current state of health. In contrast, a POLST is intended to be used only if you are seriously ill.

One advantage of advance directives is they can be done without the help of a lawyer or physician and are still able to be used to guide patient care. You can download an advance directive online and fill it out in a matter of hours. The disadvantage is that the paperwork is with you when it should be shared with medical professionals. POLST forms are available at doctors' offices, completed with the help of a physician, and created with the intent of going into your medical chart. They're standardized, easily recognizable, and designed to be transferable throughout different medical facilities.

A copy of the POLST document is available online at:

http://www.polst.org/wp-content/uploads/2013/01/POLST-2011-WA.pdf

Do you want to die at home, with the assistance of family, or in home hospice, or in a hospice facility? The National Hospice and Palliative Care Organization describes hospice care as a team approach to optimize medical care and pain management. Emotional and spiritual support are guided by the patient's requests and needs, and support is provided to family as well. Their central theme is said to be that people have the right to die with dignity and without pain. http://www.nhpco.org/

Cassius, a sixty-two-year-old physician, agreed with the above, but added some ideas such as planning for pets and assuring that there's at least one individual who has advance knowledge of where your critical papers are located.

The following two stories originally appeared on a blog I had about aging and dying:

Lessons Learned from Margie—Living Well

At the moment, Margie is still with the living and is as actively engaged in life as she has been for ninety-plus years. Margie has unapologetically approached life with gusto. Her claims to fame include a great sense of humor with a delightfully high-pitched laugh (somewhat like Julia Child's) peppered through her conversations. She is deeply spiritual yet nonjudgmental. She loves to eat and is often first in line for a buffet. She also takes pictures of particularly tasty meals so she can later reminisce on flavors long past. She was a lifelong learner well before the phrase became popular. Her apartment sports thousands of pounds of books, which she keeps close at hand to reread and as a reference for her active mind as she thinks through numerous threads. Practical and realistic, she chose to partake in far-flung world travels in her "younger" days (including her early eighties), so that as she became infirm she could travel in the U.S.A. where she'd have ready access to medical care should she need it. One of my fondest memories is of Margie revealing to me her active "practice of dying." Laughing as she related her approach, she told me that she would occasionally lie corpse-like, eyes closed, visualizing her final exit from this world.

Margie has always been frugal, true to her Scottish ancestry, but she dresses in outfits put together with flair. She tends toward bright colors and her own brand of creativity, which is delightfully original. She has never been known to follow the mandated societal style of the moment. I need to ask her which outfit she has picked for her final "unveiling," her transition into death. Even as I write this, she and her daughters have come together for a long weekend to reminisce, to be in the moment of expressed love and laughter, and to plan for her future demise. I know she has worked diligently with her daughters so they're fully onboard with her memorial wishes. Margie has given a gift of love to her daughters, extended family, and friends by being in the moment and sharing her awareness of the joy of life and the inevitability of death, planning to make the most of each and every experience.

Margie could last at least another ten-plus years, having had a father who lived to be a hundred. As with any of us, however, this could be her last day, and despite bearing a diagnosis of cancer she's applying her gusto to these moments with her girls. I've asked her to record her conversations of the weekend for anniversary playback to provide fodder for further life-lessons. I feel a sense of urgency to capture as much wisdom as I can from her on how to live and how to prepare for death. I must not allow the mundane details of my life to interfere with my sitting in Margie's presence to listen to her, laugh with her, and learn from her.

Lessons Learned from Fran—Dying Well

I knew Fran for over thirty years. She was a dear woman but somewhat reserved and self-contained. For all those years, into her eighties, I never saw her without full makeup. Her hair was always meticulously styled, and she dressed stylishly even when she wasn't planning to leave the house. Her husband had died years before she began to falter under the weight of several life-threatening illnesses. When she was told that she had little time left, she set about finalizing her plans for dying and death. I volunteered to help, ferrying her to appointments as she set about her formal planning.

Her final actions were:

- She met with her attorney to review her will and other previously prepared documents.
- She interviewed for an in-home hospice-care provider and chose the one she liked best.
- She gave the hospice-care personnel her wishes for her final days when she would likely be unable to communicate them.
- She chose her lovely bed and bedroom as the place where she wished to spend her final days.
- She chose to have both urinary and fecal catheters because she didn't want, as she said, "the indignity of someone cleaning my bottom."
- She wanted adequate pain medications because she could see no sense in, as she said, "undue suffering."

I stayed at Fran's home for the last four days of her life. She received round-the-clock hospice nursing care during that time to administer pain medication and general care of changing and bathing her.

People have asked why I chose to stay with Fran. I did it to honor my friend, and to learn from her. As I had learned much from her in the thirty years before, I knew I would receive many lessons from being in her presence as she died. Fran did not speak, eat, or drink the last four days. In retrospect, because she was mute, I presumed her to be unconscious. I'm pretty sure she was aware of her surroundings at least part of the time. Caregivers admonish us to treat supposed comatose individuals as conscious because they might well be aware; however, it's hard to remember that at the time.

I learned a lot from watching the hospice aides in their care of Fran and from the interaction of friends as they visited her. Overall, I think Fran would have been pleased with her last days. I felt good when I intuited some of what she needed to make her confinement more peaceful, comfortable, and beautiful, but it bothered me in later reflection when I realized that I hadn't been thoughtful of some of her needs.

Transition Planning

Make your plans for your final days as far in advance as possible, even in your twenties. Wills, living wills, advance directives, and medical proxies are best put in place as soon as you can. (Do not list only your significant other as a decision maker if you're unable to voice your wishes. Name several backup individuals. The reason: By the time you might need proxies, your spouse could no longer be able to make informed decisions for you based on his or her own disabilities or demise). This action assures that your wishes are followed. By making the choice to have your affairs in order you take a great burden off your family and friends.

If you don't choose in advance to have palliative care or hospice for your end-of-life care, you will likely end up in a hospital. Without prior directives, you'll likely be put through invasive and painful procedures that will rob you of dignity and peace. In harshly bright intensive care units, you and your family and friends can be robbed of the beauty and lessons of dying. You serve as mentor to your family once more by the example you set.

When in the presence of a comatose or dying patient, speak quietly unless you're told that the person is hard of hearing. Even if you think someone is unable to comprehend, he might actually hear everything that you say, so continue to identify yourself to him and continue to converse with him. You can verbalize your inner monologue, such as what you were thinking to fix for dinner or what errands you might run. Another good way to let the person know you're there and that you care is to read a book to him. This lovely gesture was done by Fran's stepson, who picked a book that he and Fran had enjoyed so that she could know he was present for her.

Explain to the person what you're going to do and why before you carry out any needed task. Example: "In a little while we will come in to change your bed." Then wait a bit and come back to it, reminding the person that you've come in to change the bed or do whatever task is at hand. It seemed helpful to talk through each step of changing or moving Fran just before the step was carried out. Ask the person to help you with the movements if he or she can. Then carry out each step slowly and incrementally so that he or she is neither hurt nor frightened.

Have someone stay in the room with the dying individual if possible. If he awakens or becomes conscious, he may be frightened. It occurred to me that the dying person might not know if he is alive or dead, so being aware that there's someone there who cares about him would be an amazing comfort.

Touching has gotten such a bad name. It can be uninvited, intrusive, and irritating, so most of us don't spontaneously touch anyone anymore. It can, however, also be incredibly comforting, so if it feels right, patting the hand or arm or brushing the person's hair might be appreciated.

Do not sit on the bed. Bouncing the bed and causing quick movements could be frightening or painful. Having a close-by easy chair in which to keep vigil is a good idea.

Arrange the furniture to accommodate the flow of visitors and caregivers. Take out furniture that's in the way. Fran's bed was a queen-size, making it difficult to change her and the bed linens. It might be better to rent a hospital bed or a twin-size regular bed unless the dying person specifically wants his or her own bed.

Fran had always craved order and beauty in both her home and her person. She had laid out lovely, lacy, colorful gowns into which hospice workers changed her each day rather than ugly hospital gowns. I also set about to keep her sickroom as clean and uncluttered as possible. Medical supplies placed haphazardly by hospice workers were moved into nearby drawers and an adjacent room. I placed potted non-scented flowers on the dressers at eye level, so that if Fran opened her eyes she would see lovely colors but not be overwhelmed by intrusive scents. Gardenia is an example of a lovely flower with a scent some people crave but that makes others gag. Fran had always kept part of her beloved artworks at floor level so she could appreciate their beauty while in bed. This propensity served her well as she lay in bed during her final days.

Fran was a skinny little gal. Something I didn't think of at the time was that her bony parts must have been uncomfortable lying on that flat bed. For comfort, egg-crate mattress covers are good for relieving pressure while a person lies in one position for a long time. Hospital supply stores have strap-on cushions such as heel pads for bony prominences. Sheepskin pillows of various sizes (not overstuffed) would be nice for support and cushioning of the body.

While cognizant of his surroundings, the dying person can choose to have more people in the room visiting if he so wishes. Once he is unable to communicate, it would be a good idea to limit visitation to one visitor at a time (plus perhaps an attendant). The tendency is for persons sitting in vigil to begin their own conversations as if the dying person were deaf, uncomprehending, or not even present. In dying, as in living, it's rude to exclude one person from the conversation. I learned this lesson, I'm sorry to say, from an oversight on my part. As two neighbors and I conversed, Fran became agitated and made a sound consistent with significant frustration. In thinking about it later, her message might have been, "Hey, you three, I'm still here! This should be about me. I'm dying—don't discuss essential oils."

Fran's presence was a gift to friends and family. The lessons learned from her insight and conscious death are a gift to all of us. Please share her wisdom and experience with those facing death—which, by the way, is all of us.

Another story was related by interviewee Lynn of her Aunt Bee:

> As she grew older and became physically ill, Aunt Bee bore up under the onslaught well on many levels. As through her life, she continued to model strength of character and courage in the face of adversity. She was sometimes cantankerous and opinionated but never unkind. Her warrior-spirited persona overlay someone who, as the old saying goes, had a heart of gold. She was known to be generous and kind and genuinely interested in the welfare of all she met. She would often dispense bits of life suggestions, including "Ladies, don't ever lose your fire," as she discussed aging beyond child-rearing years. One of many fond memories was of a trip with her toward the end of her life, in which some of the ladies of the family sequestered her for

a surprise adventure. She had always expressed a burning desire to see Boxcar Willie live in concert before she died.

Along with another of my aunts, my mother, and one of my crazy cousins, I put Aunt Bee in the car ostensibly to take her to Texarkana, Arkansas, for a visit. Unbeknownst to her, she had been ensnared for a trip to Branson instead. Each of us in turn kept her distracted as she noted our westward trajectory rather than southwest, but we were ultimately able to surreptitiously and successfully drive her to Branson instead. When we arrived, she was shocked and thrilled with our ruse on her behalf. We told her that we would reveal the agenda one activity at a time. The highlight of our day was visiting a photography shop where we had to choose the theme of our photo session from western, maybe Renaissance—not sure on this one—my memory fails, but we ultimately decided on "saloon girl" outfits. The proprietor was wonderful in not rushing us, and we spent hours picking out our outfits for the final reveal. If you've never done such an activity, you must understand that part of the hilarity is that the costumes so complete and camera-ready on the front of the body are false fronts tied onto to the body so that the posterior "nether parts" are open to the air. Anyone unlucky enough to pass in range could view our respective scantily clad derrieres. We all laughed until we cried as we chose our saloon outfits, then arranged ourselves for the photo with all the accoutrements appropriate to an 1800s saloon—fishnet stockings, feathered boas, and empty whiskey bottles. Aunt Bee was the madam with a "kick-derriere" look and a fake six-shooter. The picture is superfluous to the memory, but did record a lovely day capped by getting Aunt Bee to her front-row seat to listen to Box Car Willie that night. After the show, she flounced across the hotel bed as she announced, "Ladies, if I die tomorrow, I shall die happy."

Not many months later she did.

Planning Your Last Party

Long before it's necessary and while there's little emotional overlay, plan your sixth rite of passage, i.e., your funeral celebration. When you depart, you will thereby go out of this world on your own terms. Interviewee Lynn recently observed a gala held in honor of one woman's passage. She observed, "There were hundreds of people there, all having a great time. I had thought that the celebration was a wedding." It might be fun to plan your grand finale. I have designed the nuts and bolts of my sixth and final rite of passage, but I'm still formulating the fun stuff. [*Hmm—what about admission to the shindig only if my peeps are in costume?*]

I am ready for my final rite of passage having lived my life to the fullest. If my airplane should crash, I will be yelling, "Yee Haw!" on the way down because I have no regrets. My family and friends will know how much I loved them because I tell them often. I won't be afraid at the end. My loved ones will know that any bit of suffering I might have will be met with courage and peace.

Chapter 13

Rewriting Your Text

If you've decided that your life story might need a bit of editing or a complete rewrite, read on. Even if you're satisfied with the story thus far, these ideas might help you optimize your life trajectory. You say, "Dang it, you ask too much! I'm not an author. I can't write." But indeed you have written and are writing the book of your life, whether you're actively participating in its construction or passively absorbing it from the needs or expectations of your culture, your family of origin, your spouse, children, friends, business associates, or others. Whether you are sixteen or ninety-six, if you don't write the story of your life for yourself, this cast of characters will write it for you. Much of who you are and what you do has been incorporated from this beloved (and sometimes not so beloved) company with whom your life intermingles. Further, much of their "writing" was done without your awareness. If you don't become cognizant of their script for you, or if you choose not to edit it, then their storyline becomes yours.

Our personal story can be likened to that of Opus in the children's book *Goodnight Opus* by Berkeley Breathed:

A book was read to Opus, a young penguin, each night before bedtime. Unfortunately, the text of the story was frightening to him. The book described an unfriendly monster that lived under his bed, which made Opus fear going to sleep. This same menacing monster story was read to him each day for quite some time. One night clever Opus decided to rewrite the text of the book. In the new version, Opus changed the text to reflect the events he preferred. The scary monster was turned into a nice, large, friendly, furry individual whom Opus no longer feared. Opus changed the original author's text to become the new author of the story, changing its content and context as he wished.

You, like Opus, can rewrite the text of your story.

No matter what narrative was foisted upon you, and no matter how much of the story has already been played out, you can accept or change the current path of your story. You can write the rest of it. You can even change the beginning of your story by changing your perception of it. One thing is for sure: In the story of your life, what you do not aim for, you will never attain.

An Action Plan for Your Life

The action-plan algorithm introduced in chapter 5 can be adapted to general evaluations of various issues you might wish to examine.

1. Identify the issue to be considered.

    a. Sit down in a lovely setting with pen and paper for twenty minutes. This time might be one of the most valuable twenty-minute periods of your life. Electronic devices are not recommended here because they might distract you.

    b. In three minutes, jot down what you've liked about your life thus far: Persons, events, and/or circumstances. These may have been obviously "good" in the past and clearly still good as we look back on them now, but perhaps one or more of the listed items was not felt to be good at the time. Have you ever had an initially untoward experience become a pivotal piece of the puzzle of your life, ultimately leading to a subsequent good? Even if you feel that your life has sucked thus far, there are, no doubt, some life events that you characterize as good. If you can't think of big things such as a warm house, enough food, or loving parent(s), then think of the small things such as an ice-cream cone someone once gave you, a random person who trusted you even though she or he had no cause to, or a favorite TV show.

c. Then spend seven minutes listing the things you want to possess or achieve during your life. Put down everything that resonates with you. Don't list any obstacles—only interests, dreams, and goals. Examples are a desire to own a Ferrari or have a career as a guitarist, singer, or comedian. Others might be a wish to become a lawyer, electrician, mechanic, forest ranger, herbalist, or farmer. Other goals could be to travel to Africa or Europe or to have a spouse and perhaps children.

2. Assess the risk: Spend three minutes now listing obstacles. Don't get bummed. It's the human condition to have to overcome things, people, circumstances, or your self-generated limitations. You're just like all the rest of us humans, even the ones who you think have it all. We all have burdens to bear.

3. Arrive at an action plan: Consider alternative actions; make up your own or gather ideas to help you make your decisions.

   a. Now you have six minutes to come up with solutions to the obstacles. Remember, per interviewee Leigh, to "argue for the solution." If you argue against the possibility of a solution, you have no alternative but to remain stuck and unfulfilled in your life.

b. Finally, take one minute to quickly jot down an age by which you would like to accomplish each of the things you want to own or achieve as listed above.

4. Carry out the action plan.

a. Now, or later today, read back what you just wrote. Read your answers once a day for the next twenty-one days, which is supposedly how long it takes to form a "good" habit. If you form a habit of thinking about your life trajectory, it will make it a lot easier for you to "hit the mark." [*Isn't it a bit of a cosmic joke on us humans that we can form a bad habit in about ten minutes, yet it takes twenty-one days to form a good one? The reason I keep asking you not to blow through this book without answering the questions is because I have a really bad habit of doing just that. Okay, so I'm projecting a bit, maybe you can model good habits for me ☺.*]

5. Adjust the plan as needed based on changing circumstances.

An exercise such as the above, in which you view the longitudinal perspective of your life, can be enlightening. Through tools like this simple, quick assessment or by playing your own "What If?" game, you can discover much about yourself. You might notice that such things as seeing your funny, friendly, or curmudgeonly barista at the coffee shop each day is in fact an unrecognized high point. As you analyze what you like or dislike and what you wish to accomplish, you can begin to lay the groundwork for the structure of your life. Self-focused exercises can result in more clarity of purpose, enhance appreciation of things previously taken for granted, and help you chart a clearer path for your future experiences.

The following ideas for your personal party preparation come either directly from your party planner, *moi*, or they might come from the interviewees, as noted. The reflections, words of wisdom, and cool ideas from these folks are either directly quoted or paraphrased. You might find some of the ideas similar to those on your own list. Other ideas might be inspirational enough that you wish to adopt them as is, or you might find that your creativity is sparked to spin off to totally different concepts.

Before you start reading, however, you might want to turn on your favorite music and dance around the house a bit. Maybe pop the cork on some champagne or sparkling cider. If you wish to vie for the title of world's best party animal, try the following: Become the most interesting 16 to 96+ year-old in the world. Challenge your assumptions. Travel, write a book, volunteer for Habitat for Humanity or for international disaster efforts. Become a FEMA community volunteer, or engage in other worthy activities. Be so interesting that people seek you out. You can go big or go small.

M.T. told the story of a man she called The Hummingbird Man: "A former mathematician whom I knew retired. He lived in the middle of nowhere, and started feeding hummingbirds. He became so enamored of them that he began to study them. It gave him a reason to get up in the morning. Ultimately, The Hummingbird Man became such an expert that he gave lectures at state parks. People began to trace him to his secluded home. They valued his knowledge and his commitment to these amazingly resilient little birds, and in being with him they valued the man himself. Even into his nineties, when he could no longer travel, people came to him."

Remember: If you're not interesting to you, then no one else will be interested in you either. Get going. No excuses. No fear.

V.M., age thirty, bemoaned, "I wish I had gone skydiving when I was younger, before I had children. Now I can't skydive until I get them through college." She went on to suggest, "Do something that you fear at least once a week" (even if it's something as simple as going to the movies alone). "If you're already older, throw fear to the wind. What do you have to lose? It would be incredibly liberating to do scary things. You are going to die at some point anyway; why not do the exciting things, take the chances?"

It's a great thing to be able to party alone, but sometimes having other party-worthy individuals makes it a lot more fun. If you're a newbie to partying, or if you have only a couple of friends, start small with one or two; however, you'll be partying so much for the long term that you'll need some backups in case your core buddy is unavailable. If you haven't already developed a cadre of friends, here are some thoughts about attracting more.

V.M. suggested that people should have such deep friendships that the friend becomes a "shovel buddy," a term V.M. coined to describe her friends who would care enough about her and trust her to such an extent that they'd help her "bury" any of her problems with no explanation needed or judgment given.

Develop deep and abiding friendships that you nurture and grow. Take them forward in your life, especially before you become rich and famous. The motives of other friends you acquire later might be less that noble. Such individuals could be just hangers-on.

M.T., at age sixty-two: "I have two major friend groups: College and bridge. My college friends recently gathered at the college we graduated from forty years ago. We spent a marvelous weekend reliving the old times and creating new memories. My bridge group of eight women started getting together over thirty years ago. We've changed through the years. We had small children and careers. Now we have adult children, some of us have grandchildren, some of us are retired. The financial circumstances of some have changed. A few were very well off and some struggled financially, but for a few the circumstances have reversed. Originally, we met once a month in someone's home. It was really labor-intensive. In later years, we began to meet at restaurants when hosting became more trouble than we'd originally hoped. For a while there was some fighting between two members of the group. We unofficially disbanded. I treasured these women, so after a few years I thought *Move on!* and I reached out to everyone. The group was too important to lose."

If you just can't get out of the house, call old friends who are shut-ins to cheer their day, or call relatives to check on them. Give them reasons to look forward to your calls. Finally, make your conversation about your caller, not just about generalities (like the weather), but addressing the specific interests, joys, and sorrows of their lives. In other words, let them know that their lives are important to you. Ask questions about them. Lend a compassionate ear to their troubles. If they don't answer the phone, leave sweet messages for them just to brighten their day. If they do call you, be excited and use a voice tone that matches your words—sound happy and excited. Don't use the whiny "Eeyore voice" of the cartoon character from Winnie-the-Pooh when he laments, "Thanks for noticing." Make it such a pleasant, guilt-free call that they will want to call you back (see Resources – Topics of Interest – How to Avoid Eeyore Conversations).

What is the venue for your party?

The Party is wherever You are.

Local and regional venues can be tons of fun. There are usually amazing places to see and much to do within two to four hours of your home. Most people never explore what's right around them. The important goal is to pay attention. It sounds odd, but check in with yourself. Are you actually having fun? Sometimes we spend so much time fretting about our real or imagined troubles that the stress hormones override the light and joyful feeling of having fun. We lose interest in having fun and even the ability to recognize fun. Hmm. I wonder if your brain's capacity to have fun get's pruned if it's not used? Spontaneous and multiple fun events in childhood inevitably give way to work and other adult responsibilities. Adults must plan for fun activities or they are highly unlikely to occur. By having fun, you may just plump up the brain lobe responsible for cavorting about which surely must be helpful in retaining overall brain health.

Make your own space beautiful. Paint is inexpensive and can be applied by do-it-your-selfers. A coat of paint will add beautiful color to your indoor or outdoor space. Or if you're a minimalist, white makes any space look cleaner. One interior designer paints his front door a different color at least once a year.

Make your home, balcony, or yard a lovely functional habitat.

Interviewee T.M., age sixty, personally did most of the work on creating a habitat in the front and back yards of her aging parents. She took out the grass because it required watering and mowing. Her father, age eighty-five, had always had a garden as she was growing up. She hired some folks to bring in organic topsoil, compost, and mulch, and to help her with the heavy lifting to create a 20×40-foot raised garden space in which her father planted tomatoes, onions, okra, and cucumbers. It gave her father a project to keep him tied to his past as his cognitive abilities declined. T.M. planted fruit trees, berry bushes, flowers, and herbs for her mother. All the plants were appropriate to the growth zone, so little watering or maintenance was required. She laughed when she said, "It fulfills my Gaia-ist tendencies."

Every home, balcony, patio, or yard can become a habitat. You're limited only by your imagination. Even if your neighborhood association won't allow vegetables in your front yard, you can plant edible and medicinal herbs, replace shrubs with blueberry bushes, and add fruit trees. Vegetable gardens in the backyard are good to supplement your food budget, and gardening is a terrific skill to pass on to your children (explore permaculture, biochar, and other such topics). Tiny yards, balconies, and sunny in-home locations are good for container gardening. A.B. enjoys her composting worm farm which she keeps on the balcony of her New York City apartment. You could train to become a Master Gardener, which serves you well in several ways.

1. The study keeps your mind active.
2. You will meet like-minded motivated people who might become friends, another source of fun. Making new friends has the upside of making you live longer and again provides stimulation to stave off dementia.
3. These activities of beautification including tree, shrub, and flower planting can be done to honor the planet and as part of a continuous Earth Day celebration.

If you don't move, you hurt more. If you hurt more, you sleep less. If you sleep less, you hurt more and you move less—talk about a vicious cycle. You'll also want to look and feel your best as you party, and you especially need to be in good shape for walking if you head to an international destination. Don't relegate exercise just to the gym or a scheduled walk or bike ride. Focus on CPI—Continuing Performance Improvement—that is, constant exercise with intention. As you go about your chores realize that you are doing exercise—the intention evidently improves the exercise benefits of even routine movement.

No matter what your limitations, you can still get some form of exercise by being creative. Chair yoga was developed for people in wheelchairs. Be creative: bed yoga, chair yoga, car yoga, toilet yoga, garden yoga, laundry yoga, or yoga dance—whatever is available to you. Channel your "Inner Ellen"—break into dance. Offer no apologies. If a store puts on music, expect to have dancers. Don't look around to see if someone is watching. Do it for you, not for show. By the way, two items on my bucket list are to dance with

Ellen and to talk to Oprah. I don't need the stage—ha, ha, ha . . . who am I kidding? I would love to be on the stage to dance, but the conversations would be best over a cup of coffee with a gluten-free organic donut. I want to thank Ellen for the laughter and dance moves and to reflect with Oprah on her amazing life, her generosity, and her gratitude toward her viewers. She recently developed a free program to encourage meditation. Who knows, maybe our fellow humans like Ellen and Oprah have been partly responsible for getting us to resonate above 200 on Hawkins's scale. Like the members of Whoville, in Dr. Seuss's book *Horton Hears a Who,* if we all independently work on resonating at a higher level, who knows how high we can go?

If possible, get out of your home every day, even if only for five minutes or to stand three feet from your door. Hopefully there'll be sunshine, which is good for vitamin D levels. Get your vitamin D levels tested. By living indoors and covering themselves for protection from the bad effects of overexposure to the sun, many folks are now vitamin D deficient, which can play a role in multiple illnesses.

Schedule haircuts, physician appointments, or a coffee date with a friend in the mornings so that you have a reason to get up, get dressed, and get out of the house. If you just can't get out, open the drapes. One excellent, non-pharmaceutical and relatively inexpensive means to improve mood is to use a 10,000-lux full-spectrum light to simulate the sun's light. This sunshine therapy is used for depressed pregnant women who chose not to take anti-depressant medications. Talk to your doctor about this possibility, and follow your doctor's directions if you purchase one.

What sort of entertainment is available for the party?

The answer depends on where you and your party are located at any one time. If you're partying at home, pick your television programming wisely. Does it make you think? Does it empower you? Does it make you laugh? Combing the Internet for interesting subjects can be fun and educational. Consider interactive board games with your family (they might be a bit antiquated but are still a means to bond through quality face-to-face interaction and fun). And finally, don't forget the value and joy of reading for yourself and reading aloud to family. Read not only to your children but also to your spouse or significant other. Rather than being siloed with separate books, read to each other, share the book, and engage each other in discussion. My husband and I have read several books together including Jonas Jonasson's The Hundred-Year-Old Man Who Climbed Out the Window and Disappeared. The book is absolutely hysterical (at least we think so).

Maintaining that party glow can get difficult if the caterer doesn't show up or your band cancels. So how can you stay in the party mood? You might consider doing at least four categories of good deeds per day. My categories are to do at least one good deed for a random person, a friend or co-worker, a member of my family, and for the planet each day. J.G., seventy-six, opened a door at the library for me one day. I thanked him with a beaming smile, which he beamed back, as he said "Oh, but thank you. By letting me open the door for you, I was able to do the seventh of my ten good deeds today. That's my daily goal. I never miss it."

Your party planner won't always be with you; how do you plan to make every day a celebration?

Reflect on your life to determine what makes you the happiest. Whether it's work or recreation, whatever makes you want to get out of bed or out of a chair, do it. If it's worthy of your thought, it's worthy of your time and effort. Anything you really love to do, try to do for at least thirty minutes a day, whether it's listening to music, performing music, gardening, caring for animals or people in shelters, writing, repairing small engines, fishing, or walking your dog. If you love what you're doing, you deserve to let yourself have at least a little of the reward you'll feel.

Cherish the good times, persevere through and learn from the bad times, and look forward to it all. Prophecy of doom is a cruel joke perpetrated on us. Could it be a cosmic joke that prophecy truly is self-fulfilling? Remember Oedipus: Had he rejected prophecy he wouldn't have fulfilled the foul prediction of the prophecy that he would dishonor and harm his parents. He believed the prediction, left his home, and lost years of parental love. When he returned home years later, he did in fact harm his parents because he didn't recognize them. Had he refused to fear the prediction and remained at home with his beloved parents he wouldn't have fulfilled the prophecy.

Sensory Actualization

As we pass through In Utero II, we experience this world through our senses. How should we seek to maximize the experience? As a nod to Abraham Maslow, whom we discussed in chapter 7, I propose a process of "sensory actualization" modeled after Maslow's seventh level of human need, "self-actualization." According to *Simply Psychology,* self-actualization refers to the necessity for personal growth and discovery present in people throughout their lives. Maslow's theory of human needs is depicted as a pyramid, with fundamental requirements of food, shelter, and clothing at the base and the most advanced at the pinnacle. The seventh level, self-actualization, proposed by Maslow is characterized by the need for meaningful accomplishment during our lives (www.simplypsychology.org/maslow.html).

In a similar light, consider the senses. Can we achieve "sensory actualization" by desiring to accomplish the highest level of sensory input we can? The term "sensuous" means "of the five senses," i.e., what we can feel, taste, smell, see, or hear. Eating delicious food and relaxing in a warm bath are sensuous activities. (Something intellectually satisfying, like doing a crossword puzzle, is not sensuous, even if you really like it. I'm also not talking about the term "sensual," which has a totally different meaning.) The best use of the word "sensuous" is to describe the stuff that makes your senses happy.

Scent: Notice the scents around you. You can determine your favorites. That's the basis of aromatherapy. Try using essential oils like peppermint, which can brighten your mood, or lavender, which is mellowing.

Touch: Humans require touch. Why would adults, we tall children, have any less need? A friend of an eighty-four-year-old widower, Warner, said he'd approached her with a *Reader's Digest* article which suggested that the average human needs twelve hugs daily. The friend became tearful as she shared that she and her family began to be diligent about embracing Warner, but wished they had hugged him even more before he died. Therapeutic touch, Reiki, massage, and hugs, given with permission, of course, can be soothing (Resources – Topics of Interest – Reiki). Whole body or if you're busy a foot massage for your children before bed is a loving way to say goodnight. Start when they are babies and continue as long as they will allow. One interviewee said, "My teenagers might get irritated with me, but even they would usually allow and secretly welcome the touch of a massage. We can talk of the events of the day or just be comfortable together in silence."

Hearing: Hearing is a disproportionately important sense. Music is a gift to the essence of who we are. Hearing is evidently perceived in multiple places within the brain. Processing and recall of music can therefore be accessed through multiple sites in both halves of the brain. I think of it like dropping multiple lines of "breadcrumbs" to follow back to the source at some later time. If one line of crumbs is subsequently lost, other pathways can easily be followed back to the source memory. Due to this diversity in perception, an amazing treatment for Alzheimer's disease has emerged. Some patients with severe Alzheimer's have been found to respond significantly to the music of their youth. The memories of who they are as people can in some individuals be reconnected to reclaim their sense of self.

> This stirring documentary . . . demonstrate[s] music's ability to combat memory loss and restore a deep sense of self to those suffering from [memory loss].

(Resources – Scientific, Philosophical or Psychological Concepts – Alzheimer's – Alive Inside)

Cherish and protect your hearing. Seek periodic hearing checks, and if hearing loss is suspected seek evaluations with physicians trained in preservation of hearing and treatment of hearing loss. Remember the pruning of unused brain pathways. Evidently the acoustic nerve and brain receptors can lose the ability to perceive sound if hearing loss remains untreated for any length of time. If you have any hearing loss, seek treatment immediately. People desperate to hear sometimes fall prey to sales of expensive hearing aids, which cannot help due to nerve degeneration, so always start with medical specialists first to see if the hearing loss is neurologic and thus not helped by even the most expensive hearing aid.

Hearing loss is a profound disability for those who were born with the ability to hear. Those born deaf can become fluent in their lovely language of signing. Those who acquire deafness late in life are likely never to learn sign language and can become isolated and bereft as they lose the ability to interact with friends and family. Animated conversations are often conducted over and around the deaf person as if that individual were not in the room.

If you are in the presence of a hearing-impaired individual, make eye contact, slow down your speech, and pitch your voice higher (speak with more resonance, bringing your voice from deeper in your throat). Watch the hearing-impaired person's eyes. You can usually tell when they "check out" due to inability to hear and understand. As T.M. said of her elderly grandmother who was deaf, "as much as people fear losing their sight, hearing loss is far worse. Loss of sight is tragic, but loss of hearing isolates you from communication with humanity."

Taste: Tastes can be savored by eating more slowly, trying new spices, and seeking new textures and flavors.

Sight: The sensual benefit of sight can be maximized by gazing on flowers or other objects of beauty. Regarding those who can't see certain colors, I wonder if their color spectrum is just as gratifying? Maybe those of us who see color never perceive the contrast, depth, and texture masked by our "normal" color spectrum.

Mixed Sensory Input

Ayurveda: Ayurveda is a component of yoga practice. The emphasis is upon working to maintain health through recognition of an individual's personal characteristics. Ayurveda was developed thousands of years ago as a healing system and is still relevant to modern medicine. To further study how Ayurveda is viewed by Western medicine, see www.webmd.com/balance/guide/ayurvedic-treatments.

Author's Note: When I had an Ayurveda evaluation, of the three doshas (Pitta, Kapha, and Vata), which are roughly the physical, emotional, and energy aspects from which we draw, I learned that I am primarily Vata. Vata's tend to be "in their heads". These doshas have some relationship to the five elements of earth, wind, fire, water, and ether. Vatas are more influenced by wind and ether and are well served to carry out activities which are grounding—literally! It seems that there are also corresponding dosha times of day. The most problematic for me is the Vata hours which occur in the wee hours of the morning, making sleep difficult for Vata's. I was encouraged to rub my feet with oil at night to ground me for peaceful sleep. I went one better and named all my toes, e.g. my left great toe is Toe Main and my right is Toe-tal to hopefully keep me in a more earth-anchored perspective.

Movement: Cognitive, physical, and sensory input culminates in movement. Dance, sports, and recreational activities are energizing and help stave off emotional distress. I suggest dance for all occasions: gratitude dance, a victory dance, a good-report-from-the-doctor dance.

Laughter: Laughter, especially the sound of infectious, unrestrained baby laughter, is a boon to the spirit for babies and those who hear their joyful sounds. There is a yoga practice that involves laughter, and many Internet sites provide information on the importance of laughter for health. Some feel that laughter can help heal the body. What if you were to target laughing as a daily vitamin? I wonder at what level you would resonate?

Your party is limited only by your imagination. I hope these ideas spark your creativity. Share your ideas with friends and family or even random strangers. Send the ideas to me so that we can add a book to the Encyclopedia of Humanity called Human Humor. Maybe MN26X could even give us a hand from his copy of the Martian Manual of Mirth.

After you've read back through your thoughts from your rewrite and have instituted even a few of the Rewriting Your Text party suggestions, you can look to appendix 6 for an informal template from which to fashion your own.

[*You are, according to this humble party planner, ready for your grand gala! On second thought, who am I kidding? Using "humble" in the same sentence as "party planner" is an oxymoron.*]

Congratulations, party animal: you've arrived!
Let's get going with the party games!
Anyone for pin the antenna on the Martian?!

Chapter 14

Let's Throw a Block Party!

As you recall, a karass is a group of people who share a thought or are carrying out a similar action, but are unaware that there are others, sometimes many others, who are thinking or acting similarly. If you get excited by the ideas that describe how to get your party started, you might unknowingly be a part of a karass of people linked through shared intent to change the way each of us perceives his or her own life cycle. Do you in addition wish to help realign our societal perceptions of youth, middle age, and elder years to get the party started for everyone? It's still all about you even if you wish the best for everyone else as well. Solutions resulting in the good of the many start with your personal happiness.

For those who've suffered more and received less, consider that you might be the very individuals best able to serve as role models and mentors for humanity. By living an unhappy, unexamined, or constricted life, you cheat yourself as well as your friends and family. If some of the previously mentioned authors are right, your personal unhappiness affects everyone. By honoring the treacherous journey you've thus far navigated, can your life struggles be considered not as negative endpoints but rather as the starting line of the good you can give to yourself and humanity?

What if by helping others we help ourselves even more? Helping others may require minimal effort. No matter your financial, behavioral, or relational circumstances, you can reach out in some way to help others. You can help someone open a door as he struggles with packages and will have just done one of your good deeds for the day. An unconditional good deed is not dependent on any return currency of being acknowledged or thanked. In other words don't get ticked at the driver you let into traffic if he or she does not wave in thanks. The one you helped or others who observe your gracious action might then be inspired to similar acts of unconditional kindness.

You mentor others by the full life you live. You don't need anyone to align himself with you if what you espouse is your examined truth. By living your truth you might, along with enough of the karass, cause a Tipping Point, which Malcolm Gladwell discusses in his book of that name. Per Gladwell, a few like-intentioned people, once they reach a relatively small percentage of an overall population, can ultimately tip the scale of thought in a new direction.

Whereas the rewrite chapters contained ideas specifically intended to spark your imagination for your personal journey, this chapter is devoted to "you-can-make-a-diffeence" ideas. I'll share some questions, personal suggestions, and business ideas that might just go over big.

What are some of the many things that a karass of people, who wish the world to be a better place for all, might set out to accomplish? Our karass just might stir each of us to undertake an introspective examination of our lives. Darn—that just gave me another thought: What if this idea of celebrating all of life's component parts starts a "movement?" We need a term for the endeavor, like the "Awesome Life Cycle Movement." Wow, that's way too clunky. So, go for it team; come up with a refreshingly vibrant title. Remember that this is a dialogue, so you have some obligation to make this undertaking work. What could this movement look like for each of the respective age groups? Hmm. Since part of the problem is that age groups are isolated (in silos, so to speak), the movement would likely be best served if all of the sage-groups were represented. Interested young, middle-saged, or elders could formally start think-tank groups to address some of the concerns, challenges, and opportunities in each sage group or across sage groups. Informal think-tank groups could gather for frivolity through pretty much any venue, for example pot-luck meals, board games, book clubs, gaia earth celebrations, worm appreciation groups, and knitting or quilting clubs at which the topics introduced in this book could be discussed and expanded upon. Formal clubs, churches,* government agencies, and charitable organizations could take a portion or the whole of the innovations of these think tanks to get their party started.

*Oh, my religious buddies, please don't brand me as a heretic. What about "secular" churches, not to displace well-established terrific houses of worship but to address the need for a "church" for folks whose lives are not religious? Maybe these secular churches could be termed multi-generational singing, sharing (conjoining of disparate ideas), volunteering (celebrating differences)" community centers that mirror a portion of what religious churches offer.

Formalized groups who wish to help humanity with charitable monetary contributions or volunteerism could be formed. For example, such groups could sponsor, in a crowd-sourcing manner, the overwhelming student debt that clouds the lives of so many folks. Another idea would be to underwrite a year's overhead for an artist, musician, writer, or craftsman to ply his or her trade unfettered by everyday expenses. I propose that such groups could be called Rennaissance Mentors in a nod to the benefactors who underwrote artists like Michelangelo. What do you think?

In addition, elders could form a group known as a Guild of Elders to discuss ideas for improving cross-generational ties. They could sponsor or give grants to younger, not-as-financially-viable people who would like to participate in improving communication. Under another heading, "Egalitarian Contemplators," elders could sponsor seminars of cross-generational participants to tackle any issue, thorny or otherwise, to assess the issue, propose solutions, and volunteer to help accomplish potential actions.

Children's books could be written aimed at the positive aspects of reaching each of the pivotal ages throughout life. These books could begin to build significant positive links with elders, and could load children's little computer-bank brains with pre-information about growing up, aging, and dying so that when death occurs, whether family, friends, or pets, the passage is viewed from a more naturalistic perspective. Children's books regarding celebrations of the earth with positive everyday rituals rather than one Earth Day per year could reconnect us with the beauty and majesty of our planet and our responsibility to protect Earth (please check out the book entitled *Last Child in the Woods*).

Books about pubertal rites of passage written for children could give form to their eventual life paths. Children could look forward to the accomplishment of reaching each birthday for another privilege earned. For example, at sage eight, a child could earn sleepovers or dance lessons. At sage eight the child would also earn additional responsibility. This year the child could assume the responsibility to plan from scratch one family weekend outing and could accept the responsibility for gathering the daily recyclables and placing them in the appropriate container.

One interviewee noted that she had gifted "treasure chests" to her children, into which she placed items the child was aware of and to which he or she did not have access until a stipulated sage. When her children had children, she again gifted treasure chests, which she prepopulated with books in which she wrote a message such as "Here is a copy of *The Call of the Wild,* which my dad (your great grandpa) read to me when I was eight years old. Congratulations on attaining your eighth birthday. Love you, Your grandmother." Be sure to date the messages. Later, these dates greatly enhance the meaning of the message. She added "The same is true for my own purchases; I record locations purchased, dates of purchase, and from or to whom books, works of art, and furniture were gifted (typically on the back of the item in my own handwriting). Years later this has proven to be great fun as these 'messages' are rediscovered."

Rites of passage allow children to be children, at times delaying certain events until the child has earned the privilege at an appropriate sage. An example: choosing not to pierce your child's ears, but allowing him or her at puberty to make the decision of whether to undergo piercing. If your child voiced that she'd likely want piercings, earrings could be added to the treasure chest starting in her eighth year, but not become available until her twelfth birthday when she could make the final decision as to whether to pierce. Children could help plan for their pubertal rites of passage. The very young would have the opportunity to strive; that is, to study and perform designated acts whose culmination could herald both increased privileges and increased responsibility for charting a life they ultimately consider well lived.

The following is an example of a pubertal rite of passage for one young man of the Jewish faith. The boy, who worked weekly for a year to learn the tasks pertaining to the bar mitzvah, delivered his address to the members of the synagogue. He thanked his parents for having raised him. The rabbi stated that the boy had become a man and as such was responsible for his own life. As a spectator this freaked me out; I thought no, he's too young to pronounce him a man. The rabbi went on to explain that the young man was indeed responsible for his subsequent actions in that he could choose to follow his parents' directives or elect to openly defy or sneak around to disobey. The rabbi reminded the young man that he alone would bear the burden of any poor choices he made, whether of drugs, excess alcohol, or irresponsible behaviors, and that the parents could not be blamed for his future actions. The autonomy earned by achievement of the landmark age was accompanied by increased privileges, but tempered with the caveat that such autonomy also created more inherent responsibility.

For those lacking a specific cultural or religious rite of passage, a personal one could be formulated. Resources include organizations (such as the Boy Scouts) and websites that can help you or your child create milestones appropriate for any age. If you're already a teen and did not experience a formal recognition of your entry into adulthood, there's nothing stopping you from formulating your own event, which could be private or shared with significant people in your life. [*By the way, if you're a teen reading this, I'd welcome the privilege of interacting with you about this concept of self-generated pubertal rites of passage. We could coauthor a book; that is, you write it, and I'll appear as a guest author, mentor, or pearl-of-wisdom resource.*]

As one of the karass of celebrants, you might consider architectural interventions that could maximize the benefits of all phases of the life cycle. For elders, what about a pod-type living arrangement with private quarters but a central common room? Those elders who are single could form men-only, women-only, or coed groups. They could use their private spaces or join with others in the common room. The individuals could collaboratively buy the domicile, rent from one or more of the tenant owners, or rent from a businessperson who invests in building such a shared structure. Monthly dues could split all expenses for utilities, housekeeping, caregivers, cooks, gardeners, and home health purveyors. Collective buying of groceries, utilities, and hiring staff (cross-generational-aged cooks, gardeners, masseuses, nurses, and housekeepers, among others) could be shared to extend fixed incomes.

A similar model could be adapted for cross-generational pod living so that the small "f" family could be created. A specific plan could be to have tenants from each of the decades so that twenty-somethings would have the stability and advice of forty to one hundred-somethings, and the older age group would be exposed to and naturally emulate the enthusiasm and activity of the younger decades. This style of pod living would have many cross-generational benefits, but one of the most important would be to allow children to experience individuals of all ages, including elders. The crossover benefit would allow adults of advanced years to serve as surrogate grandparents for the children whose "F" grandparents live far away or who are no longer alive. Such an arrangement would also provide older tenants access to grandchildren equivalents should they either have none of their own or if their biological grandchildren live far from them.

Another model of life-cycle karass living arrangements is to construct a tiny-home village with the homes arranged around a central green space. The campground model could be applied so those with wanderlust could meander around the country, traveling from camp to camp. A note to recreational vehicle manufactures: I have a great idea. You've already made RV interiors amazingly compact and organized; now just adapt the outside to look less like a bus but more like a woodland cottage or meditation retreat (Zen-mobile). Such a vehicle could be customized as prospective buyers come in with cool ideas for the exteriors of their tiny houses. In a nod to Gaiists, add solar panels, small windmills, and rainwater cisterns. Work with brilliant folks to develop electric engines and, in the interim, consider natural gas. Back to campgrounds, you could offer dump stations that effectively compost "humanure." This concept is included in a book earlier referenced called *The Scoop on Poop: Safely Capturing and Recycling the Nutrients in Greywater, Humanure, and Urine.* A communal building in the middle of a green space, about which utility hookups are spaced, could provide an opportunity for group interaction. (Note: It's likely that innovative architectural resources have already put some of these ideas into motion. Maybe you could mine the Internet to find them.)

The above-described imaginative ideas are just a few of the many that could build cross-generational bridges, but as the interviews demonstrated, there are as many good ideas as there are people to conceive them. The next step is to bring this creativity to fruition in action steps. Those most acutely aware of the need for a new paradigm for sage-ing are those of us who are moving into the later years of our lives. We will model how future generations perceive aging, dying, and death. We have a unique opportunity to reject what's been fashioned for us not by design but by default. We can reject the direction of our life path if not of our choosing and thereby improve our lives and all other future lives in the process.

This is what the baby boomers (those born between 1946 and 1964) have been doing since the 1960s. This generation did not opt to maintain the status quo. Boomers petitioned for more environmental protection after years of chemical pollution. Boomers rejected sterile hospital births and sought out more natural birth and Eastern preventive medicine approaches. Boomer women rejected the decades-long use of hormone therapy at and after menopause. How about we "boomer ladies" take on our responsibilities as elders of our human tribe? The term "crone" used to designate great respect for matriarchs in a culture. The word is now used as a term of pejorative marginalization. Let's pick a new term or even an old one (some women's organizations are currently using the term "crone" hoping to revive its historical relevance). How about matriarch? We can share our legitimate power for the benefit of our children and all future children. Here's an interesting thread of inquiry for social scientists: Compare the personalities of flappers, beatniks, and hippies of days gone by to our current crop of "The Greatest Generation, boomers, Y2Kers, and Millennials." Is it just me, or does it seem like we keep reinventing the same wheel? Are these fluctuations in mental attitude generationally random, or is there a repeating pattern every three to four generations?

When I discussed the mindset and activism of boomers with one member of that generation, he said boomers were the children of the Age of Aquarius and therefore had a more cosmic consciousness. He bemoaned, however, that their time is now over and that boomers lack the need or ability to embrace their lifelong activism. I disagree. Baby boomers have the critical opportunity to continue to impact the world. What if they joined with "The Greatest Generation," Millennials, Generation X, and successors to rewrite our conjoined texts? Who knows . . . those representatives of all age groups who are standing on the planet right now have the opportunity to leave a gift for all time. Perhaps the Age of Aquarius can be attained by reintegrating all portions of the human life cycle, which might be our greatest legacy and the launchpad for future generations.

Chapter 15

Exit Stage Left

"Exit stage left!" delivered with a verbal flourish was the catchphrase of an animated lion named Snagglepuss. Quite histrionic and a bit of a ne'er-do-well, Snagglepuss treated his life as if he were on a theater stage. With vocal delivery akin to Shakespearean-trained actors, he would gaze directly at the camera, his perceived audience, to explain with exalted oratory the particulars of some predicament. It seems this lovable cartoon character was always getting into some sort of self-inflicted entanglement. When the ramifications of his actions were about to make his life too difficult, Snagglepuss would bemoan his situation to the audience, at the end of which he would strike a pose, raise one leg, and with arms akimbo utter his trilling cry, "Exit stage left!" (on occasion, stage right, up, or down), then disappear off-screen in a whirling pattern. In this manner, he successfully extricated himself unscathed from his deserved consequences.

As I exit "stage left," I thank you, dear reader, for being the inspiration for my writing journey. Once I no longer feared dying and death, it seemed a service to share the questions that helped me reach my personal truth. On the other hand, I've avoided sharing my answers for the questions raised. My personal answers aren't important in the grand scheme of things, since they constitute my truth, i.e., my opinion without the possibility of substantiation. This book was in the making during a lifetime of experiences, both good and bad, with the aid of thousands of people met along the way.

I have grown up, am aging, have come close to dying, have "worried" about my memory, and am a recovering naysayer. I've made most of the mistakes, oversights, and untoward decisions discussed in this book. When experiences and perceived pearls of wisdom that occurred to me from questioning and reflecting on my missteps resonated so loudly that they had to be put to paper, it took twelve consuming months to write the book. One of my IPA Friends takes exception to my adding the word "perceived" to pearls of wisdom (see appendix 2 for the definition of an IPA Friend). Granted, I think I'm pretty wise, but I countered, "As is the case for beauty, it is the observer who decides if there's any sincerity or wisdom in a thought or observation." You might think me wise or think me full of baloney. It's your call.

The interviews were primarily performed over the first four months, although some were from years past. All were included in aggregate, and some specific interviewees—whose names have been changed for purposes of privacy—have been quoted. The full measure of the insights gleaned from the interviews would fill another book with funny stories, poignant remembrances, epiphanies, and astute observations. At a later date, I hope to include more of the interviewees' wonderfully wise observations via a subsequent book, blog, short story, or article. Since the editing began, it has seemed that the book would repeatedly be finished in "just two more weeks." Invariably, it seemed, some serendipitously found new source of inspiration or an interview with a chance stranger would add more valuable information, delaying completion once again "just two more weeks."

So, as Snagglepuss puts it, "Exit stage left!" I truly hope I have herein fulfilled my dharma. Dharma can be understood as simply the idea of doing on this planet what you were meant to do. I find that the fire in the belly is burning low. I might or might not author another book after I gain back some weight and catch up on my chores, long neglected, like cleaning my house. This book has been a great deal of fun to write and has changed my life for the better. Maybe I can just share future cogitations or old ones accidentally left out of this book in essay or blog format. But let's focus on you.

What you feel is vitally important to you and likely to the world. Write down your stories. Share them or not, but in the writing you will gain perspective. If you share them, your wisdom and great ideas can help us all to live more fulfilling lives. Let's collaborate. If you write a book to which I might contribute, let me know—maybe this book could become one volume in *The Encyclopedia of Humanity* to which we could all contribute. Perhaps we could coauthor a subsequent volume (as long as you do all the work—LOL) into which I could drop some pearls of perceived wisdom. Since our thousands of thoughts each day are often on a recurrent loop, we rarely have the opportunity to unwind the loop to see the end of a thought, that is, reach a reasoned conclusion. An applicable metaphor is: If you hold on to a rope, you can float out into a stream knowing you'll be able to get back to shore. The anchored position allows you to float, but not be swept away as you watch the water flow past you. You might notice beautiful fallen leaves float by, or sometimes you might get poked by random floating sticks. Because you're anchored by the rope (your lifeline), you can move freely from side to side, give yourself some slack in the rope, pull yourself back to shore, or add more rope to bravely traverse the rapids downstream.

In writing this book, I've been able to unwind loops of thought, thereby allowing me to observe my thoughts floating past, move back and forth from perspective to perspective, and even allow myself more rope to safely explore the "rapids" of innovative, creative, and controversial ideas and then include them in this book. It's now time to pull myself back to shore (before I get jabbed with too many sticks). Intensively exploring my own ideas accrued over a lifetime of inquiry, then going out to solicit the wisdom of a cadre of wise and inspiring folks, and ending with a search of some of the mass quantities of available literature has inspired me to live the most evolved life I can imagine. I'm thrilled to get on with the adventure. Maybe it will be as a "Halt and Reverse Alzheimer's Warrior" or a volunteer in Namibia, or maybe it will just be as an organic gardener doing garden yoga and ministering to my worms.

During my writing experience, "my book" evolved into "this book" as it seemed to grow a life of its own. From the outset, I resisted putting my name and credentials on it, because this book was written from the perspective of a fellow Earth traveler, not as an expert—on anything! Since it was felt that the book might reach a broader audience if my certifications were included, I acquiesced, but only if I could add those that I truly think give me a bit more legitimacy to speak on our human condition (such as worm wrangler).

From the moment we arrive on the planet, whether we're aware of it or not, we are on the quest for the meaning of life. I've heard the candle analogy used in all sorts of contexts, and I'm sure my use is not an original thought, but it's worth revisiting. If you haven't studied a lone candle, imagine this: In a darkened room, strike a flame and touch it to the wick of the candle. Watch it flare and then go steady. Unseen, unexpected drafts of air cause the burning taper to wriggle and dance.

The flickering candlelight speaks to me in the following way. Since we come in and out of this existence alone, each of us must light her or his own candle of understanding. But as you illuminate your own being, your inner light might be the candle in the darkness for others. The light is no longer yours alone because it shines forth beyond you so others might see. People can choose to light their own candles or not. They can stand close to join their candles' glow to that cast by yours, or they can move in a different direction. Each successive light can bring about myriad patterns, each a nidus of illumination for them and their fellow travelers.

We can cajole others to see the same light we see, or cajole them to light their own candles by the flame of ours. In so doing we must tip our candle to start their flames. Tipping the lighted candle can cause the hot wax to splash. Thus one or the other of us can be burned. But in holding up our light without a sense of entitled illumination or manipulation of their path, others can see more clearly to strike the tinder of their own flames. Each of our individual lights can shine forth as our own torch of understanding. Each successive candle lit is additive; the world gets brighter, and all our paths become easier to see. Even if we walk alone, our light can offset the darkest of nights for ourselves. In taking responsibility for lighting our own flame we share the light and thereby encourage others to strike their own. With illumination and the different lenses to gaze through (created by your answers to the questions this book posed) you can chart your life journey. As this book ends, I'm more convinced than ever that it merely provides food for thought for your own unique and precious life. You truly are the expert when you listen to your inner wisdom and give voice to the essence of who you are.

If we are each courageous, loving, and in search of enlightenment, the world, which is truly a wondrous place, will be more apparent to us all.

APPENDICES

Appendix 1

Excerpts from the Martian Manual

This is MN26X. Just to help you humans out, here are a few excerpts from our manual and since I have been observing you folks since at least the 1960s, I've added comments that seem pertinent to your human condition.

The Martian Manual: Perspective on Aging

What has been your theme? Has it been "It's all about me!" or "It's all about them!" or "It's all about us!"? Martians make no judgment on any of these choices, but wouldn't it be intriguing to try another path for a while? Have you identified what the work of your life (your dharma) was, is, or will be if you have not yet achieved it? Could it be that you have not yet identified and/or attained your life work or your passion and that you have a few or a bunch of years left to make "it" happen?

You can choose to be an elder or you can become elderly. An elder, in Martian parlance, sees life as a continuum, remembers, learns from, and cherishes the past; is able to look forward to and plan for the future, and joyously embraces the present. You earthlings have come to the realization that your present moment is most important. Our Martian perspective is in general agreement, but as usual, you tend to throw the baby out with the bathwater. This all-or-none thinking has some discouraging outcomes.

Could ignoring or negating the past be similar to human dementia? To erase our memories is to obliterate the essence of who we are as individuals. Similarly, do we erase the collective essence of civilization if we do not value and preserve the history of humanity? Our Martian precedent is to value what those who have come before us have done, the good and bad, to celebrate the good events and learn never to repeat the missteps of the past.

Can you be "in the present," that is, in the moment, if you are only observing what is happening? If you suspend thought (which is judgment) to become fully absorbed in the senses, whether by painting, running a backhoe, mindless doodling, coloring, dancing, playing music, playing a musical instrument, watching bees, or being present as you observe a child, do you become absorbed fully into the moment? Is this a form of meditation?

Older Martians are considered elders (note small "e") to connote their having passed through their first six millennia. The term is a marker of chronologic age that does not necessarily imply wisdom gained in the journey. Martians elders who become venerated as Elders (note capital "E") display, among many other positive traits: integrity, honesty, perseverance, resilience, humor, gratitude, and *Weltgeist* (world spirit). We look to them for perspectives on the long-term opportunities found in short-term challenges as well as the long term ill consequences of short term "great" decisions.

We try to discourage our elders from becoming "elderly," which is tough on them and tough on the rest of us, by periodically administering a test (much like a human driving test). For Martian purposes, answering the following questions in the affirmative places an elder into the realm of elderly.

- If you were to tally your thoughts in a day's time, would most them be complaints and negative statements?
- Are you a help-rejecting complainer?
- Are your topics of conversation centered on your aches, pain, and failing health?
- Since you're going to hurt anyway, do you reject any enjoyable activities?
- Do you feel compelled to chronicle your doctor visits?
- Are there more doctor visits than enjoyable activities marked on your calendar for the coming months?
- Do you complain that no one calls or comes to visit you?
- Do you complain to those who do call or visit you that no one ever calls or visits?
- Are you bored?
- Are you boring?
- Are you fixated on your bowel movements?
- Do you consider yourself a victim?
- Do you nurse grudges and old injuries?
- Do you limit your activities because you consider yourself too old to do such things as exercise, run, or travel?
- Have you abdicated responsibility for your life to your spouse, children, doctors, or caretakers?

We give the above test to elders who start to act elderly. They either get mad or start laughing because they recognize themselves;

either way they clean up their act to become one of our venerated Elders (note capital "E").

You third-trimester humans have an opportunity. As your Yogi Berra said, "When you come to a fork in the road, take it." I am not saying any of your earth heroes, humorists, or philosophers were Martians, but some of them have channeled a modicum of our native wisdom. Yogi's humorous twist on the idiom regarding choice is brilliant. A split in the road implies that you have a choice to proceed along the left or right fork, the up or down path, or the larger or smaller of two distinct possibilities. He may have been admonishing you to not stop at the fork, frozen into place due to indecision or fear. Yogi might have just been trying to make us keep moving forward, think in a completely different way, or maybe he was implying that there are events beyond our control that can divert us onto a fork not chosen. Even within events or collective perceptions that are not of our choosing, there are immediate forks or choices that appear for each of us to consider. In the case of aging, do you choose to cringe with society's collective angst toward this "tragically inevitable outcome of living," or do you choose to run toward, embrace, and celebrate a time that can be the greatest of your life stages?

The Martian Manual: Perspective on Naysayers

In a nod to an Earth-based humorist named Foxworthy, you might be a naysayer . . .

If you are generally disagreeable about anything with which you disagree,

If you never question that with which you do agree,

If you think you are smarter than most everyone else,

If you confuse truth with your tightly-held opinions,

If you think your opinion is so important that you must voice it,

If you think that others who get quiet are in awe of your opinion,

If it has not dawned on you that those who grow quiet might instead think that you are an arrogant, condescending curmudgeon who lacks the creativity to think in an expansive manner,

If you believe that because a cohort of naysayers all agree that you are all correct,

If you think that your ends-focused agenda justifies any means you utilize to achieve it,

If you throw the term pseudoscience about in order to denigrate dissenting opinion,

If you use the term pseudoscience to assess those ideas which did not propose to be science in the first place, or

If your science, religion, manner of teaching, or manner of thinking has become dogma.

The Martian approach is to lock each individual naysayer in a roomful of naysayers who disagree with them, so he or she is rehabilitated by being on the receiving end of the naysayer creed noted above. It is a painstakingly slow and controversial treatment because some feel that this method is cruel. Martian pragmatists, however, have prevailed with their opinion that letting a random naysayer run amok among the rest of us stymies creativity and limits our possibilities.

The Martian Manual: Perspective on Yaysayers

We Martians are wary of the thought processes of yaysayers. The Martian phrase "reactive attachment to agreement" sums up these individuals who are immediately onboard with an opinion or call to action without a systematic assessment of the short- and long-term consequences. The upside is that they are agreeable folks; however, to readily agree with prevailing thought without applying their own critical analysis leads to potentially negative outcomes. This is the stuff of lynch mobs. The emotion-laden rhetoric of one individual or a cohort of like-minded people can sway others in a manner that they would not likely choose on their own.

Appendix 2

How to Grow a Friendship

A friend is generally defined as someone bonded, not by sexual or family relation, with whom there is shared affection. A friend is someone whose company you enjoy. If friendship is important to you, you might wish to reflect on what you consider your personal definition of a friend.

> *Friendship is unnecessary, like philosophy, like art. . . . It has no survival value; rather it is one of those things which give value to survival.*
>
> C.S. Lewis, The Four Loves

> *Friendship is the hardest thing in the world to explain. It's not something you learn in school. But if you haven't learned the meaning of friendship, you really haven't learned anything.*
>
> Muhammad Ali

Some people describe friends as more important than family because of the depth of a relationship that is non-transactional. Neither owes the other commitment based on genetics or obligation to the family unit.

The Eskimo language has up to fifty words for our single term "snow." We have only one word for it, with a few descriptors like wet or heavy snow. Similarly, we have only one term "friend," which can have very different meanings to those who use it. In fact the term is often misused when *friend* is used to describe mere acquaintances a person interacts with. Like "wet" snow, we add descriptors such as *dear* friend or *true* or *real* or *best* friend. These, however, merely describe a friend, but don't define the essence of what a friend is to us. Wouldn't it be nice to have separate terms to more accurately reflect what we mean when we designate someone a friend? Maybe we can adopt a few terms from other languages, but in the interim, what if we define friend on a continuum much like we do when we describe beer:

Beer Continuum / Friend Continuum	
pre-beer	Contains the makings of beer; i.e., hops, barley . . .
pre-friend	Contains the makings of friendship; i.e., mutual interest, personality . . .
3.2 beer	Short for 3.2% alcohol, (a beer wannabe)
3.2 friend	One with potential but not quite there yet . . .
beer-lite	Plug in your favorite brand name followed by "lite"; not as much taste but fewer calories.
friend-lite	Someone you can have fun with, but can't count on in a crisis. These friendships are easy to have because there's no commitment.
Beer	Full bodied, 5% alcohol, more flavor, and more calories
Friend	(Notice capital "F") Full friend, one you can count on, but known to you less than five years.
IPA Beer	Brewed longer to be full-bodied; higher alcohol content and intensity
IPA Friend	True best and real friend, with a distinct and full presence, known longer than five years.

Friendship is important to most humans, but if you don't want or need friends, it's not for the rest of us to judge. To avoid misunderstanding, it might be nice if you made your lone-wolf tendencies clear to anyone who makes overtures of friendship. To move forward toward friendship, at least two people must be involved. A "Grow a Friendship" suggestion is that the two pre-friends clarify the desired level of friendship. If you assume a friendship to be at or going toward a full beer level and eventually even an IPA level, but the recipient of your overtures can only muster a 3.2 level, you will give them loyalty beyond what they deserve or want, and you'll feel betrayed if they don't reciprocate at your level. It takes time to brew a full friendship. IPA Friends develop from friends who stand by each other whatever comes their way, who tolerate or even celebrate the differences, faults, or idiosyncrasies of the other. It takes time to develop IPA Friends, but is well worth it because they are precious gifts in this life. By the standards of alcohol tolerance, the higher alcohol content of a full beer suggests that you don't have as many of them as you do beer-lites. Similarly, most people have even fewer IPA Friends because the commitment and depth of the friendship is too important to dilute. If you would like to "brew" a friendship, you might wish to apply the adage "You must be a friend to have a friend."

> *You can't stay in your corner of the forest waiting for others to come to you. You have to go to them sometimes.*
>
> A.A. Milne, *Winnie-the-Pooh*

So, the ball is in your court. The suggestions below might mirror your own approach or suggest new approaches for you to clarify your definition of friendship. If you're interested in doing so you can thereby extend your group of personal friends. Plug in one of your friends' names below and see if you can say the following about your commitment to the friendship:

- I am interested in who my friend is, what has shaped his or her life, and what my friend's dreams entail.
- I am concerned for my friend's welfare and that of the persons he or she cares about.
- I am willing to go out of my way to support my friend in a spirit of shared joy or sorrow. I'm prepared to help physically with chores or errands if my friend is in a difficult situation. The spirit of my generosity is not strained by any expectation of gratitude but is motivated by the privilege of being able to be of service to my friend.
- I am available to my friend. Even when I'm busy, I can preface answering his or her phone call with "I'm super busy but I wanted to pick up your call to make sure you're okay." If I must sign off quickly, I make a specific action plan to call back.
- I am always respectful of personal privacy, never revealing any of my friend's thoughts given in confidence.
- I am always honest with my friend, and will gently offer my opinion if it seems appropriate.
- I strive to make my friend's day better for having interacted with me. I don't dump my problems on him or her, and I don't "share" tales of sadness or woe for which my friend can do nothing.

One of the reasons I'm a party animal is because I am privileged to have exceptional friends. Their qualities embody my perception of an IPA Friend. I deeply treasure my friends, all of whom have overcome adversity but have emerged as some of the kindest, most loving people on the planet. Admirable attributes of these women and men would include intelligence, strength of character, deep enlightenment, eclectic interests, humor, and courage. They have quirky natures and are funny, wise, hardworking people who are willing to sacrifice for their own success and willing to help their fellow man. My friends make me "feel felt," as Siegal notes in his book *Mindsight,* in which he describes the human capacity to empathize. My friends are honest with me. I cherish their counsel, solicited or otherwise. If I ask their help with a problem, I want them to always give me their honest opinion, even if their opinion is contrary to mine. My friends make me think and make me laugh. They support and challenge me to be the best me. Their emotional support and affection adds zest to the good times and buoys me during the hard times. It's humbling to be cared about by friends I respect and admire.

How to Develop a Friendship

A chance acquaintance can present an opportunity to develop a friend-lite, but not calling them friends prematurely can keep you from being trapped into giving the same loyalty to them that you bestow upon a quality beer Friend. Strike up a conversation. You might be rejected, but you need feel bad only if you choose to. I've been known to say to fellow airplane passengers, cab drivers, and random people in restaurants: "Since we're sitting next to each other for the next few hours, if you prefer I'll quietly read my book so you can read or sleep. However, if you're interested, I'd enjoy exchanging a one-sentence synopsis of the book that each of us is reading or some cool thing that happened to us. In this manner, if we have some common thread of interest, we won't miss an opportunity to talk." To not engage the individual for even a moment could lead to a missed opportunity. By engaging strangers, I've made friends around the world and from all walks of life. [*How cool is it to think of all the elements of my life and the traveler's that* had to align to make the meeting possible. These elements include such variables as the choices of travel dates and times, airline carriers, and individual decisions of why and when to fly. Such a random meeting represents the culmination of an incredible number of forks in the road that have ultimately led to our "chance meeting." All told, the probability of our meeting could be one in a billion.]

Be more interested in listening to whomever you are conversing with than in delivering a narrative of your own accomplishments. Once you've gone beyond a chance meeting to a shared interest, you can exchange contact information. Make it a habit to send a follow-up email or handwritten note to potential friends you meet. If they follow up with you, you're off and running toward a pleasant acquaintance.

Interviewee T.M. met Rosie, sixty-seven, a native of Australia, on Rosie's return flight from Memphis to her home. Rosie was greeted by a "cheeky" American who was intrigued by her accent. Rosie had traveled all the way from Australia to visit Graceland—the home of Elvis, her favorite singer. T.M. shared: "After nineteen years, Rosie and I still write and exchange small gifts from our respective homelands. She sends me little gifts like tea towels or pictures of her family from Griffith, New South Wales. I send her Elvis memorabilia—Christmas ornaments, key chains, and magazines. We don't often talk via phone due to the sixteen-hour time difference, but we send notes a few times a year. A chance meeting has resulted in a lifelong friendship."

Friends are not limited to any category be it Chinese, old, young, African American, Nigerian, Muslim, Buddhist, rich, poor, Christian, agnostic, Bahá'í, spiritual, atheist, or religious. They are the cohort of individuals with whom I am privileged to share my life. A funny and endearing story comes from my Friend, S.N., who when asked about her friends stated that she did not have any white ones, but then realized that two of her very best friends would in fact be considered white. S.N. is so dear that it did not dawn on her to think of her friends under a color category. S.N. relayed the story of her six-year-old daughter asking about "white" skinned individuals. S.N. told her daughter that in fact there is no such true delineation in that people are varying shades of brown from deep mahogany to the lightest beige. Further demonstrating her wisdom, my Friend assured her daughter that each person has rich additional shades from ebony to red, yellow, or a mixture of all, but that each is a treasured portion of our human race.

Shared interests, shared or similar experiences, and an appreciation of differences lend toward the development of an "early friendship." Be careful: Early friendships are fragile. If you or the acquaintance don't like each other initially, you might give each other another chance in five to seven years after many of your bodies cells have been replaced and each of you has had a chance to become more friendable. Without a long period wherein consistency of action and clarity of motivation prove you a worthy friend, actions you take may be misperceived. This is true to some extent with telephone conversations wherein you can't see facial expressions and body language to let you know if your message is being received. With abbreviated emails and snippets of text, however, not even tone of voice is available to assess whether communication is proceeding well. Especially beware of emoticons: What they mean to the sender might be completely different than what the receiver perceives. Be careful to proceed stepwise. Sadly, some individuals have borderline personality disorder, which is characterized by reactive attachment. These sometimes-volatile individuals demand an inappropriate depth of relationship over much too short a time to be considered healthy.

If a new friendship is developing, it might be worth clarifying, e.g., "I think we're exploring whether we'll become friends. Let's communicate openly, and let each other know right away if either of us chooses not to develop a more lasting friendship." Pursuing a friendship that's not reciprocal is uncomfortable and off-putting, so honest communication can turn the relationship back to a pleasant acquaintance. If, on the other hand, the relationship is collaborative, now is the time to apply your friendship parameters. If you're in need of advice or a bit of old-fashioned sympathy regarding your plight, be careful—friends are too precious to whine to them. A good Grow a Friend strategy is to determine first for yourself whether you have a problem and what your potential action plan is. Only then is it appropriate to solicit a friend's advice if you wish it; however, a complainer, particularly a help-rejecting complainer, establishes grounds for a friendship divorce.

Just because you're a friend to a new acquaintance doesn't mean that he or she is a friend to you. If you consistently feel worse during or after being in the presence of a "friend," run away—quickly. He or she may be one of the dreaded energy vampires. Perhaps the best way to determine that you have a friend is to ask yourself: "Would I want this person on my sinking ship?" Would their presence be calming? Would this individual try to help me keep the ship afloat? And, if we were unsuccessful, would he or she have the presence of mind to not whine on the way down?

Appendix 3

Disaster Preparedness Protocol

This protocol was originally drafted many years ago when I was working as a medical director for emergency services at a regional hospital, and was updated after hurricane Katrina displaced thousands of people from their homes. A disaster is defined as "a sudden calamitous event bringing great damage, loss, or destruction," which could be natural or manmade. We think of disasters in terms of many people being affected; however, a disaster could happen to a few people or even you alone. An example would be a house fire. Please see resources for the Federal Emergency Management Agency (FEMA) official government recommendations for disaster preparedness.

The following suggestions are not complete but are meant to stimulate your thought on preparing for potential adverse events.

1. Safe houses

   a. Consider cooperative agreements with people in the four cardinal directions locally and at a distance from your location such that you can go their way or vice versa in the event of an emergency that displaces you from your home. Do this in advance of any disaster; you might not be able to call to let them know you're coming. This would have been a great deal of help in hurricanes Katrina and Rita when thousands of people were displaced and area hotels were full.

b. Stock enough food to feed your family and the additional family for at least one week, preferably for a month.

c. Keep multiple paper maps with marked routes out of your area. GPS technology might not work.

2. "Go Bag"

a. Keep a go bag for each member of your family in an appropriate-sized sized backpack that contains essentials such as changes of clothing, food, diapers, and formula. Parents' packs should contain a flashlight, extra batteries in all sizes, emergency radio, compass, hiking shoes, food, and water in case of a sudden disaster from which you and your family need to rapidly flee.

b. Commit to reading a good disaster preparedness manual, then keep it in your go bag.

c. Keep a go bag in both your home and car.

3. Medications

a. Keep at least a three-month supply of medications (preferably up a six-month supply). Insurance might not cover the cost in other than one-month increments. You must decide how important having the medication is to you should the supply be unavailable for an indeterminate time. If you decide the cost is worth it, continue to get your usual monthly allotment on time, but use the six-month supply first and keep the subsequent monthly meds in sequence.

b. Pharmacies will quickly sell out of key medications in the event of a disaster.

c. Pharmaceutical supply lines could be disrupted for an extended period.

4. Water

   a. Set aside as much water as you can, preferably in glass containers. Replace the water on a regular schedule.

   b. Should a disaster event occur, immediately fill bathtubs, toilets, washing machines, sinks, and containers with water in case tap water becomes unavailable or contaminated.

   c. Water bottles/filter

      i. Various water bottles with filters are available through sporting goods, camping stores, and other outlets. Berkey water bottles are available from their website. These will filter contaminated water, which might be the only water available.

      ii. There are filters such as Katadyn filters, which provide even more advanced filtration and purification of contaminated water.

5. Food

   a. Stock up and rotate your food supply. Food packets can be purchased from food-insurance sites on the Internet.

b. MREs (Meals Ready to Eat) have a good shelf life and are available on multiple websites.

c. Dry packaged products, often sold for camping, also provide reliable long-term food sources. Canned foods must be rotated because of expiration dates. Freeze-dried foods can last for many years in storage.

d. Depending on your storage capacity, you might wish to have food to last for a minimum of one to three months.

6. Communication

   a. Emergency radios are available, which can use battery, solar, or manual power.

      i. Pre-event communication: Talk to people now so that in the event of an emergency, if you can't reach them, they'll know what you're doing by protocol. For example, you would know that you could expect your adult child and his or her family to travel via highway 40 (alternate state route 117 if 40 is blocked) to arrive at your home within twenty-four hours. If they didn't arrive, you'd know which routes to take should you begin to search for them.

      ii. Cell phones: These would be beneficial if they work. Should electricity be down, extended batteries and solar chargers can extend your phone usage. You might not be able to use your cell phone, since the microwave towers could be damaged or overloaded by cell phone traffic for local calls. Try calling long distance in the event your local tower is overtaxed. Distant contacts might be able to call back in to your local contacts for you. Print a copy of your contact list to keep in your go bag. Numbers not memorized will not otherwise be available to you if your cell phone doesn't work.

7. Personal Protection
   a. If there's a catastrophe, there will be different needs for specific emergencies. Nuclear fallout from a dirty bomb is unique in that, initially, if you're in the immediate vicinity, it might be best not to flee, but to stay in the center of buildings and away from windows.
   b. In all disasters, you can expect to see a breakdown of the social order, so be prepared to safeguard your life and supplies.
   c. Establish a local neighborhood association to plan a cooperative defense strategy. You will not be safe from marauding well-armed individuals or gangs. Attend your local community and local government meetings to ask what measures are in place for emergencies in your area. Look at any disaster protocols to see if they appear adequate. If they're not, get involved to help draft appropriate protocols. As an example, if water supplies are disrupted, is there a central place to which the local government would truck in water supplies.
   d. Establish a meeting place for the neighborhood if the usual lines of communication aren't working.
8. Immediate Reaction—It is essential to react immediately to any emergency. Plan to take full responsibility for your lives. Government agencies, police departments, and fire departments will be so overwhelmed that you must presume they won't be available to help you.

9. First Aid

   a. A well-stocked first-aid kit is vital in the event of a disaster. It's also beneficial in the event of any serious injury that might occur.

   b. Consult a good disaster-planning manual for details of needed supplies.

   c. Stay up to date on your tetanus shots.

10. Resources—Assemble a library of helpful books, e.g., *When Technology Fails, Dare to Prepare,* and the Foxfire books are a good start, as are government websites such as Federal Emergency Management websites, which are listed in the resources.

11. Cash—Banks might be inaccessible. Have as much coin and paper money in small denominations as you feel safe holding. If the disaster is for an extended time, be prepared to barter with extra food, batteries, or medical supplies.

12. Miscellaneous

    a. Permanent markers—keep these in your go bag

       i. In the event of a disaster, you could write on your skin (or that of family members) your last name, allergies, blood type, medications, and emergency contact(s) in case you're subsequently injured or unconscious and can't give the information.

       ii. Marking a child's name and contact information on his or her forearm would have avoided the horrible situation of being unable to rapidly reunite lost children with their families when they were separated during the chaos of Katrina.

b. Mark Your House

i. If you leave your home, for example to go to a safe house, leave information as to where you're going so family seeking you at the home will know your plans.

ii. If you have agreed on a particular route, they can follow your trail.

c. Consider physically marking your route by writing your name, the date and time, and your next planned destination on the first public building you pass as you travel through towns on your route. That way, people who might care to join you—or rescue you—will know how far you've gotten and where you're heading.

13. Insurance

a. Most people have homeowners, fire, and auto insurance; and don't expect a return for the money they've spent. In fact, you hope you never have to use it, but it is sure nice to have the insurance if it is needed.

b. Emergency supplies should be purchased in advance of untoward events. The resources in number 10, above, provide detailed recommendations.

c. Engaging your thinking skills and taking the time to prepare is true disaster insurance.

The above is to give you some ideas of the measures you can take in advance of a disaster. It's your responsibility to choose whether to prepare and what measures you feel would be important. Taking it a grocery shopping at a time, in which you purchase a few needed items and a few supplies to add to your disaster preparedness stock, can be instituted if it seems too expensive or overwhelming to take all measures at once. Think of it as getting ready for an adventure; grab it with gusto—hunkering down will just not work out well.

Appendix 4

How to Grow a Group

If you consider yourself a part of the karass to improve societal perception of growing up, aging, and dying, and wish to solicit like-minded people to participate, you might wish to grow the group as follows:

1. Ask prospective members whether they've participated on committees in the past, what roles they filled, how long they served, and why they left.
2. Seek out egalitarian contemplators. Ask the potential group members how they feel about issues that could be considered gray areas. Ask how they would seek to resolve a conflicting opinion within the group. You might wish to steer clear of potential group members who are paternalistic or naysayers. (see discussion below).
3. Pre-write your committee bylaws, which can be adapted as the group forms but will serve in the interim to guide you on the mission you wish to pursue. Having provisional bylaws in place can avoid unnecessary misunderstanding, conflict, and potential disruption of the group, resulting in failure to achieve the mission and vision.

4. Even though you might start the group, would you be willing to step back from leadership for the good of the whole?

5. Study resources on group dynamics.

6. Follow Robert's Rules of Order.

7. Articulate the vision and mission of the group.

The Community Tool Box is a public service of the University of Kansas. In chapter 9, section 7, there's a helpful overview of the importance of bylaws, a guide to what should be included, example bylaws, and how your organization might use them.

http://ctb.ku.edu/en/table-of-contents/structure/organizational-structure/write-bylaws/main

Appendix 5
Interviews

I interviewed over one hundred individuals for this book. Some were well known to me; others I met randomly on airplanes, in restaurants, while shopping, or at large events. Some I sought out because of their age, experience, or reputation. Interviewee identities have been concealed to protect their privacy. There are interviewees representative of each decade. The interviews consisted of twelve questions:

1. Do you or did you ever imagine being the age that you felt was old?
2. As a young person, what age felt (or feels) old to you?
3. Now, at your current age, what do you consider to be old?
4. Do you have friends in the age group whom you consider to be old?
5. If you don't know anyone in that age group, why not?
6. What's is your perception of society's attitude toward aging? Dying? Death?
7. What's your attitude toward aging? Dying? Death?

8. How did you come to feel this way?

9. What's your current age "in your head"? How old do you feel if you don't look in a mirror?

10. Would you be willing to be a mentor, either for those younger or older than yourself?

11. Do you have a close relationship with your extended "F" family? If so, please describe it. If not, would you be interested in creating a "f" family?

12. Have you experienced personal rites of passage during your life? Please describe. If not, would you consider this an action that might be helpful in appreciating our life continuum?

These questions were posed without further explanation. Each interviewee was encouraged to expand on any topic that occurred to her or him. All interviews were important and considered in aggregate for trends of thought. Each interview contained valuable content, but not all are quoted in this book due to the volume of information shared. I intend to continue to mine the wisdom of these interviews for the messages to us all.

To those of you who graciously allowed me to interview you:

I'm honored that you granted me access to your deepest, not-often-expressed thoughts concerning aging and dying. I appreciate your willingness to share your emotions and wisdom. Whether you expressed sadness or joy, stagnation or creativity, inadequacy or ability or any other unique perspective—your voice is important.

We have all benefited from your insights.

Appendix 6

Additional Party Games

The following party games are provided to serve as an informal template on which you can fashion your own unique celebration. Party games are a way to exercise both body and mind while enjoying the experience.

One way to exercise your mind is to formulate your own answers to questions that occur to you before you solicit the opinions of others. In this manner, you can think of actions that resonate with you alone. You can make a tentative plan and then solicit advice, which you can choose to incorporate into your life or not. By doing so you don't give up your personal power. If, however, you don't choose to work your mental muscles, you're not only shirking the responsibility to make your own decisions but also putting the burden of your ultimate decision on the advice giver. You thereby lose your power of decision-making (critical thinking). Your brain goes to mush, and if the plan doesn't work you can inappropriately put the blame on the advice givers because they failed you. Seeking advice is not an opportunity to whine and reject good ideas. Such an action reaffirms your card-carrying victim status as a "Help Rejecting Complainer." This mental health phrase describes the behavior of a set of individuals who perceive their circumstances to be suboptimal and who monotonously detail their situation to others with whom they interact. In *Psychology Today,* a paper entitled "Complaining," by Robin Kowalski, Ph.D., discussed help-rejecting complainers, who complain to others but reject any help that's offered. A constructive suggestion such as "Why don't you try . . .?" is met with resistance that the advice is useless. If you're facing a help-rejecting complainer, you might feel frustrated when they scoff at the folly of your suggestions. Acknowledging the complaint rather than offering solutions might be a healthier option for both you and the complainer. In addition, asking what he or she intends to do transfers the decision-making responsibility back to the source, which encourages their objective review of prior experiences, and thus enables empowered life planning.

https://www.psychologytoday.com/blog/the-happiness-project/201101/assay-useful-term-the-help-rejecting-complainer

Per *Psychology Today,* help-rejecting complainers present themselves as among the most victimized and mistreated persons. Instead of the usual competition of "one upsmanship", the author coined the term "one downsmanship" to describe this type of competitive suffering.

https://www.psychologytoday.com/blog/the-couch/201410/whats-the-best-way-deal-help-rejecting-complainers

As you consider a rewrite of a portion or all of the text of your life, you might want to apply a more assertive approach. The following is not a prescription of what you "should" do (CBT considers a "should" statement to be a cognitive distortion!) but rather is a list of ideas that might help get your own creative ideas to flow:

Rewriting Your Text—Template

1. Question everything at least once. The first suggestion is to question your absolute truths. A great example of

re-examining your truths can be found in the story called the "Streetlight Effect," which describes observational bias.

A policeman asks a drunken man what he is looking for. Standing under a streetlight, the drunken man replies that he has lost his keys. The policeman begins to help look for the keys under the streetlight, but after several fruitless minutes asks the man if he is sure he lost them there. The drunk replies "no" and explains that he lost his keys in the park. Incredulous, the policeman asks why the drunk is searching so far from the keys, to which he replies, "I can see better where there's light" (see Resources – Definitions – Streetlight Effect). If you look for your answers only in the places lighted by others, you might miss your chance at finding your personal path to an enlightened and examined life.

2. Stay curious. Even regarding those things, ideas, or events you're an expert about, you might gain some really interesting viewpoints. Always consider the perceptions of those you disagree with. Any conflicting perspective inevitably enhances your depth of thought. Such awareness is similar to the situation of a race in which top-flight runners have a pacer to push them to a higher level of competition.

3. Watch for the lessons to be learned by reflecting on every event, good or bad or mundane. Sometimes the coolest ideas can come from the most unlikely places. Remember the worms.

4. Live as if you'll live just one more day, so you're present and mindful of the day's events, and as if you'll live to be a hundred, so you'll sink deep roots to hold you strongly against adversities over time.

5. Form an opinion on everything; you can always change it. Try not to denigrate others for having differing opinions.

Opinions are just perspectives; compromise can't happen without dialogue.

6. Live intentionally. Make choices rather than let events unfold unbridled.

7. Recognize the power of one. Remember the Starfish Story (resources). Helping even one person in need helps not only that person but also provides a significant benefit to the one providing help.

8. Create impenetrable defenses. One interviewee, S.N. age forty-one (who is not a narcissist) uses the following internal reminder when she comes up against people who say derogatory things of her: "I am perfect. I have no need of your permission or approval." Memorizing such a statement to repeat to yourself when someone is unkind is an excellent defense against believing that the other person (who could just be jealous or mean-spirited) is correct.

9. Surround yourself with people who make you feel good. If you notice you're feeling good but that after an interaction with someone you feel drained, tired, and defeated (especially if you notice this feeling each time you interact with that person), you may have met an energy vampire. Try to give an energy name to all the people you interact with. If you call them liquid yoga or wise owl you might want to keep them as friends, but if you mentally name them energy siphon or angry tiger you might want to keep them at bay.

10. Live with animated exhilaration. Why not? You can have a lot of fun cavorting. Plus, it's also fun to observe the confused expressions of people who used to know you by the trappings of your practice life, especially if you used to be a complainer or curmudgeon.

11. Draw your lines in concrete, not in sand. As you enter any relationship (spouse, girlfriend, job, boss, boyfriend), establish standards of behavior that cannot be breached. This approach creates lines of acceptable behavior in concrete. If that person crosses the line of acceptable behavior even once, terminate the relationship. The one wronged needs to be strong. If you accept a phone call, letter, or text from the perpetrator, you will most likely be persuaded to rescind your decision to avoid further contact. The line in the concrete becomes a fading line in the sand. In fact, the injured individual might have thought she would never tolerate being addressed in a verbally demeaning way; however, at some point she began to be addressed by the "loved one" in a belittling manner. The partner apologized and was forgiven. The relationship is "good" for a while, but then the partner slips into controlling, angry, or demeaning behavior once more. Once the behavior is accepted again, it becomes a gateway to verbal abuse (Resource – References – Books – Dixon). The line is repeatedly moved, allowing worse and worse treatment. Eventually the relationship might become physically abusive as well. Sadly, verbal abuse can be worse than physical abuse because the tracks of abuse are hidden from sight. The abused individuals are then surprised at being the recipients of behaviors they never dreamed they would tolerate.

12. Don't let others muddy the waters of your clear mind. One young woman, Ann, age twenty-five, said she thinks of her mind as a pool of crystal-clear water. She chooses not to taint it with thoughts, movies, or books that make her sad, angry, frustrated, or frightened. Ann said that when someone wishes to "share" a tragic tale with her, she stops the person gently and requests her or him to pause. She then

asks if the storyteller feels that there is something Ann can do to help the situation. If told no, Ann respectfully requests that she not be burdened with details of sad or tragic events that she can't positively impact. Ann considers such random sharing of grisly or tragic tales as a type of voyeurism. She compares it to throwing mud or garbage into the beautiful clear waters of her mind.

13. Marry a friend: Character and intellectual honesty are requisites for a healthy long-term relationship. (Seriously, folks, if you have an affair with an unfaithful, married individual, do you really think your paramour will later be faithful to you?)

14. Try on some "Egger skin." Take acting lessons at a community college or a local group and learn to act and dress in other roles. It might help to know that you can temporarily assume the identities of other people if you are considering that you can choose to change your own life story.

    a. The "Egger Skin" reference comes from the movie *Men in Black*. A giant space bug confronted by Edgar ("Egger") not only dispatches Edgar but also feels uncomfortable and frustrated as he tries to wear Edgar's skin as a disguise.

15. The concept of a message in a bottle might have started with early ocean travel, and to this day fascinates people. There are websites that detail both how to send messages and relate stories of messages later found by others.

    a. Write down your thoughts even if you're not a "writer" or don't have a high level of education. Those are external implied constraints, which you must buy into for them to be true.

b. Write letters. Personal writing is becoming a lost art. Handwritten pieces are by nature more poetic, reflective, and complete than email or text messages. Cursive writing is an art form. This type of communication is as individualistic as fingerprints. Sadly, the school budget for teaching art has been diminished or totally abandoned as non-vital. Similarly, the time necessary to teach cursive writing has been eliminated in some schools. I wonder how society expects people in the future to be able to write their own unique signatures?

c. Leave a quick note to someone you don't know to cheer their day. For example, you might leave a note saying: "I enjoy the effort that you put into your beautiful lawn, which I have the privilege to see each day as I drive to work."

16. Be where you are. One interviewee said she hated to commit to anything because of a fear that she was missing something better.

17. Spin through the universe. Grab each situation to the fullest. It would be helpful if restaurants or food courts had an area marked SURE, I WOULD LOVE TO TALK TO YOU. Similarly, I'm always interested to see if fellow airplane travelers will engage in conversation. In trying to avoid the occasional adjacent traveler who talks incessantly, how many people fail to meet others who are truly amazing? A chance encounter might never occur again. If in a safe place . . . meet people. There are some bad guys out there, but a whole lot more good ones.

18. Value your time. On reflection, we're often surprised with how we spend our time. If you feel you don't have enough

time to accomplish something you aspire to, it might serve you to make a chart of your time use. Per the American Time Use Survey, the average number of hours per year per worker in the U.S. is 1,789 hours. Government statistics reveal that we spend on average 5.8 hours in leisure activity daily. Over a year that's 2,117 hours, of which 1,022 hours are spent watching television (Resources – Supporting Data – American Time Use Survey Summary). If you want to learn a skill or hobby, want to take online courses, or work overtime for vacations, travel, or to build funds for retirement—you have the time to spend.

> *The human race is a monotonous affair. Most people spend the greatest part of their time working in order to live, and what little freedom remains so fills them with fear that they seek out any and every means to be rid of it.*
>
> —Johann Wolfgang von Goethe,
> *The Sorrows of Young Werther*

19. Trust your instincts. If something feels wrong it probably is. Per T.M., "Anytime I override my instincts, things don't turn out well. It's so hard to resist someone who keeps insisting I do something that just doesn't feel right. The last time I overrode my instincts was in a kickball game. My finger was broken by a hard-kicked ball within two minutes of going to an infield position at the insistence of an infielder who wanted to move out to my position. It's a silly example, but I'm still irritated when my crooked finger prevents me from doing something I wish to do."

20. Practice gratitude, in thought, in words, or notes of thanks to those who did a good deed for you, the nation, or the planet.

21. Reading is a high-level activity. It engages the brain in thought and sparks the imagination. Many people no longer read books for pleasure, especially the young.

> *A person who won't read has no advantage over one who can't read.*
>
> Mark Twain

If you wish to be able to continue your exploration of possible ideas, philosophic challenges, and absolute fun, read, read, read. Reading allows you to pace your intake of ideas and to pause to reflect or re-read passages which resonate with you. In the resource section are some book titles you might enjoy, but there are thousands of others available. Ask your friends for their favorites.

Appendix 7

Supplemental Information—Alzheimer's Disease and End-of-Life Planning

This appendix includes additional statistical and research information about Alzheimer's disease. [Author's note: Much like the Black Plague, Alzheimer's disease does not respect any boundaries; social, racial, or economic. Every human is at risk.]

First, consider the scale of the economic challenge for the U.S. alone. As Guy Eakin, Vice President of Scientific Affairs for BrightFocus Foundation, an organization that provides funding for early stage, investigator-led research, points out, the total US healthcare cost for Alzheimer's is expected to grow to $1.1 trillion per year by 2050. Noted previously but repeated here to emphasize the scope of 1.1 trillion is the example as follows: a million seconds is 11.6 days; a billion seconds is 31.7 years; a trillion seconds is 31,709 years.

In an article written by Leslie Goldman in 2013, she states:

> The exact causes of Alzheimer's disease are still unknown, but experts have identified a host of contributing factors: diabetes, smoking, saturated fats. Now a theory points the finger in a different direction: a variety of metals that can build up in the body over time.

Scientists have identified structural abnormalities in the brains of patients who have died due to Alzheimer's disease. These include tiny clusters of protein called beta-amyloid plaques. When these were analyzed, they included metals . . . not only aluminum but also iron and copper. As cited in Goldman's article, Neal Barnard, M.D., an adjunct associate professor of medicine at the George Washington University School of Medicine, explained, "These metals produce free radicals, which are like little sparks that damage brain cells." Iron is an essential element for hemoglobin, the substance that carries oxygen in our blood cells. We might, however, be exposed to excessive iron. Research has shown that people with elevated levels of iron might be three times as likely to develop Alzheimer's as people with normal levels. Goldman goes on to provide practical suggestions, including decreasing the consumption of red meat (high in iron) and transitioning from cast-iron cookware to stainless steel. Due to the potential link of aluminum to Alzheimer's disease, Goldman also recommended decreasing possible exposure to the aluminum present in many antacids, aluminum soda or beer cans, and through water supplies.

Consider the following abstract from the National Institutes of Health (citation included).

Aluminum and Alzheimer's disease: after a century of controversy, is there a plausible link?

> The brain is a highly compartmentalized organ exceptionally susceptible to accumulation of metabolic errors.

> Alzheimer's disease (AD) is the most prevalent neurodegenerative disease of the elderly and is characterized by regional specificity of neural aberrations associated with higher cognitive functions. Aluminum (Al) is the most abundant neurotoxic metal on earth, widely bioavailable to humans and repeatedly shown to accumulate in AD-susceptible neuronal foci. In spite of this, the role of Al in AD has been heavily disputed based on the following claims: 1) bioavailable Al cannot enter the brain in sufficient amounts to cause damage, 2) excess Al is efficiently excreted from the body, and 3) Al accumulation in neurons is a consequence rather than a cause of neuronal loss. Research, however, reveals that: 1) very small amounts of Al are needed to produce neurotoxicity and this criterion is satisfied through dietary Al intake, 2) Al sequesters different transport mechanisms to actively traverse brain barriers, 3) incremental acquisition of small amounts of Al over a lifetime favors its selective accumulation in brain tissues, and 4) since 1911, experimental evidence has repeatedly demonstrated that chronic Al intoxication reproduces neuropathological hallmarks of AD. Misconceptions about Al bioavailability may have misled scientists regarding the significance of Al in the pathogenesis of AD. The hypothesis that Al significantly contributes to AD is built upon very solid experimental evidence and should not be dismissed. Immediate steps should be taken to lessen human exposure to Al, which may be the single most aggravating and avoidable factor related to AD.
>
> https://www.ncbi.nlm.nih.gov/pubmed/21157018

Copper has also been found in Alzheimer's beta-amyloid plaques. The above-cited article by Leslie Goldman also shared that individuals whose high-fat diets included 1.6 or more mg of copper a day experienced a loss of mental function equivalent to an extra nineteen years of aging, compared with those who took in an average of 0.9 mg a day. Other sources of potential exposure to excessive levels of copper include vitamin supplements with high levels of copper, and copper tubing used in plumbing in many homes. The above authors' and scientists' speculations are a matter of public record and can be reviewed as you choose an action plan. (The sources for the above information on the causes of Alzheimer's disease are included in Resources – Scientific, Philosophical or Psychological Concepts – Alzheimer's Resources.)

Alzheimer's resources

Alive Inside. N.p., n.d. Web. 13 Dec. 2016. http://www.aliveinside.us/ [*Author's note: It has been found that music, particularly of the era in which an elder was born and grew up is helpful for re-engaging people suffering Alzheimer's with the world. Please visit the alive inside website to view a two-minute trailer that could change your life or the life of someone you love.*]

"Aluminum and Alzheimer's disease: after a century of controversy, is there a plausible link?" National Center for Biotechnology Information. U.S. National Library of Medicine, n.d. Web. 18 Oct. 2016. https://www.ncbi.nlm.nih.gov/pubmed/21157018

"Alzheimer's Disease: Facts & Figures." BrightFocus Foundation. N.p., 2016. Web. 03 Dec. 2016. http://www.brightfocus.org/alzheimers/article/alzheimers-disease-facts-figures [*This interesting article provides details on the incidence of Alzheimer's, and suggests that by 2050 over 130 million people worldwide could have the disease if breakthroughs are not discovered*]

"Alzheimer's Research Spending vs. Annual Care Costs." Alzheimersnet. N.p., 2015. Web. 18 Oct. 2016. http://www.alzheimers.

net/2013-12-19/research-spending-vs-annual-care-costs/ [This article looks at the costs of Alzheimer's disease in the US, noting that despite the cost to society and governmental agencies, Alzheimer's research has not risen to a level of top priority. The government is currently spending millions of dollars on Alzheimer's research, which sounds like a lot of money; however, current costs of the disease already exceed $200 billion per year, and are projected to rise to $1.1 trillion per year by 2050.]

Campbell, Don. "Increase Alzheimer's Research Funding: Column." *USA Today.* Gannett, 2013. Web. 18 Oct. 2016. http://www.usatoday.com/story/opinion/2013/09/16/nih-alzheimers-research-funding-column/2822817/ [Author's note: Don Campbell provides an insightful analysis of the current state of the battle against Alzheimer's disease]

Changing the Trajectory of Alzheimer's Disease: How a Treatment by 2025 Saves Lives and Dollars; https://www.alz.org/documents_custom/trajectory.pdf [Author's note: This article notes that in 2015, the costs to all healthcare insurers for Alzheimer's disease was an estimated $226 billion, with governmental programs (Medicare and Medicaid covering most of the cost). The author also looks to the future, noting the staggering cost of future care.]

Goldman, Leslie. "3 Metals That Might Cause Memory Problems." *The Huffington Post.* TheHuffingtonPost.com, n.d. Web. 30 Nov.2016 http://www.huffingtonpost.com/2013/12/18/metal-dangers-memory-loss-alzheimers-disease_n_4413511.html

"Medical News Today." Medical News Today, MediLexicon International, http://www.medicalnewstoday.com/articles/311731.php [Author's note: This article discusses the feasibility of a *vaccine for Alzheimer's disease, which could potentially be available within 3–5 years.]*

Moyer, Melinda Wenner. "Controversial New Push to Tie Microbes to Alzheimer's Disease." Scientific American. N.p., 2016. Web. 18 Oct. 2016. https://www.scientificamerican.com/article/controversial-new-push-to-tie-microbes-to-alzheimer-s-disease/ [*Author's note: This article looks to a potential connection of herpes virus and the bacteria causing Lyme disease as etiologies for Alzheimer's disease.*]

"Potential Alzheimer's Vaccine Undergoing Pre-clinical Trial Tests." *Alzheimer's News Today.* N.p., 2016. Web. 18 Oct. 2016. https://alzheimersnewstoday.com/2016/07/18/progress-alzheimers-vaccine-preclinical-tests/ [*Author's note: This article also looks at the potential benefit of a vaccine for Alzheimer's disease.*]

2016 Alzheimer's Disease Facts and Figures, Alzheimer's Dement. 2016 Apr;12(4):459-509. https://www.ncbi.nlm.nih.gov/pubmed/27570871 [*Author's note: This report describes the public health impact of Alzheimer's disease, including incidence and prevalence, mortality rates, costs of care, and the overall impact on caregivers and society. It also examines in detail the financial impact of Alzheimer's on families, including annual costs to families and the difficult decisions families must often make to pay those costs.*]

End-of-Life Planning and Documents

1. **Life and disability insurance:** Obtain insurance before you acquire some medical condition that precludes coverage.

2. **Will:** A will allows you to direct your assets (including those most meaningful to you) to those persons whom you want to receive them.

3. **Living Will or Advance Directive:** A living will, also called an advance directive, is a legal document that allows you to state your intent for end-of-life medical care in case you become unable to communicate your decisions. The need for a living will has arisen in part because of the advances in medical care as well as the public's awareness of life-sustaining treatment they might not desire. Typically, people will indicate that they don't want certain treatments such as tube feedings, being placed on a ventilator, or certain invasive treatments in the event that they are in a terminal state.

4. **General Power of Attorney:** A general power of attorney gives broad powers to a person you designate as your agent to act on your behalf. The agent has power to handle financial and business transactions.

5. **Durable Power of Attorney for Healthcare:** This document lets you name someone else (your designated agent) to make decisions about your health care in case you are not able to make decisions yourself. It also provides your agent with direction regarding the kinds of medical treatment you desire. Note: Always name a successor agent in case your primary agent is unable to act on your behalf.

6. **POLST:** If you are acutely ill, with a life expectancy of less than one year, clarification of Physician Orders for Life-Sustaining Treatment (POLST) is of benefit (as detailed in chapter 12). You or the person you designate in your Durable Power of Attorney for Healthcare can collaborate with your physician to clearly indicate the care you want before expected changes in your condition take place. Even

if you're not acutely ill and don't need to execute the POLST, it's worth reading for ideas you might wish to include in your advance directive.

7. **Estate Planning Documents:** Most financial planners suggest that the best time to execute these documents is "at least ten years ago." In other words, just get it done.

Appendix 8

Message in a Bottle—Suicide

Once the book was finished and ostensibly off to start the process of publication, it seemed there were a few topics left uncovered that my initial readers wished I had included. I plan to address most of these topics later; however, one was too important to postpone.

T.T., age forty-one, asked if I would include the topic of suicide, and Charlie, the sixteen-year-old interviewee, related her struggles regarding her best friend's suicide. I mentioned to T.T. that I had in fact addressed the terrifying number of youngsters who've considered suicide in the last six months. As well, I had indirectly addressed suicide across all age groups in discussing that our thought processes, which result in emotions, lead us to actions. This same process of thought, emotion, and action is engaged to carry out acts of self-harm. I had not, however, directly addressed suicide in a book that encourages each of us to celebrate life. Over the next several months the thought that something in this book might be of benefit for those who consider self-harm made me reconsider. What better way to celebrate life than to decide that, despite all the reasons to end your life, there are even more reasons to continue your life's journey?

If you are in crisis or considering harm to yourself, please call 911. The people available to speak to you at all times of the day or night are trained to assist you. Other options are to contact the National Suicide Prevention Lifeline through their phone center (1-800-273-8255) or website.

The National Suicide Prevention Lifeline is a national network of local crisis centers that provides free and confidential emotional support to people in suicidal crisis or emotional distress 24 hours a day, 7 days a week. They are committed to improving crisis services and advancing suicide prevention by empowering individuals, advancing professional best practices, and building awareness.

http://suicidepreventionlifeline.org/

If you are considering suicide, you have options. If you decide not to ask for help to prevent harming yourself, you won't likely receive help. Family, friends, and strangers don't know that you're considering self-harm if you don't tell them. There are others who would like to prevent your suicide, whether family, friends, or strangers who care enough about you to answer the 911 and suicide crisis lines. It's your decision to give them a chance to help you find reasons to continue your life.

Suicide is a permanent solution. Rather than act right away, can you give yourself and others a bit of time to see if this is what you truly want? Ultimately, no matter how many medical personnel, police, or family members try to help you, the final decision rests with you.

If you're brave enough to face the fear and pain of death, can you turn that bravery to doing just the opposite? Could you use your bravery to embrace life for at least the next six months? Could you be brave enough to do those things you fear to do—even at the risk of life?

During those six months, could you seek help of physicians or counselors, talk to friends and family, and investigate alternatives to suicide? Before you would take that last step to self-harm, consider whether a treatable illness is what's making you feel that suicide is your only option. If you haven't yet chosen to seek help because you fear the stigma of being labeled mentally ill, can you entertain the notion that anyone who would look down on you is an idiot? People with diabetes or heart disease aren't disparaged for seeking treatment, so why in the world would treating the chemical and structural problems of the brain, which make you consider self-harm, result in labeling and denigration? Some of the bravest, strongest, and most admirable people I've met have had mental illnesses.

Before you make your final decision, could you take the time to read about suicide and mental illness, not only for you but also to see what effects your suicide will have on the many people who know and care about you? There are many websites that can get you out of your persistent loop(s) of thoughts to explore other options:

National Suicide Prevention Lifeline https://suicidepreventionlifeline.org/

Emory University http://www.emorycaresforyou

National Alliance on Mental Illness www.nami.org/

Survivors of Suicide http://www.survivorsofsuicide.com/faq_suicide.shtml

> Author's note: This site is for those people whose lives have been impacted by the suicides of people they loved. If you're considering suicide, it's an excellent site to visit to help you understand the impact your death will have on others.

Here are a couple of "What ifs?" to consider: What if there are more reasons to live than not? What if there is one person or even many people who care about you? What if there's meaning for your life and you just haven't yet found it? What if there's a unique reason that you're are here on the Earth, and if you check out of this life early, your dharma will never be fulfilled? What if there's a next life and you launch into it without having developed in this world what you need for the next? What if you give up too early on this life and have to come back in a similar circumstance and try it again? Yep, wouldn't that suck?

You're not alone. Many people have occasional thoughts about suicide, but for some it becomes an intrusive thought. According to Emory University, it's estimated that 3.7% of the US population (8.3 million people) had thoughts of suicide in the past year, with 1.0% of the population (2.3 million people) developing a suicide plan and 0.5% (1 million people) attempting suicide. A long time ago I was one of those 2.3 million people. As one of my close encounters with death, this one was the only one I had control over. Ultimately, only the thought of the trauma and guilt my action would have created in my family and friends, and that suicide would have increased the chance that they would have also then considered suicide, kept me from carrying out my plan. It's currently estimated that committing suicide increases the risk of family and friends attempting suicide by 65% (http://www.medicaldaily.com/suicide-bereaved-self-destruct-371022).

All these years later, I'm glad on many additional levels that I decided not to end my life. Because I chose to stick around a while longer, I've had many adventures, even silly ones with my chickens. The tough experiences have given me the chance to forge my philosophic path on this journey. Had I bowed out early, I'd have missed the opportunity to meet such amazing people and the privilege to have fulfilled my dharma. For all the hard times, I wouldn't have wanted to miss the good ones, but that's just me. What about you? Are you willing to give your life a chance to get better?

RESOURCES

I hope you will look through this section. There's a lot of information that might be helpful to you. I've included several [*Author's note:*] entries to share my perspective.

Organization of Resources

1. Definitions
2. Quotations
3. Topics of Interest
4. Scientific, Philosophical or Psychological Concepts
5. Supporting Data
6. References
    a. Books
    b. Funny and/or Philosophical Movies
    c. Web Sources

Definitions

English is an old language. There are many sources for definitions and many different interpretations of meaning within each source. Even common words, phrases, and old sayings can be interpreted differently by the deliverer of an idea and the recipient. Lest there be any misunderstanding, please note: for the purposes of this book, these are the specific definitions I intended to convey.

Amyotrophic Lateral Sclerosis (ALS)

ALS, or amyotrophic lateral sclerosis, is a degenerative disease of that leads to a progressive loss of muscle control. The disease attacks the cells of the brain and spinal cord and typically has a very poor prognosis.

Angst

Angst is a term from German that describes a feeling of deep anxiety, particularly with respect to broad societal or global issues.

Apoptosis

Apoptosis refers to controlled cell death, which is part of the normal human developmental process, where some cells are "culled" to enhance function. In the brain, apoptosis occurs particularly in toddlers and adolescence.

Bias

Bias denotes prejudice against persons, things, and concepts. There are several types of bias. The types of bias relevant to the discussion in this book include:

1. Situational bias: the tendency to explain behavior as being due to external influences rather than our internal attributes. While we can often "explain away" our own poor choices or behaviors as being due to external influences, when we observe the same behaviors in others, we can attribute it to their "poor character."
2. Confirmation bias: the tendency to select observations to confirm previously held views (Note: this is said to be a problem in research. Hmm. Could this be fueled by descent into dogma?)

[*Author's note: It's hilarious how biased we are about our own biases. Figuratively speaking, we can obviously see the wart on someone else's nose—for gosh sakes look at that wart—but we humans physically lack the ability to see our own noses unaided. Without reflection, we can't see our own warts.*]

Bon vivant

The term bon vivant is usually used to describe bright and happy individuals, often with refined tastes for fine food and beverage.

Brain plasticity

Brain plasticity pertains to the ability of the brain to adapt to changes, even significant injuries, by reforming itself. *Plasticity* metaphorically refers to the ability of plastic to be molded and remolded into various shapes. Following an injury, cells in the brain can form new pathways and connections to recover function.

Bucket list

The term *bucket list* is used to represent a compilation of those things a person wants to do before he or she dies or "kicks the bucket."

Cliché

This term typically applies to a phrase or description that's too often applied to describe a particular situation.

[*Author's note: Cliches are tired, lazy ways of saying something—so much better to come up with something creative—like Martians.*]

Cognitive

Cognitive refers to the conscious functions of the brain, such as reasoning, cogitating (thinking) or using one's memory.

Connectome

Connectome is a term that has been applied to the overall neural mapping of the brain. The human brain has numerous types of cells, each with numerous types of connections to other cells, forming an extremely complicated network. Connectome has been used to describe a theoretical map of all these nerves and connections.

Contemplator

Contemplator, as used in this book, refers to a person who thinks before acting, one who considers multiple perspectives and has the depth to consider alternatives.

Critical thinking

The author's compilation of attributes of critical thinking include:

- To think critically is a learned process that results in mental flexibility and confidence to act.
- Critical thinking is the mental process we use to interpret novel observations or actions and thereby make sense of our daily experiences.
- Critical thinkers can reference historical information and experiences, ones that they can apply to current observations, to anticipate future events.
- Using numerous apparently disjointed bits of information that might or might not be related, critical thinkers can arrive at new ideas.
- When thinking in an analytical manner, the critical thinker can organize and construct action plans, make decisions, and evaluate ideas.
- Critical thinkers have the ability to think beyond currently accepted lines of thought.
- Critical thinkers are not threatened by fear of "failure" but consider the process to be attempts which have not yet been successful.

[Author's note: Thomas Edison when asked about his 1000 failed attempts to invent the light bulb said, "I didn't fail 1000 times. The light bulb was an invention with 1000 steps."]

Dharma

The word "dharma," derived from Sanskrit, has various meanings. To some, the term encompasses living your life in a manner consistent with the laws of nature. A more expansive perspective, and the one applied in this book, is doing in your life what you were meant to do during your lifetime.

Egalitarian

The term *egalitarian* is defined because of the use in this book of the term egalitarian contemplator. Egalitarian is a quality of those individuals who recognize that all people have equal rights and are of equal value.

Egalitarian contemplator

Author's definition: I coined this phrase to signify a person whose thoughts regarding any issue are guided first and foremost, by the principle that all people are equal, possessing the same value and rights. An egalitarian contemplator considers issues in a thoughtful and reflective manner, pondering the perspectives of all sides as related to both immediate impact and long-range potential consequences of an action.

Elder

Elder, as used in this book, applies to a person who has garnered authority and respect due to his or her wisdom, knowledge, and experience.

Elderly

Elderly, as described in this book, refers to older individuals who have taken on the persona of those who are victims of their age, rather than those who celebrate every day of their lives. "I am a victim of having not died yet."

Family

Family is a term that can have many meanings. The following definitions provide additional characteristics:

Nuclear family

Nuclear family refers to the basic social unit of parents and their children.

Extended family

Extended family refers to the nuclear family plus, to a variable extent, related individuals such as grandparents, aunts, uncles, cousins and so on—basically those who show up at a family reunion.

Friend

Friend is a very broad term typically applied to someone a person knows, likes, and spends time with (excluding family or sexual relationships)

[Author's note: please see appendix 2 for a full definition and how to grow a friendship.]

Gaia

The Gaia hypothesis was developed in the 1970s by chemist James Lovelock and microbiologist Lynn Margulis. The hypothesis proposes that we are not isolated creatures living on a planet, but rather highly integrated, synergistic parts of a greater organism that includes the planet. In recent decades, much of society has gained greater appreciation of the importance of diversity of species, interactions among species, and the importance of clean air and water for survival not just of humanity but of the planet as a whole. Some perceive Gaia as a single living organism of which we are a part.

[*Author's note:* There are many sources for the further study of Gaia, which I hope you will explore. Every little bit each of us does for sustaining our ecosystem benefits all inhabitants of the Earth. A book that details the basis of the Gaia theory is *Wulf's The Invention of Nature: Alexander von Humboldt's New World*. For a particularly intriguing and frankly unsettling discussion of Gaia, see the discussion thereof by Buhner in his book *Plant Intelligence* (see Books, below).]

Gamma waves

Gamma brainwaves are the most recently discovered of the major classes of brain waves. These fast waves are very important for communication among various parts of the human brain and are felt to be essential for higher-level functions, including love and virtues. Recent research has demonstrated that those who meditate or have higher levels of spirituality have greater Gamma wave function.

Gestation

Gestation refers to the process and the time period during which a woman carries a child in her womb.

Industrial Revolution

The Industrial Revolution was brought about by the development of power-driven industrial production. The power sources included steam, coal, and oil. The Industrial Revolution was also characterized by major societal changes as people moved from the farm to cities disrupting family structures which had the precedent of thousands of previous generations.

Infantilize

Infantilize refers to treating a person in such a manner as to deny their growth, maturity, or intelligence, akin to treating the adult individual as if they were a child.

In utero

Present in the uterus. The uterus is the female organ in which offspring are conceived and carried until maturation and birth.

Joie de vivre

Joie de vivre, a term from the French, describes an overall excitement for and enjoyment of life.

Karass

Karass is a term referring to a group of people, who may be unaware of each other but who share an idea, action, or motivation.

This term, originally coined by author Kurt Vonnegut, has been used to explain why the ideas of like-minded individuals, once achieving critical mass, can spontaneously coalesce into significant forces for societal change.

Law of attraction

The law of attraction is at term applied to the concept that "what you put out there, you tend to get back." Perhaps more eloquently stated, "like attracts like." The concept is that when an individual focuses on positive or negative thoughts, corresponding positive or negative experiences are likely to follow.

[*Author's note:* Interestingly, the scientifically based Cognitive Behavioral Therapy of psychologist Aaron Beck has some similarities to the tenets of the "Law of Attraction." Beck posits that thought patterns, particularly negative thoughts, bring about negative emotions. The concept of the "Law of Attraction" is not a scientific law, but rather a metaphor for the observation that "like attracts like." We see the validation of this hypothesis in observing that people who give off negative "vibes" are offensive not only to others but often to themselves as well. The converse is also true. People who give off "positive" vibes are attractive to each other. Further, individuals who positively envision an outcome may bring that outcome to fruition at least in part due to their mindset.]

Mentor

A mentor is an individual who provides guidance to a less knowledgeable or less experienced individual. While traditionally mentors are viewed as older individuals, as used in this book a mentor could be older or younger than the mentee. The key characteristic is not age, but rather one who has knowledge sharing with one who desires such knowledge.

Metaphysical

Metaphysical points to those things that are thought to exist, but which are not subject to proof either through direct observation or scientific analysis, although some concepts, originally considered to be metaphysical have subsequently become physical laws.

[Author's note: Some scientists go all "pseudoscience" on things of the mind. Hmm. What of Einstein's thought experiments that allowed him to imagine what was not possible to prove in a linear scientific-method manner?]

Millennial

In reference to humans a *Millennial* describes a generation who reached adulthood around the year 2000.

Naysayer

A naysayer is a person who is negative, particularly about the ideas or thoughts of others.

Object permanence

Object permanence refers to the concept, developed by philosopher Jean Piaget, that at about the age of eight or nine months, children begin to be aware that objects exist even if they can't see them. This contrasts with earlier in development when children cannot conceptualize any object which is not subject to their direct observation.

Parasympathetic nervous system

See Sympathetic nervous system (below)

Plasticity

Plasticity refers to the quality of being able to be shaped, sometimes repeatedly, and thus assuming a new form.

Brain plasticity

Brain plasticity denotes the ability of the brain to adapt to changes, even significant injuries, by reforming itself. The term plasticity metaphorically refers to the ability of plastic to be molded and remolded into various shapes. Following an injury, cells in the brain can form new pathways and connections to recover function.

Power

The capacity to influence or control.

Referent power

Referent power refers to the power one has based on one's characteristics. Natural leaders tend to gain referent power due to their personal characteristics which earn respect or admiration.

Legitimate power

Legitimate power is power gained due to one's position. Individuals with legitimate power often wear the uniform of their position, such as a general, a policeman, or a surgeon. Legitimate authority is based on formal power associated with the position.

Pseudoscience

Pseudoscience is a term which is often used to describe ideas or claims which have not been validated by formal scientific proof.

[*Author's note: "Pseudoscience" is a label, assigned in a pejorative sense, often to a concept with which one disagrees. For a full discussion by the proponents and denigrators of the use of the term, I recommend an Internet foray down that rabbit hole of investigation. Some metaphysical constructs are presented as science and thus subject to the scientific method; however some metaphysical constructs are not presented as science and cannot be disproven through application of the scientific method*]

Retirement

Retirement, as used in our society, refers to leaving one's life work typically at approximately the age of 65. The concept was introduced by Otto Von Bismarck, Chancellor of Germany in 1883. As a shrewd political maneuver, Bismarck leveraged Marxist support by offering a pension to non-workers over the age of 65. It should be noted that workers living to that age was somewhat uncommon. This construct, developed for political reasons almost 150 years ago, continues as a dominant concept in society today, even though we may live thirty years longer on average than we did at that time.

Rheostat

A rheostat is a common electrical device used to incrementally increase or decrease an electrical current [such as a volume control on a radio].

As used in this text, a rheostat is a device that can adjust the effect of a given force.

Sage

Sage refers to a person who is wise. Elders, as defined in this book could also be called sages. Sage is also an adjective which is characterized as showing judgment, wisdom, logic, and reason.

Sage-ing

Sage-ing is a term introduced by Zalman Schachter-Shalomi and Ronald Miller to describe in a positive way the process whereby the young and the old both acquire experience and knowledge.

Sea legs

Sea legs refers to the ability developed by those at sea to adjust to the motion of a ship, allowing the ability to walk and to avoid seasickness.

Sensuous

Sensuous describes "things of the senses." Sensuous describes the very positive experience of enjoying high quality food, drink, aroma, sound, and touch. Eating delicious food is a sensuous experience. The term, as used in this book, is contrasted with sensual which is usually used in a sexual context.

Sympathetic nervous system

The sympathetic nervous system is that part of the nervous system which causes increased heart rate, increased blood pressure, and the release of specific hormones.

[Author's note: The sympathetic nervous system triggers what is known commonly as the "fight or flight" response. If you were to see a snake, the sympathetic system would dilate your pupils (to enhance vision of said snake), increase your heart rate so you could run away, and shuts down functions not needed at that moment, such as your digestive system.]

The parasympathetic nervous system, on the other hand, slows the heart rate, lowers blood pressure and increases the activity of the digestive system and various glandular functions.

[Author's note: This is the system you use when you are lying around, eating potato chips and watching the TV.]

Venue

The place where an event occurs, especially an organized event such as a concert or party.

Yaysayer (or yeasayer)

The opposite of a naysayer, yaysayers tend to react positively, supporting just about any thought or idea, without critical evaluation.

Quotations

[*Author's note: Some of the following authors were not referenced in the book but have made significant contributions to man's search for meaning in life.*]

Campbell, Joseph (1904–1987)

Joseph Campbell was an author who linked cultural myths to societal development.

"We must let go of the life we have planned, so as to accept the one that is waiting for us."

Hawking, Stephen (b. 1942)

Stephen William Hawking, one of the world's most brilliant individuals, was diagnosed with amyotrophic lateral sclerosis, a slowly progressive neurologic disorder. He has become increasingly paralyzed over his life. His life expectancy at the time of his diagnosis was two years. At the time of this writing, he is 74 years old (surviving more than 50 years longer than expected). Part of his life story was depicted in the 2014 film The Theory of Everything.

"I'm not afraid of death, but I'm in no hurry to die. I have so much I want to do first."

Keller, Helen (1880–1968)

Helen Keller was born in 1880. At the age of 19 months, she suffered a severe illness resulting in complete loss of vision and hearing. The story of her struggle to overcome these losses and become a spokesperson for the disabled has been well documented. Her teacher, Anne Sullivan, unlocked Helen's creative potential by establishing communication. Keller wrote multiple articles and had twelve books published.

"Your success and happiness lies in you. Resolve to keep happy, and your joy and you shall form an invincible host against difficulties."

Rogers, Will (1879–1935)

Will Rogers, born to a Cherokee Nation family in Oklahoma, had an extensive career, including having made numerous movies and having written thousands of nationally syndicated newspaper columns. His earthy anecdotes have been widely quoted. There is a wonderful movie about Roger's life if you are interested.

"Half our life is spent trying to find something to do with the time we have rushed through life trying to save."

Twain, Mark (1835–1910)

Mark Twain, whose actual name was Samuel Langhorne Clemens, was a prolific writer, hometown philosopher, and humorist.

"The fear of death follows from the fear of life. A man who lives fully is prepared to die at any time."

Topics of Interest

Earthworm Society of Britain

http://www.earthwormsoc.org.uk/earthworm-information/earthworm-information-page-3.

[*Author's note: Leave it to the British! When I was going down the rabbit hole of inquiry regarding the global status of my worm-buddies, I came upon this website. It's truly delightful.*]

Elder Athletes

Ernestine Shepherd is a remarkable 80+ y.o. body builder who started bodybuilding at age 67. You can read her story on the following websites:

https://www.yahoo.com/beauty/80-old-fitness-trainer-prove-000000042.html

http://www.boredpanda.com/oldest-female-bodybuilder-grandma-80-year-old-ernestine-shepherd/

In 2015, Harriette Thompson, a 92 y.o. woman, finished the San Diego marathon. Read her story at:

http://www.cnn.com/2015/06/01/us/san-diego-marathon-oldest-woman-finishes/

http://womensrunning.competitor.com/2015/05/inspiration/92-year-old-runs-to-break-marathon-record-in-san-diego_40956

Also in 2015, N.K. Mahajan, to celebrate is 96th birthday, trekked up Sinhagad Fort in India. His story is told on the site below:

http://indianexpress.com/article/pune/96-year-old-celebrates-birthday-by-climbing-sinhagad-fort/

Eeyore

Eeyore is a character in the Winnie-the-Pooh books. A. A. Milne, the author, depicted Eeyore as a gloomy, negative, whiny-voiced pessimistic donkey who carried the weight of the world on his shoulders (or at least that was his perception).

> Author's note: If you wish to avoid Eeyore conversations, do the following:
>
> Do not make a habit of complaining or whining.
> Do not cast yourself as a victim.
> Do not whine. Use your "big girl" or "big boy" voice.

FEMA (Federal Emergency Management Agency) Disaster Resources

The following links include documents that you can download for disaster preparedness and planning. Navigating the main site can be a little unwieldy. Going direct to the sites that might be the most helpful is the way to start.

http://www.fema.gov/media-library-data/1390846764394-dc08e309debe561d866b05ac84daf1ee/checklist_2014.pdf

[Author's note: This site is excellent. It contains a one-page checklist for basic supplies needed and an addendum for secondary needs.]

http://www.fema.gov/media-library/assets/documents/7877

[Author's note: This site contains an in depth guide for disaster preparedness. There is also a discussion of becoming a part of the Community Emergency Response Team CERT which involves 20 hours of training should you wish the training for yourself or for being available to assist in your community should the need arise.]

https://www.fema.gov/recovery-resources

[*Author's note: I like this site because it contains practical information on a number of vital topics including how to locate family members if they are scattered during a disaster. There's information about taking care of pets in a disaster. Tragically, in Hurricane Katrina, rapidly evacuating pet owners had to abandon their pets. This site gives practical advice to let you know in advance the measures to have in place for your pets' safety.*]

https://www.fema.gov/pdf/areyouready/areyouready_full.pdf

[*Author's note: This FEMA website contains a fifty-five-page downloadable document for emergency preparedness.*]

Many other sites are available within the main FEMA website; your time would be well spent to explore them, some of which include the building of safe rooms for tornado and hurricane areas.

Kant, Immanuel (1724–1804)

Author's note: It is often said that a person may be either "ends justified" or "means justified." I take this to mean that someone who is ends justified will utilize any means necessary to achieve their desired outcome. So, a laudable outcome could be the result of unconscionable intermediary actions. This is the stuff of despots and villains. A means justified individual is one who takes the high road of ethical behavior at each decision point, even if it means accepting a lesser outcome.

Prayer and Meditation

Herbert Benson, M.D., compared prayer and meditation across the spectrum of multiple religious beliefs. He has applied a scientific investigative approach to the subject using MRI brain scans to observe what happens when individuals meditate (or pray in a similar manner).

Benson, Herbert, MD. "Can Prayer Heal?" WebMD. WebMD, n.d. Web. 14 Nov. 2016.
http://www.webmd.com/balance/features/can-prayer-heal?page=2

Reiki

Reiki is a healing technique which involves channeling universal energy through the touch of a Reiki therapist (functioning as a conduit, rather than the source, of the energy) to an individual to restore physical and emotional well-being. Reiki is also used more broadly for the benefit of society, the earth, and beyond.

[*Author's note:* The following citation demonstrates that Reiki is now being introduced into the curricula of many leading academic medical centers. Please see references – Books – Barnett.]

"Libby [Barnett, Reiki Master] has presented Reiki to medical and nursing students at Harvard, Brown, Tufts, and Yale as well as staff at Massachusetts General, Beth Israel, Mt. Auburn, Emerson, Dartmouth-Hitchcock, Southern New Hampshire, New York Foundling, and New York Columbia Presbyterian."

Barnett, Libby. "Reiki I Notebook." Wilton, NH: Reiki Healing Connection, 2012. Print

Science Fiction

[*Author's note:* Science fiction is my favorite genre of literature. It is full of imagination, impossible ideas, improbable actions, and ultimately oft-time visionary in that many such impossible ideas have come to pass. Think of Roddenberry's Star Trek tricorders . . . they became flip-phones. I think science fiction is an excellent genre for teens who are exploring their universe and are not constrained by impossibilities. Among many others, the following are some of my favorites.]

Bradbury, Ray

Fahrenheit 451, Something Wicked This Way Comes, The Martian Chronicles, The Illustrated Man, among others.

Card, Orson Scott

Ender's Game, Ender's Shadow, Speaker for the Dead, Xenocide, Shadow of the Giant, Shadow of the Hegemon, Children of the Mind, Shadow Puppets, First Meetings in the Enderverse, Earth Unaware, The Call of the Earth, Earth Afire, and *Shadows in Flight* among others.

Heinlein, Robert (1907–1988)

Robert Heinlein was a prolific author of over a hundred books. My favorite is *Stranger in a Strange Land.*

Orwell, George (1903–1950)

Nineteen Eighty-Four; Animal Farm; and The Road to Wigan Pier

Socrates (469–399 BC)

Socrates who was born in Greece in 470 BC is recognized as one of the greatest philosophers of all time. He was forced to drink a beverage containing hemlock, a lethal poison. The reason? He articulated an opinion that others disagreed with . . . vehemently.

The Starfish Story

The Starfish Story: one step towards changing the world
By Peter Straube; adapted from *The Star Thrower,* by Loren Eiseley (1907–1977)

To read the Starfish Story, see

https://eventsforchange.wordpress.com/2011/06/05/the-starfish-story-one-step-towards-changing-the-world/

Author's Note: An additional thought on this story. An old man wonders why a boy is trying to rescue some of the thousands of starfish stranded on a beach since he could only save a small portion of them. The boy obviously wishes to make a positive effort on behalf of the starfish but could become overwhelmed with the enormity of the task as had the old man. The boy could say that there is no point to helping one of the starfish since in aggregate he could not help the tens of thousands in need. He could feel hopeless and helpless to impact the situation. I think that the effort by the boy is helpful to him as well the one starfish in that the boy was not giving up in despair. He chose to at least try to impact a few which included himself as he did the best he could under the circumstances.

Scientific, Philosophical or Psychological Concepts

Alzheimer's resources

Alive Inside. N.p., n.d. Web. 13 Dec. 2016.

ALIVE INSIDE is a joyous cinematic exploration of music's capacity to reawaken our souls and uncover the deepest parts of our humanity. Filmmaker Michael Rossato-Bennett chronicles the astonishing experiences of individuals around the country who have been revitalized through the simple experience of listening to music.

This stirring documentary . . . demonstrate[s] music's ability to combat memory loss and restore a deep sense of self to those suffering from [memory loss].

http://www.aliveinside.us/

[Author's note: Please visit the alive inside website to review a two-minute trailer that could change your life or the life of someone you love.]

"Aluminum and Alzheimer's disease: after a century of controversy, is there a plausible link?" National Center for Biotechnology Information. U.S. National Library of Medicine, n.d. Web. 18 Oct. 2016.
https://www.ncbi.nlm.nih.gov/pubmed/21157018

The brain is a highly compartmentalized organ exceptionally susceptible to accumulation of metabolic errors. Alzheimer's disease (AD) is the most prevalent neurodegenerative disease of the elderly and is characterized by regional specificity of neural aberrations associated with higher cognitive functions.

The hypothesis that Al significantly contributes to AD is built upon very solid experimental evidence and should not be dismissed. Immediate steps should be taken to lessen human exposure to Al, which may be the single most aggravating and avoidable factor related to AD.

"Alzheimer's Disease: Facts & Figures." BrightFocus Foundation. N.p., 2016. Web. 03 Dec. 2016.

Every 66 seconds, someone in America develops Alzheimer's. It is estimated that nearly 500,000 new cases of Alzheimer's disease will be diagnosed this year.

Worldwide, 46.8 million people are believed to be living with Alzheimer's disease or other dementias. By 2030, if breakthroughs are not discovered, we will see an increase to nearly 74.7 million. By 2050, rates could exceed 131.5 million.

http://www.brightfocus.org/alzheimers/article/alzheimers-disease-facts-figures

"Alzheimer's Research Spending vs. Annual Care Costs." Alzheimersnet. N.p., 2015. Web. 18 Oct. 2016.

http://www.alzheimers.net/2013-12-19/research-spending-vs-annual-care-costs/

Alzheimer's disease affects more than 5 million Americans. It's the fifth leading cause of death in the United States overall, and care costs for Alzheimer's patients exceed $200 billion. But somehow the government hasn't made research into this disease a top priority.

Campbell, Don. "Increase Alzheimer's Research Funding: Column." *USA Today.* Gannett, 2013. Web. 18 Oct. 2016.

http://www.usatoday.com/story/opinion/2013/09/16/nih-alzheimers-research-funding-column/2822817/

"It's time we launched a serious war on Alzheimer's disease. Right now, we're pursuing a "national plan to address" Alzheimer's, passed by Congress two years ago. It's a timid plan, having produced a lot of bureaucratic boilerplate but only a paltry increase in federal funding for research into the insidious disease.

It includes a goal of being able to prevent and treat Alzheimer's by 2025, but without the means to achieve that goal. Why is it so difficult to get the war launched?"

Changing the Trajectory of Alzheimer's Disease: How a Treatment by 2025 Saves Lives and Dollars;
https://www.alz.org/documents_custom/trajectory.pdf

"Medical News Today." Medical News Today, MediLexicon International,
http://www.medicalnewstoday.com/articles/311731.php

"A Vaccine for Alzheimer's disease could be trialed in humans within the next 3-5 years, after researchers from the United States and Australia have uncovered a formulation that they say successfully targets brain proteins that play a role in development and progression of the disease."

Moyer, Melinda Wenner. "Controversial New Push to Tie Microbes to Alzheimer's Disease." Scientific American. N.p., 2016. Web. 18 Oct. 2016.
https://www.scientificamerican.com/article/controversial-new-push-to-tie-microbes-to-alzheimer-s-disease/

Controversial New Push to Tie Microbes to Alzheimer's Disease

A journal article says herpes virus and Lyme disease bacteria are behind the mind-robbing illness, but not all researchers are convinced.

"Potential Alzheimer's Vaccine Undergoing Pre-clinical Trial Tests." *Alzheimer's News Today.* N.p., 2016. Web. 18 Oct. 2016.
https://alzheimersnewstoday.com/2016/07/18/progress-alzheimers-vaccine-preclinical-tests/

Scientists have developed a novel form of vaccine targeting the two main proteins triggering Alzheimer's disease, amyloid-beta and tau protein.

Researchers and physicians have seen an increase in Alzheimer's disease, with more than 7.5 million new cases diagnosed worldwide per year. There is an urgent but still unmet need for a vaccine and effective treatment for dementia, one of the most detrimental features of Alzheimer's disease.

2016 Alzheimer's Disease Facts and Figures, Alzheimer's Dement. 2016 Apr;12(4):459-509.
https://www.ncbi.nlm.nih.gov/pubmed/27570871

This report describes the public health impact of Alzheimer's disease, including incidence and prevalence, mortality rates, costs of care, and the overall impact on caregivers and society. It also examines in detail the financial impact of Alzheimer's on families, including annual costs to families and the difficult decisions families must often make to pay those costs.

Watching the essence of those you love disintegrate is akin to standing on the bank of a pond just watching them drown.

Pert, Candace

The following are a few of the many, many references for Dr. Pert. She had an incredibly diverse career and has both avid supporters and detractors. Some of the written content focuses more on her struggles in the academic community and not as much on the specifics of her research. It is challenging to find a good summary book or article either written by Dr. Pert or her reviewers and considerable time must be spent if one desires to understand her work.

Pert, Candace B. Molecules of Emotion: Why You Feel the Way You Feel. New York, NY: Scribner, 1997. Print.

[Author's Note: I have to admit that I was somewhat disappointed in the book in that she covered her theories, but spent more time on her challenges.]

On February 22, 1993, Bill Moyers engaged a number of experts in a panel discussion, including Candace Pert. The transcript of that conversation can be read at:

http://billmoyers.com/content/mind-body-connection/

In that discussion, Dr. Pert described her research on neuropeptides. These chains of amino acids are released from the brain and travel to receptor sites on cells throughout the body. She found that these neuropeptides function at least in part to mediate emotion. She suggests that these neuropeptides connect the body and mind which essentially identifies the body-mind dichotomy as an artificial construct. The mind is located not only in the brain, but throughout the body.

Other information can be gained from the following websites:

http://www.primal-page.com/pert.htm
https://www.youtube.com/watch?v=17A7aMMlfrE
https://www.youtube.com/watch?v=8CFjt4qXE-Y
http://www.smithsonianmag.com/history/review-of-molecules-of-emotion-157256854/#O5AOvk6iGGfLmERo.99
http://www.smithsonianmag.com/history/review-of-molecules-of-emotion-157256854/#FwglCsbSpFPriuGK.99
http://www.smithsonianmag.com/history/review-of-molecules-of-emotion-157256854/#O5AOvk6iGGfLmERo.99

Satir, Virginia (1916–1988)

I was privileged to be in the audience of one of Satir's conferences and would like to share my recollection. She observed a dimension of family dynamics that could benefit even the most "functional" of families. However, in that corporate, political, and job-related roles can mirror "family," it would seem to me that her work is applicable in a host of other settings beyond her original intent of assisting the family of origin to have healthier relationships.

Satir described the dysfunctional roles that people unconsciously assume within a relationship. As I recall from her workshop, these roles have been described as: placator (one who martyrs himself); blamer (one who can always find someone else to blame); computer (one who appears centered but is detached and overly logical); and distractor (one who presents an irrelevant perspective by talking about unrelated subjects). Satir proposed physical stances for each of these roles, so they could be acted out in a theater-like manner. Satir observed that the roles could shift for any one individual as the numbers of people within the relationship varied.

As an example, in a relationship encounter of only two people, e.g., in the presence of her child, the mother might be observed to take the role of computer. The child's role might be identified as that of distractor.

In a relationship encounter of three people, e.g., adding in the father and the same child, the mother might unintentionally switch to another role, e.g., placator. The fascinating observation Satir noted to the audience is that the child, when in the presence of both parents, might switch from distractor to blamer. Satir observed the undulating dynamics within families of two, three, four, and more. She noted to the audience that she had worked with up to thirteen members of an extended family in her therapy room at one time.

Satir proposed an approach to family therapy to assist first by awareness of the patterns that each member assumed. She would then have the members assume the stances to physically role-play as each person would assume the stance and demeanor of the four roles, successively. Each family member's role would shift over the course of several exercises to placating, blaming, computing, and distracting roles. Using the lessons learned during this role-playing, she helped families to restructure their relationships.

Satir had another method which was very effective, wherein she would ask people to identify why they felt a certain way. The answer gleaned would then be examined with "Why?" The secondary reason for their feelings would be put to the same scrutiny as to why and so on until she felt the core issue was identified. Thus, Satir could drill back to the core reasons for a thought or action. As an example, "I do not wish to leave my home to socialize. Why? Because I would be embarrassed. Why? Because I had a bad incident in a store as a child. Why? Because I wet my pants. Why? Because my mom was on drugs and would not take me to the bathroom. Why? She did not love me. Why? Because I am no good." Satir would, in that manner, help people to identify their core issues, which had been layered over and thus hidden from thoughtful scrutiny.

Bear in mind that the above are my recollections. Please read her book if you are interested. Hmm . . . it might be thought-provoking to combine some of her tenets with those of Beck.

Twelve-Step Program

[*Author's note: The original 12-step program designed for overcoming addiction to alcohol has been adapted for use by many organizations that help people deal with addictions, including Narcotics Anonymous and Anger Anonymous. There are secularized interpretations available. There is more information regarding the 12 Step Program in the Resources section.*]

Yoga

Yoga is an ancient practice of both art and science integrating body, mind, and spirit. Yoga not only increases personal awareness, but also awareness of the unity of creation. Essential components include physical, emotional, and spiritual growth and balance.

Supporting Data

[*Author's note: The following are quoted excerpts from the named sources.*]

American Time Use Survey Summary
From the United States Department of Labor
http://www.bls.gov/news.release/atus.nr0.htm

Leisure Activities in 2015

On an average day, nearly everyone age 15 and over (96 percent) engaged in some sort of leisure activity such as watching TV, socializing, or exercising. Of those who engaged in leisure activities, men spent more time in these activities (5.8 hours) than did women (5.1 hours).

Watching TV was the leisure activity that occupied the most time (2.8 hours per day), accounting for more than half of leisure time, on average, for those age 15 and over. Socializing, such as visiting with friends or attending or hosting social events, was the next most common leisure activity, accounting for 41 minutes per day.

Men were more likely than women to participate in sports, exercise, or recreation on a given day—23 percent compared with 18 percent. On days they participated, men also spent more time in these activities than did women—1.7 hours compared with 1.2 hours.

On an average day, adults age 75 and over spent 7.8 hours engaged in leisure activities—more than any other age group; 35- to 44-year-olds spent 4.0 hours engaged in leisure and sports activities—less than other age groups.

Time spent reading for personal interest and playing games or using a computer for leisure varied greatly by age. Individuals age 75 and over averaged 1.1 hours of reading per weekend day and 20 minutes playing games or using a computer for leisure. Conversely, individuals aged 15 to 19 read for an average of 8 minutes per weekend day and spent 1.3 hours playing games or using a computer for leisure.

CDC Suicide Data Sheet

http://www.cdc.gov/violenceprevention/pdf/suicide-datasheet-a.pdf

Cell-Phone Distracted Parenting Can Have Long-Term Consequences: Study

New research shows how cell phone distraction can deprive babies' developing brains of crucial developmental signals.

http://time.com/4168688/cell-phone-distracted-parenting-can-have-long-term-consequences-study/

Per Capita Consumption

Per Capita Consumption of Food

Category	*Annual (pounds)*	*Lifetime (tons)*
Meat	148.49	5.85
Dairy (all groups)	187.75	7.40
Added Fats and Oils	57.04	2.25
Added Dairy Fats	10.76	0.42
Fruit	133.07	5.24
Vegetables	173.57	6.84
Grain Products	135.64	5.34
Sugars and Sweeteners	99.01	3.90
All Category Total	945.33	37.25

USDA Data—2013, based on food availability data
Quantity of food consumed after adjusting for all losses
http://www.ers.usda.gov/media/134674/tb1927.pdf

Per Capita Consumption of Minerals

Category	*Annual (pounds)*	*Lifetime (tons)*
Bauxite (Aluminum)	62	2.44
Cement	638	25.14
Clays	152	5.99
Coal	4,988	196.53
Copper	12	0.47
Iron Ore	270	10.64
Lead	11	0.43
Manganese	4	0.16
Natural Gas (lbs. coal equivalent)	8,990	354.21
Petroleum Products	6,607	260.32
Phosphate Rock	194	7.64
Potash	32	1.26
Salt	477	18.79
Sand, Gravel, Stone	16,615	654.63
Soda Ash	35	1.38
Sulfur	75	2.96
Uranium	0.16	0.01
Zinc	7	0.28
Other Metals	20	0.79
Other Non-metals	471	18.56
Total	39,660	1562.60

SOURCES: US Geological Survey; Energy Information Adm.; and U.S. Census Bureau.

2015 data are preliminary. Totals may not add due to rounding.

Updated: March 2016

Author's note: These are the minerals used on behalf of each of us as individuals (per capita use per year or in a lifetime). For example, an individual can expect to utilize 10.6 tons of iron ore, which is used to make many of the products we consume, over the course of his or her lifetime.

POLST

A copy of the POLST document is available online at:

http://www.polst.org/wp-content/uploads/2013/01/POLST-2011-WA.pdf

Social Security Website Actuarial Table

https://www.ssa.gov/oact/STATS/table4c6.html

Period Life Table, 2013*

	Male		*Female*	
Age	*Remaining Life Expectancy*	*Total Life Expectancy*	*Remaining Life Expectancy*	*Total Life Expectancy*
0	76.28	76.28	81.05	81.05
1	75.78	76.78	80.49	81.49
2	74.82	76.82	79.52	81.52
3	73.84	76.84	78.54	81.54
4	72.85	76.85	77.55	81.55
5	71.87	76.87	76.56	81.56
6	70.88	76.88	75.57	81.57

7	69.89	76.89	74.58	81.58
8	68.9	76.9	73.58	81.58
9	67.9	76.9	72.59	81.59
10	66.91	76.91	71.6	81.6
11	65.92	76.92	70.6	81.6
12	64.92	76.92	69.61	81.61
13	63.93	76.93	68.62	81.62
14	62.94	76.94	67.63	81.63
15	61.96	76.96	66.64	81.64
16	60.99	76.99	65.65	81.65
17	60.02	77.02	64.67	81.67
18	59.05	77.05	63.68	81.68
19	58.09	77.09	62.7	81.7
20	57.14	77.14	61.72	81.72
21	56.2	77.2	60.75	81.75
22	55.27	77.27	59.77	81.77
23	54.33	77.33	58.8	81.8
24	53.4	77.4	57.82	81.82
25	52.47	77.47	56.85	81.85
26	51.54	77.54	55.88	81.88
27	50.61	77.61	54.91	81.91
28	49.68	77.68	53.94	81.94
29	48.75	77.75	52.97	81.97
30	47.82	77.82	52.01	82.01
31	46.89	77.89	51.04	82.04
32	45.96	77.96	50.08	82.08
33	45.03	78.03	49.11	82.11
34	44.1	78.1	48.15	82.15
35	43.17	78.17	47.19	82.19
36	42.24	78.24	46.23	82.23

37	41.31	78.31	45.28	82.28
38	40.38	78.38	44.33	82.33
39	39.46	78.46	43.37	82.37
40	38.53	78.53	42.43	82.43
41	37.61	78.61	41.48	82.48
42	36.7	78.7	40.54	82.54
43	35.78	78.78	39.6	82.6
44	34.88	78.88	38.66	82.66
45	33.98	78.98	37.73	82.73
46	33.08	79.08	36.81	82.81
47	32.19	79.19	35.89	82.89
48	31.32	79.32	34.97	82.97
49	30.44	79.44	34.06	83.06
50	29.58	79.58	33.16	83.16
51	28.73	79.73	32.27	83.27
52	27.89	79.89	31.38	83.38
53	27.05	80.05	30.49	83.49
54	26.23	80.23	29.62	83.62
55	25.41	80.41	28.74	83.74
56	24.61	80.61	27.88	83.88
57	23.82	80.82	27.01	84.01
58	23.03	81.03	26.16	84.16
59	22.25	81.25	25.31	84.31
60	21.48	81.48	24.46	84.46
61	20.72	81.72	23.62	84.62
62	19.97	81.97	22.78	84.78
63	19.22	82.22	21.95	84.95
64	18.48	82.48	21.13	85.13
65	17.75	82.75	20.32	85.32
66	17.03	83.03	19.52	85.52

67	16.32	83.32	18.73	85.73
68	15.61	83.61	17.95	85.95
69	14.92	83.92	17.18	86.18
70	14.24	84.24	16.43	86.43
71	13.57	84.57	15.68	86.68
72	12.92	84.92	14.95	86.95
73	12.27	85.27	14.23	87.23
74	11.65	85.65	13.53	87.53
75	11.03	86.03	12.83	87.83
76	10.43	86.43	12.16	88.16
77	9.85	86.85	11.5	88.5
78	9.28	87.28	10.86	88.86
79	8.73	87.73	10.24	89.24
80	8.2	88.2	9.64	89.64
81	7.68	88.68	9.05	90.05
82	7.19	89.19	8.48	90.48
83	6.72	89.72	7.94	90.94
84	6.27	90.27	7.42	91.42
85	5.84	90.84	6.92	91.92
86	5.43	91.43	6.44	92.44
87	5.04	92.04	5.99	92.99
88	4.68	92.68	5.57	93.57
89	4.34	93.34	5.17	94.17
90	4.03	94.03	4.8	94.8
91	3.74	94.74	4.45	95.45
92	3.47	95.47	4.13	96.13
93	3.23	96.23	3.84	96.84
94	3.01	97.01	3.57	97.57
95	2.82	97.82	3.34	98.34
96	2.64	98.64	3.12	99.12

97	2.49	99.49	2.93	99.93
98	2.36	100.36	2.76	100.76
99	2.24	101.24	2.6	101.6
100	2.12	102.12	2.45	102.45
101	2.01	103.01	2.3	103.3
102	1.9	103.9	2.17	104.17
103	1.8	104.8	2.03	105.03
104	1.7	105.7	1.91	105.91
105	1.6	106.6	1.78	106.78
106	1.51	107.51	1.67	107.67
107	1.42	108.42	1.56	108.56
108	1.34	109.34	1.45	109.45
109	1.26	110.26	1.35	110.35
110	1.18	111.18	1.26	111.26
111	1.11	112.11	1.17	112.17
112	1.04	113.04	1.08	113.08
113	0.97	113.97	1	114
114	0.9	114.9	0.92	114.92
115	0.84	115.84	0.85	115.85
116	0.78	116.78	0.78	116.78
117	0.72	117.72	0.72	117.72
118	0.67	118.67	0.67	118.67
119	0.61	119.61	0.61	119.61

Adapted from the Social Security Actuarial Table

References

Books

Author's note: Books are the messages from writers both to themselves and to their readers. I have always been appreciative in a generic sense to writers for their efforts, but the fruits of their labors have been what captivated me. Now that I see how tough it is to write a book, I want to get to know the following authors at least long enough to say thanks. I hope you're as enriched by their work as I've been. However, what resonates for one reader may not resonate for another, so choose wisely. There are so many books to read but limited time to read them. The following are just a few of the many that have been the food for thought during my life journey. A part of my Rite of Passage #6, my memorial service, includes an extensive bibliography of my favorite books to pass along to friends and loved ones.

Adele, Deborah. *The Yamas & Niyamas: Exploring Yoga's Ethical Practice*. Duluth, MN: On-Word Bound, 2009.
ISBN: 978-0-9744706-4-1

Aron, Elaine. *The Highly Sensitive Person: How to Thrive When the World Overwhelms You*. New York: Broadway, 1997.
ISBN: 0-553-06218-2

Austin, Miriam. *Yoga for Wimps: Poses for the Flexibly Impaired*. New York: Sterling Pub., 2000.
ISBN: 0-8069-4339-4

Becker, Gavin de. *The Gift of Fear: Survival Signals That Protect Us from Violence*. New York: Random House, 1997.
ISBN: 978-0-440-50883-0

Author's note: Most folks are nice or at least neutral, but there are some truly bad-news characters out there. This book and a book cited later by Sanford Strong entitled Strong on Defense: Survival Rules to Protect You and Your Family from Crime are excellent resources. Just as you have fire drills in your home so that all family members have an embedded automatic action plan for safety, these books help you prospectively recognize dangerous situations and give specific actions to avert crimes against you. The wisdom of these two books can save your life and the lives of those whom you love.

Breathed, Berke. *Goodnight Opus*. Boston: Little, Brown, 1993.
ISBN: 0-316-10599-6

Bucke, Richard Maurice. *Cosmic Consciousness.* New York: Dutton, 1959. (Note: original publication 1901.)
ISBN-13: 9781578989621; ISBN-10: 1578989620

Buhner, Stephen Harrod. *Plant Intelligence and the Imaginal Realm: Beyond the Doors of Perception into the Dreaming Earth.* Toronto: Bear, 2014.
ISBN: 978-1-59143-135-0

Carson, Rachel, Lois Darling, and Louis Darling. *Silent Spring.* Boston: Houghton Mifflin, 1962.
ISBN: 0395075068

Chapman, Gary. *The Five Love Languages: How to Express Heartfelt Commitment to Your Mate.* Men's Edition ed. Chicago, IL: Northfield, 1997.
ISBN: 1-881273-10-5

Chiras, Daniel D. *The Scoop on Poop: Safely Capturing and Recycling the Nutrients in Greywater, Humanure, and Urine.* Gabriola Island, BC: New Society, 2016.
ISBN-13: 9780865717879; ISBN-10: 0865717877

Cline, Foster, and Jim Fay. *Parenting with Love and Logic: Teaching Children Responsibility.* Colorado Springs, CO: Navpress, 1990.
ISBN:0891093117

Author's note: I highly recommend the original. I'm unfamiliar with subsequent iterations. These authors provide practical interventions to engage a child's developing critical-thinking skills to prepare the child for adolescence and adulthood.

Coelho, Paulo, and Alan Clarke. The Alchemist. San Francisco: Harper, 1993.
ISBN: 978-0-06-112241-5

Evans, Patricia. *Verbal Abuse Survivors Speak Out: On Relationship and Recovery.* Holbrook, MA: Bob Adams, 1993.
ISBN-13: 9781558503045; ISBN-10: 1558503048

Author's note: This is a must read. Verbal abuse, which encompasses much more than foul or loud language, injures victims in ways that are not obvious, unlike physical abuse. Much more subtle forms of verbal abuse exist and are prevalent in many relationships, including those with significant others but also very much apparent in business relationships. The power-over mentality of the abuser can be an insidious power play using techniques that undermine the recipient's sense of self and reality.

Dooley, Mike. *Infinite Possibilities: The Art of Living Your Dreams.* New York: Atria, 2009.
ISBN: 978-1-58270-232-2

Duhigg, Charles. *Power of Habit: Why We Do What We Do in Life and Business.* New York: Random House Trade Paperbacks, 2014.
ISBN: 97808129933894

Author's note: This is a very important book for everyone to read. The author's style is concise, entertaining, and approachable. He cites research on habit formation then teaches each of us how to recognize our habits and analyze them. Habits can be helpful and appropriate or problematic. Duhigg demonstrates how to tease apart habits by identifying the cue that starts the routine (aka as habit) resulting in the reward for the habit. He found that the craving which underlies the formation of a habit may not always be apparent. As an example, the habit of eating cookies each afternoon is not desirable due to weight gain. It would appear that the craving is for the cookies, but once analyzed the trigger could be craving for a break or the stimulation of talking to fellow workers in the cafeteria, not hunger. The routine or habit is to each afternoon go to the cafeteria to eat cookies. Duhigg found that the craving was for the reward of getting to talk to others in the cafeteria, not actually the cookie.

Elk, Black, and John G. Neihardt. *Black Elk Speaks: Being the Life Story of a Holy Man of the Oglala Sioux*. Lincoln: U of Nebraska, 1988.
ISBN: 0803283598

Erikson, Erik H. Identity: youth and crisis. New York: Norton, 1994.
ISBN-13: 9780393311440; ISBN-10: 0393311449

Erikson, Erik H. Childhood and society. New York: Norton, 1950.
ISBN-13: 9780393310689; ISBN-10: 039331068X

Erikson, Erik H. Insight and responsibility. New York: Norton, 1964.
ISBN-13: 9780393312140; ISBN-10: 0393312143

Foer, Joshua. *Moonwalking with Einstein: The Art and Science of Remembering Everything*. New York: Penguin, 2011.
ISBN-13: 9780143120537; ISBN-10: 0143120530

Gladwell, Malcolm. *The Tipping Point: How Little Things Can Make a Big Difference*. Boston: Little, Brown, 2000.
ISBN: 9780316346627

Gladwell, Malcolm. *Blink: The Power of Thinking without Thinking*. New York: Little, Brown, 2005.
ISBN-13: 9780316010665; ISBN-10: 0316010669

Godin, Seth. *The Icarus Deception: How High Will You Fly?* New York: Portfolio/Penguin, 2012.
ISBN: 978-1-59184-607-9

Harris, Dan. *10% Happier: How I Tamed the Voice in My Head, Reduced Stress without Losing My Edge, and Found Self-help That Actually Works: A True Story*. New York: HarperCollins, 2014.
ISBN: 978-0-06226543-2

[Author's note: Hilarious and insightful. If you do not see the value in meditating or have difficulty trying to meditate, this is terrific resource for the novice.]

Hawkins, David R. *Power vs. Force: The Hidden Determinants of Human Behavior*. Carlsbad, CA: Hay House, 2002.
ISBN: 978-1-56170-933-5

Jonasson, Jonas, and Rod Bradbury. *The 100-Year-Old Man Who Climbed Out of a Window and Disappeared.* New York: Harper-Collins, 2009.
ISBN: 978-1-4013-2464-3

[Author's note: This is one of the most intriguing and entertaining books I've ever read. Its humor really appeals to me, but the deeper impact is the treasurable, unique, serendipitous full life that this centenarian has led.]

Louv, Richard. *Last Child in the Woods: Saving Our Children from Nature-deficit Disorder.* Chapel Hill, NC: Algonquin of Chapel Hill, 2005.
ISBN-13: 9781565126053; ISBN-10: 156512605X

[Author's note: This book is important for parents to ponder for their children and themselves.]

Nerburn, Kent. *Wisdom of the Native Americans.* Novato, CA: New World Library, 1999.
ISBN: 1-57731-079-9

Petersen, Timothy J., Susan E. Sprich, and Sabine Wilhelm. *The Massachusetts General Hospital Handbook of Cognitive Behavioral Therapy.* New York: Springer, 2016.
ISBN: 978-1-4939-2604-6

[*Author's note:* This is a text for healthcare providers. Please check the Internet and bookstores for CBT references if you're interested in further reading or seeking such therapy.]

Saradananda. *The Power of Breath: The Art of Breathing Well for Harmony, Happiness, and Health.* London: Duncan Baird, 2009.
ISBN: 978-1-84483-812-7

Satir, Virginia. The New Peoplemaking. Palo Alto, CA: Science & Behavior , 1988.
ISBN-13: 9780831400705; ISBN-10: 0831400706

[*Author's note:* See commentary on Satir's techniques in Interesting Stuff]

Schachter-Shalomi, Zalman, and Ronald Miller. *From Age-ing to Sage-ing.* New York: Warner Books, 1995.
ISBN: 0446671770

Seligman, Martin E. P. *Authentic Happiness: Using the New Positive Psychology to Realize Your Potential for Lasting Fulfillment.* London: Nicholas Brealey, 2003.
ISBN-13: 9780743222983; ISBN-10: 0743222989

Seligman, Martin E. P. Flourish: *A Visionary New Understanding of Happiness and Well-being.* New York: Free, 2011.
ISBN 9781439190760

Seligman, Martin E. P. *Learned Optimism: How to Change Your Mind and Your Life.* New York: Vintage, 2006.
ISBN-13: 9781400078394; ISBN-10: 1400078393

Seligman, Martin E. P., Karen Reivich, Lisa Jaycox, and Jane Gillham. *The Optimistic Child.* Boston, MA: Houghton Mifflin, 1995.
ISBN-13: 9780618918096; ISBN-10: 0618918094

Seuss, and Seuss. *Horton Hears a Who!* New York: Random House, 1954.
ISBN-13: 9780394800783; ISBN-10: 0394800788

Author's note: Dr. Seuss books, in my opinion, contain some spot-on wisdom and assessments of the folly of human action from which lessons can be learned; but a few of the books seem to be more geared to adults. Some children can be frightened by characters like the Grinch. I very much enjoyed Horton Hears a Who!, which illustrates that one person can and does make an impact. (There is even a part in Horton's book that I, as a parent, found off-putting, so I abridged the story as I read it to my children).

Siegel, Dan. Mindsight: *The New Science of Personal Transformation.* New York: Bantam Books, 2011.
ISBN: 9780553386394

Stein, Matthew R. *When Technology Fails: A Manual for Self-reliance, Sustainability, and Surviving the Long Emergency.* White River Junction, VT: Chelsea Green Pub., 2008.
ISBN: 978-1-933392-45-5

Strong, Sanford. *Strong on Defense: Survival Rules to Protect You and Your Family from Crime.* New York: Pocket, 1996.
ISBN: 0-671-52293-0

[Author's note: Most folks are nice or at least neutral, but there are some truly bad-news characters out there. This book and the book cited above by Gavin Becker entitled The Gift of Fear are excellent resources. Just as you have fire drills in your home so that all family members have an embedded automatic action plan for safety, these books help you prospectively recognize dangerous situations and give specific actions to avert crimes against you. The wisdom of these two books can save your life and the lives of those whom you love.]

Taylor, Jill Bolte. *My Stroke of Insight: A Brain Scientist's Personal Journey.* New York: Plume, 2009.
ISBN: 0452295548

Tolle, Eckhart. *The Power of Now: A Guide to Spiritual Enlightenment.* Novato, CA: New World Library, 1999.
ISBN: 1577313364

Vonnegut, Kurt. *Cat's Cradle.* New York, NY: Delta Trade Paperbacks, 1998.
ISBN: 038533348X

Weiner, Eric. *The Geography of Genius: A Search for the World's Most Creative Places from Ancient Athens to Silicon Valley.* New York: Simon & Schuster, 2016.
ISBN-13: 9781451691672; ISBN-10: 145169167X

[Author's note: I swore months ago that I would not pick up a new book to read until I finished writing mine. I failed. I haven't even finished Mr. Weiner's book, but the first 183 pages are too important not to mention. First, he's funny. Second, he's inquisitive about everything. He takes nothing at face value, but drills for the nuggets of cause and effect and the mined pearls of wisdom. (Hmm, I think I just mixed my metaphors.) Third, in my opinion, future generations are going to recognize him as a modern-day philosopher.]

Whyte, David. *Consolations: The Solace, Nourishment and Underlying Meaning of Everyday Words*. Langley: Many Rivers, 2015.
ISBN-13: 9781932887341; ISBN-10: 1932887342

Wulf, Andrea. *The Invention of Nature: Alexander von Humboldt's New World*. New York: Alfred A. Knopf, 2015.
ISBN-13: 9780345806291; ISBN-10: 0345806298

[Author's note: This book is excellent. See the body of the text in chapter 8 for details.]

Funny and/or Philosophical Movies

[*Author's question:* Is it just me, or did movies and television programming used to be more optimistic overall? Innocent and informative roles played by child actors, who worked with and respected their adult mentors, showed how to overcome adversity, learn life lessons, and have fun while doing so. Children's movies and television programming provided examples of child hero roles in shows like *Sky King*, *Lassie*, and *My Friend Flicka*. Even entertaining cartoons such as Snagglepuss, Foghorn Leghorn, and Super Chicken often taught lessons while making you laugh.]

City Slickers. Dir. Ron Underwood. N.p., n.d. Web.

Crash. By Paul Haggis. Perf. Sandra Bullock, Don Cheadle, Matt Dillon. N.p., n.d. 2004.

[*Author's note:* *Crash* is one of the most thought-provoking films I have ever seen.]

Defending your Life. By Albert Brooks. Perf. Albert Brooks, Meryl Streep. N.p., n.d. 1991.

Men in Black. Dir. Barry Sonnenfeld. N.p., n.d. Web.

Monty Python and the Holy Grail. N.p., n.d. Web.

[Author's note: Monty Python is a very funny movie other than the last few minutes, which I always skip. It is the source of several notable quotations.]

Short Circuit. By Paul Terry. N.p., n.d. Web.

The Princess Bride. Twentieth Century Fox Film Corp., 1987.

Web Sources

"An Age-Old Problem: Who Is 'Elderly'?" NPR. NPR, n.d. Web. 13 Nov. 2016. http://www.npr.org/2013/03/12/174124992/an-age-old-problem-who-is-elderly

"At What Age Does the Brain Stop Developing? | Reference.com." N.p., n.d. Web. 21 Oct. 2016.
https://www.reference.com/science/age-brain-stop-developing-fcc9a17b5c52f5ef

Andrews, Sally, David A. Ellis, Heather Shaw, and Lukasz Piwek. "Beyond Self-Report: Tools to Compare Estimated and Real-World Smartphone Use." Plos One 10.10 (2015): n. pag.

"Average U.S. Gasoline Usage Lowest in 3 Decades, Study Says." Automotive News. N.p., n.d. Web. 30 Oct. 2016.
http://www.autonews.com/article/20150325/OEM06/150329911/average-u.s.-gasoline-usage-lowest-in-3-decades-study-says

Benasich, April. "Effect Of Gamma Waves On Cognitive And Language Skills In Children." ScienceDaily, n.d. Web. 12 Dec. 2016.
https://www.sciencedaily.com/releases/2008/10/081021120945.htm

Benson, Herbert, MD. "Can Prayer Heal?" WebMD. WebMD, n.d. Web. 14 Nov. 2016.

http://www.webmd.com/balance/features/can-prayer-heal?page=2

Brown, Dennis C. "Web commentary on Jill Bolte Taylor's text My Stroke of Insight: A Brain Scientist's Personal Journey" (citation under Taylor's name, below)

https://www.amazon.com/My-Stroke-Insight-Scientists-Personal/product-reviews/0452295548/ref=cm_cr_arp_d_viewpnt_rgt?ie=UTF8&filterByStar=critical

Dobbs, David. "Zen Gamma." Scientific American. N.p., 17 Mar. 2005. Web. 11 Mar. 2017.

https://www.scientificamerican.com/article/zen-gamma/

"Don't Believe Everything You Think" ClevelandClinicWellness.com. N.p., n.d.

http://www.clevelandclinicwellness.com/programs/NewSFN/pages/default.aspx?Lesson=3&Topic=2&vUserId=00000000-0000-0000-0000-000000000705

Erikson, Eric. Generativity—see

McLeod, Saul. "Erik Erikson." Simply Psychology. N.p., 2016. Web. 08 Sept. 2016.

http://www.simplypsychology.org/Erik-Erikson.html

http://www.facebook.com/AboutPsychology. "What's the Difference Between Generativity and Stagnation." Verywell. N.p., n.d. Web. 08 Sept. 2016.

https://www.verywell.com/generativity-versus-stagnation-2795734

Fry, Richard. "For First Time in Modern Era, Living With Parents Edges Out Other Living Arrangements for 18- to 34-Year-Olds." Pew Research Centers Social Demographic Trends Project RSS. N.p., 2016. Web. 30 Oct. 2016.

http://www.pewsocialtrends.org/2016/05/24/for-first-time-in-modern-era-living-with-parents-edges-out-other-living-arrangements-for-18-to-34-year-olds/

Garrett, Mario, Ph.D. "Brain Plasticity in Older Adults | Psychology Today." N.p., n.d. Web. 21 Oct. 2016.

https://www.psychologytoday.com/blog/iage/201304/brain-plasticity-in-older-adults

Goldman, Leslie. "3 Metals That Might Cause Memory Problems." *The Huffington Post.* TheHuffingtonPost.com, n.d. Web. 18 Dec. 2013, updated 25 Jan. 2014

http://www.huffingtonpost.com/2013/12/18/metal-dangers-memory-loss-alzheimers-disease_n_4413511.html

"Hebbian Theory." Wikipedia. Wikimedia Foundation, n.d. Web. 08 Nov. 2016.

https://en.wikipedia.org/wiki/Hebbian_theory

Hensch, Takao K. "Critical Period Plasticity in Local Cortical Circuits." Nature Reviews Neuroscience 6.11 (2005): 877-88. Web.

http://www.nature.com/nrn/journal/v6/n11/full/nrn1787.html

How Many Pounds of Food Does the Average Adult Eat in a Day?" Reference. N.p., n.d. Web. 30 Oct. 2016.

https://www.reference.com/food/many-pounds-food-average-adult-eat-day-3f49d34cd3d872cd

"How Much Sleep Do Babies and Kids Need?", Excessive Sleepiness. N.p., n.d. Web. 12 Nov. 2016.

https://sleepfoundation.org/excessivesleepiness/content/how-much-sleep-do-babies-and-kids-need

Huffington, Arianna. "It's Time to Retire Our Definition of Retirement" N.p., n.d. Web. 21 Oct. 2016.

http://www.huffingtonpost.com/arianna-huffington/its-time-to-retire-our-definition-of-retirement_b_5774878.html

Hutton, John, M.D.
@NeuroscienceNew. "Reading to Children Promotes Brain Development." Neuroscience News. N.p., 2015. Web. 30 Oct. 2016.

[Author's note: This is a terrific article for parents of toddlers and children regarding the benefits of reading and interacting with children to engage their critical-thinking skills and thereby stimulate brain development.]

"Is There a Perfect Age to Start Music Lessons?, Today's Parent." Todays Parent. N.p., 2016. Web. 11 Nov. 2016.
http://www.todaysparent.com/kids/start-music-lessons/

"Kübler-Ross model." Wikipedia. Wikimedia Foundation, 24 Feb. 2017. Web. 04 Mar. 2017.
https://en.wikipedia.org/wiki/K%C3%BCbler-Ross_model

[Author's note: Dr. Kübler-Ross was a prolific author who originally described five stages of the grieving process regarding death, including denial, anger, bargaining, depression, and acceptance. She wrote about working with terminally ill children, the elderly, AIDS patients and others. Her works have attained international acclaim.]

Lange, Catherine De. "How to Live Longer—the Experts' Guide to Ageing." The Guardian. Guardian News and Media, 2013. Web. 13 Nov. 2016.
https://www.theguardian.com/science/2013/sep/08/how-to-live-longer-experts-guide-ageing

Lee, Jae Rhim. "My Mushroom Burial Suit." N.p., n.d. Web. 19 Oct. 2016.
http://www.citationmachine.net/bibliographies/133200814?new=true

"Livestock a Major Threat to Environment." Livestock a Major Threat to Environment. N.p., n.d. Web. 30 Oct. 2016.
http://www.fao.org/Newsroom/en/news/2006/1000448/index.html

Madhu, B. Web commentary on Jill Bolte Taylor's text My Stroke of Insight: A Brain Scientist's Personal Journey (citation under Taylor's name, below)
https://www.amazon.com/My-Stroke-Insight-Scientists-Personal/product-reviews/0452295548/ref=cm_cr_arp_d_viewpnt_rgt?ie=UTF8&filterByStar=critical

Mother Earth News
https://www.motherearthnews.com/store/offer/EMEGOGCA?gclid=CjwKEAiA1ITCBRDO-oLA-q_n8xYSJADjBQfGj0yGGNjECnIGYj75eLgdMTo8o3WbHfz-EOJo-oPwPRoCHIfw_wcB

[*Author's note: Mother Earth News is a magazine that has over forty years of back issues available on CD, that promote sustainable living and earth friendly lifestyles. I wish that the magazine and their quarterly fairs held in the four main US regions would be advertised on college campuses. I think youth would enjoy being exposed to the programming to learn skills not likely to have been taught to them previously.*]

Nemko, Marty. @PsychToday. "Ten Underrated Jobs." Psychology Today. N.p., n.d. Web. 26 Oct. 2016.
https://www.psychologytoday.com/blog/how-do-life/201610/ten-underrated-jobs

Onink, Troy. "College Costs Could Total As Much As $334,000 in four years." Forbes
http://www.forbes.com/sites/troyonink/2015/01/31/college-could-cost-as-much-as-334000-total-in-four-years/#3e6a8dd9679f

"Parenting and Cell Phones: Science Shows the Harms Of Digital Distraction." Time. Time, n.d. Web. 06 Mar. 2017.
http://time.com/4168688/cell-phone-distracted-parenting-can-have-long-term-consequences-study/

"Per Capita Consumption of Poultry and Livestock 1965 to Estimated 2016, in Pounds." National Chicken Council
http://www.nationalchickencouncil.org/about-the-industry/statistics/per-capita-consumption-of-poultry-and-livestock-1965-to-estimated-2012-in-pounds/

"POODWADDLE WORLD CLOCK." THE WORLD CLOCK. N.p., n.d. Web. 02 Dec. 2016.
http://www.poodwaddle.com/worldclock/

Author's note: Please check out this website, which shows in real time the moment-to-moment increase in the world's population, currently increasing at over 225,000 per day. As well, the amount of deforestation and garbage dumped into the sea is displayed as they accrue.

Pulling the plug: ICU 'culture' key to life or death decision
http://vitals.nbcnews.com/_news/2013/05/21/18382297-pulling-the-plug-icu-culture-key-to-life-or-death-decision?lite

Robinson, Sir Ken. "Do schools kill creativity?" TED Talk
https://www.ted.com/talks/ken_robinson_says_schools_kill_creativity?language=en

Seligman, Martin. "The New Era of Positive Psychology." N.p., n.d. Web. 11 Nov. 2016.
https://www.ted.com/talks/martin_seligman_on_the_state_of_psychology?language=en

Shermer, Michael. "Afterlife for Atheists." *Scientific American* 314.2 (2016): 73. Web.
http://www.michaelshermer.com/2016/02/afterlife-for-atheists/

Steele, Christopher, et al. "Early Musical Training and White-Matter Plasticity in the Corpus Callosum: Evidence for a Sensitive Period." *Journal of Neuroscience*. N.p., n.d. Web. 11 Nov. 2016.
http://www.jneurosci.org/content/33/3/1282.full?sid=91a5e9d3-1520-4bef-9da6-cf8123a0d50c

Taylor, Jill Bolte. TED Talk
http://www.ted.com/playlists/171/the_most_popular_talks_of_all?gclid=CjwKEAjw97K_BRCwmNTK26iM-hMSJABrkNtbPz6j6BcGNFAB4t-B4i0_YPS1GiXui259YgMxPxvU7RoCshjw_wcB

[Author's note: Dr. Bolte and I have something in common. We both had an AV malformation of the brain. Arteries have a muscular wall allowing them to withstand the pressure of blood pulsing from the heart. Veins, on the other hand, are non-muscular because the venous side of our circulation is under no pressure. Normally between arteries and veins there is an elaborate series of progressively smaller blood vessels that allows a smooth transition from the high arterial pressure to the very low venous pressure. Some people have a malformation in which an artery joins directly to a vein, putting the venous side at risk for rupture since veins do not have the strength to withstand arterial pressure. Dr. Bolte's AVM ruptured; mine has not. I did, however, have one of my expert dier episodes when a diagnostic procedure gone awry induced spasm in the arterial supply to the posterior part of my brain. The stroke knocked out all short-term memory, some long-term memory, disrupted my balance, and caused blindness. Fortunately, I recovered from these significant deficits.]

TED Talks—General Website
https://www.ted.com/about/our-organization

The following is an excerpt from the website:

TED is a nonprofit devoted to spreading ideas, usually in the form of short, powerful talks (18 minutes or less). TED began in 1984 as a conference where Technology, Entertainment, and Design converged, and today covers almost all topics — from science to business to global issues — in more than 100 languages. Meanwhile, independently run

TEDx events help share ideas in communities around the world.

TED is a global community, welcoming people from every discipline and culture who seek a deeper understanding of the world. We believe passionately in the power of ideas to change attitudes, lives and, ultimately, the world. On TED.com, we're building a clearinghouse of free knowledge from the world's most inspired thinkers — and a community of curious souls to engage with ideas and each other, both online and at TED and TEDx events around the world, all year long.

"The Only Way to Change Diapers Is One Baby at a Time." Real Diaper Association. N.p., 2015. Web. 13 Nov. 2016.
http://realdiapers.org/diaper-facts

Thuret, Sandrine: "You Can Grow New Brain Cells. Here's How." N.p., n.d. Web. 11 Nov. 2016.
https://www.ted.com/talks/sandrine_thuret_you_can_grow_new_brain_cells_here_s_how?language=en

Wikipedia. "World Population." N.p., n.d. Web.
https://en.wikipedia.org/wiki/World_population#cite_note-LongRangeProjections2003KeyFindings-14

Young, Shinzen. "Practical Steps for Transforming Physical Pain Into Spiritual Growth." N.p., n.d. Web.
http://www.shinzen.org/Articles/artPain.htm

Acknowledgments

I am grateful to family, friends, teachers, and the many people with whom my life has intersected. Each deeply evolved relationship and chance tangential interaction has impacted the course my life has taken. Whether our interaction has been considered "good" or "bad," the inspiration and lessons learned have shaped my philosophy and have lent meaning to my life.

My thanks go out to many people. To the authors of the thousands of books I've read, I wish I could meet you to say thanks in person. As to the writing of this book, my thanks go to the two coaches who challenged me to put pen to paper and author a book that has been in the making over most of my lifetime—Izzy Lanahan and Aruni Nan Futuronsky. For the people kind enough to grant interviews, to my Millennial cheerleaders, Greg Weygandt and Bree Barton, to my IPA (see appendix 10 for definition) friends Lee (artist), Dr. Rhonda, Dr. Cassius, Dr. Melissa, and Sherri for their years of affection and support, and to those who have assisted me with the nuts and bolts of the publishing process—Mayapriya Long, Bree Barton (again), Ken Benson, Cynthia Frank, and Charles

Chappell, Ph.D., I express my deepest gratitude. My heartfelt appreciation goes to my editor and husband, Paul Weygandt. Final thanks go to the readers who have given me such valuable feedback, encouragement, support, and counsel.

About the Author

Blue and White Gingham Collar:

Some people are considered "blue collar" due to their livelihood in the trades. Others are noted to be "white collar" due to a livelihood dependent upon academic credentials. My life has bridged the two.

The Blue Collar refers to my roles as a loving granddaughter of subsistence farmers and an intensely proud daughter of a military father who became a barber and a farmer's daughter who became a beautician. My first job was in third grade, as a waitress. Subsequently, I worked as a babysitter, started a yard service and housekeeping business, was employed as a department store clerk, and later a clothing salesperson. I was pretty much continuously employed in one of the above jobs through college.

The White Collar refers to my roles as a physician trained in emergency medicine and psychiatry. My first desire to become a physician was expressed at age three.

The Gingham Collar refers to my life as a synthesis of the blue- and the white-collar backgrounds. My current positions include wife, mother, and grandmother. I am a physician, writer, and farmer, and, as you're aware by now, a yoga instructor, Reiki teacher, bee watcher, worm wrangler, party animal, and right-brained metaphysical wanderer.

But there is more yet to come. Perhaps I could set a world record for the number of friends I make in the coming years. My life plan includes at a minimum further development as a world traveler (to visit all the friends I will make from among you readers), an adventurer, a disaster volunteer, an athlete, an elder role model, a speaker . . . I want to develop my farm as a place of learning (a place where instructors could come to teach bee, chicken, and worm husbandry, meditation skills, how to weld, or how to can vegetables). I'm looking for help to establish the first chapters of the Egaliatarian Contemplators, the Guild of Elders, and the Renaissance Mentors.

My bucket list, which is immense, includes:

- To launch the first of what will hopefully be many regional chapters of a Guild of Elders whose charge will be the reintegration of individuals from all life stages.
- To get a "rescue elephant"—which I might add is being opposed by a certain adult male member of my immediate family. Maybe I'll just join the wonderful organizations that are working to save these majestic creatures.
- As mentioned earlier to philosophize with Oprah and to join Ellen and her audience in a dance.
- To meet those individuals who will be recognized as historical luminaries such as Albert Einstein, Mark Twain, and Mother Teresa.
- To study Buddhist principles, world religions, and philosophies and to meet the Pope and the Dalai Lama.

- To meet the authors of all the books which I have read to thank them for their efforts, and to read every article and see every science-based episode on such channels as National Geographic, Science, and the like.
- Oops! I realize that to finish this list could turn in to another book-sized document. Suffice it to say, I would like the words on my tombstone to say, "Darn it! Despite all the items I have checked off, I still have a few more to add to my bucket list."

As I exit stage left from this life, I would like to leave my farm, which is only on loan as it has been to previous owners, to posterity as a legacy for all to enjoy. My final aspiration is to emulate Aunt Margie, who is now transitioning. Even though we have just found out that she has but a very short time left, she is making lists of people she wants to say goodbye to, completing her own eulogy (per the request of her children), apportioning her worldly goods, and inspiring those around her. Recently Margie stated "I shouldn't feel this good as I am dying." I hope that I can be as courageous, curious, and joyful as Aunt Margie so that I may, as well, become a truly *expert dier*.